FREEDOM OF CONSCIENCE IN (POST)SOVIET SPACE

A volume in the NIU Series in

Slavic, East European, and Eurasian Studies

Edited by Christine D. Worobec

For a list of books in the series, visit our website at cornellpress.cornell.edu.

FREEDOM OF CONSCIENCE IN (POST)SOVIET SPACE

LEGACIES OF MICHAEL BOURDEAUX AND THE KESTON ARCHIVE

EDITED BY
JULIE K. DEGRAFFENRIED,
MICHAEL LONG, AND
XENIA DENNEN
Preface by Rowan Williams

NORTHERN ILLINOIS UNIVERSITY PRESS
an imprint of
CORNELL UNIVERSITY PRESS
Ithaca and London

Open access funding was received from Keston Institute, a UK charity.

First published 2025 by Cornell University Press

Library of Congress Cataloging-in-Publication Data

Names: Bourdeaux, Michael, honouree. | deGraffenried, Julie K., editor. | Long, Michael, 1957– editor. | Dennen, Xenia, 1944– editor.
Title: Freedom of conscience in (post)Soviet space : legacies of Michael Bourdeaux and the Keston Archive / edited Julie K. deGraffenried, Michael Long, and Xenia Dennen.
Description: Ithaca [New York] : Northern Illinois University Press, an imprint of Cornell University Press, 2025. | Series: NIU series in Slavic, East European, and Eurasian studies | Includes bibliographical references and index.
Identifiers: LCCN 2024049555 (print) | LCCN 2024049556 (ebook) | ISBN 9781501782718 (hardcover) | ISBN 9781501782725 (paperback) | ISBN 9781501782732 (epub) | ISBN 9781501782749 (pdf)
Subjects: LCSH: Liberty of conscience. | Communism and religion. | LCGFT: Essays.
Classification: LCC BV741 .F7925 2025 (print) | LCC BV741 (ebook) | DDC 261.7/20947—dc23/eng/20250216
LC record available at https://lccn.loc.gov/2024049555
LC ebook record available at https://lccn.loc.gov/2024049556

GPSR EU contact: Sam Thornton, Mare Nostrum Group B.V., Mauritskade 21D, 1091 GC, Amsterdam, NL, gpsr@mare-nostrum.co.uk.

To all who defend freedom of conscience

Contents

Illustrations

FOREWORD

In the 1980s, Michael Bourdeaux began his review of a newly published and lavishly illustrated book on Russian Orthodoxy with the words: "This book will tell you everything you want to know about the Russian Orthodox Church except the truth." Nothing could be worse, in Michael's eyes, than such a failure. He fought as consistently as anyone could against any kind of instrumentalizing of the facts. Selective reporting had to be resisted, whatever the embarrassments this might bring for interested parties. A depiction of injustice, corruption, and suffering that tacitly absolved certain parties or privileged the sufferings of one group over those of others was not defensible. All that Michael did with and for Keston College was based on this unflinching commitment to an inclusive account of the facts emerging. Those who unthinkingly cast him as some sort of Cold War apologist completely misread him. If his reporting of religious persecution in Communist countries could be used by some on the political Right to serve their purposes, his own impartiality was unchallengeable, and the painstaking documentation of the deep dishonesty at the heart of the Soviet system was, along with much else, a robust challenge to any on the political Left who might be inclined to give a moral free pass to governments claiming progressive credentials. He was, in that sense, stubbornly nontribal. The interests he served were truthfulness and justice, and he would have worked with no less energy and courage to expose tyrannies of the Right.

As several of these essays make clear, he was for decades a virtually unique figure in the English-speaking world simply in the depth and professionalism of his knowledge of religion and communism. He was a crucial conduit for amplifying in the Western world the voices of those silenced by a hostile state. We would have known immeasurably less about dissident literature in the Eastern bloc of the middle to late twentieth century without the patient—and often highly risky—labors of Michael and his colleagues. And the fact that Keston was trusted without qualification by dissidents and minorities of such diverse kinds speaks volumes. Keston's publications have always sought to do justice to any and every religious group under pressure, Orthodox, Catholic, Baptist, Buddhist, Muslim, Jehovah's Witnesses, and this is a large part of why Michael's work remains so significant. He is not the chronicler simply of injustices or atrocities inflicted on the group with which a researcher identifies; he is the chronicler of one of the great political pathologies of the modern world—the ambition to control consciences by force, not (as in the pre-modern world) in the name of a dominant moral or spiritual system but in the name of a sheerly political claim for the state's omnipotence. His work and that of Keston throughout its life can be seen as a sustained attempt to point clearly to the cost of the totalitarian mindset in terms of insecurity, pain, and gross violence, but also in terms of public corruption and mendacity and the resentment or cynicism that this breeds.

The present volume offers an excellent perspective on this aspect of his and Keston's research, and it also takes forward the same agenda through searching analyses of the condition of post-Communist, especially post-Soviet, society in Eastern Europe. The relation of the state to civil society in general and religious communities in particular is not any more straightforward than in the heyday of Keston's work in the pre-perestroika years (as the history of the Russian Orthodox Church in the last couple of years amply and tragically demonstrates). This book is a great deal more than the celebration of an exceptional figure of the recent past. Practically every contribution here can and should be read as potentially casting light on a contemporary world in which resurgent varieties of ultranationalism or open fascism, nostalgia for the supposed security of past tyrannies, and the mobilization of selective narratives of victimhood by powerful and untruthful interests are everywhere to be seen. We are still urgently in need of voices and minds like Michael's to reinforce for all of us, religious or secular, Western or Eastern, Christian or non-Christian, the imperative of truth, a truth that will set us free.

Rowan Williams, Baron of Oystermouth and
former Archbishop of Canterbury

ACKNOWLEDGMENTS

This book was made possible by the generous and thoughtful contributions of scholars whose essays appear here, all of whom responded not only with alacrity but also with genuine, warm enthusiasm when we proposed such a volume. From start to finish, working with such cooperative, willing colleagues from around the world has been an enjoyable experience. Michael Long deserves credit for the idea for the volume, and the Keston Advisory Board at Baylor University and Keston Institute (UK) deserve the same for their wholehearted support of our project. Kathy Hillman and Larisa Seago at the Keston Center for Religion, Politics, and Society at Baylor University have been essential partners along the way, and we are grateful to them. Rowan Williams, Baron of Oystermouth and former Archbishop of Canterbury, has lent his support to Keston Institute in a myriad of ways over the years; we thank him for his willingness to write the foreword. We owe a special debt of gratitude to Amy Farranto at Cornell University Press for her patient, incisive counsel at many points along this journey, to the CUP production team for their professionalism and guidance, to the editorial board for useful suggestions, and to two anonymous reviewers who provided enormously insightful feedback. Undoubtedly, the volume is better because of it. Julie wishes to thank the Keston Center, Sergo Grigorian, the Thursday morning Muses, and, as always, her family, for their support in bringing this work to fruition. Michael thanks the Keston Center, the coeditors Julie deGraffenried and Xenia Dennen, Sara Alexander, and other colleagues who have offered advice on how to assemble a volume of collected essays.

NOTE ON TRANSLITERATION

Transliterations in this volume conform to the most recent standards of the Library of Congress (LOC), although diacritic marks have been omitted. For well-known names, the spelling most commonly familiar to readers has been used (for example, Aleksandr Men instead of Men' or Andrei Sinyavsky instead of Siniavskii), except in quoted material. Bibliographic references in other languages have also been transliterated using the LOC standard unless the original source differs from that system.

FREEDOM OF CONSCIENCE IN
(POST)SOVIET SPACE

Introduction

On Tributes and Truth-Speaking

Julie K. deGraffenried

When Reverend Canon Dr. Michael Bourdeaux passed away in 2021, the most obvious tribute to his life and work was the production of a book. For decades, Bourdeaux and his creation, Keston College, championed freedom of conscience. He earned the 1984 Templeton Prize for his work to "examine and explain the systematic destruction of religion in Iron Curtain nations" and for his defense of "the rights of faiths in these countries to worship as they chose."[1] As Keston Institute chairperson Xenia Dennen recounts in her biography of Bordeaux (see Appendix), Keston College was founded, first and foremost, to encourage the study of religion and religious life under Communism. Bourdeaux himself wrote or edited over a dozen books and countless articles on the subject, while Keston's holdings supplied critical material to scholars such as Jane Ellis, Michael Rowe, Philip Walters, and Marite Sapiets. Their analytical and editorial work helped establish religion in the Soviet Union and other Communist countries as an academic topic worth pursuing, focusing in particular on its persistence despite unjust persecution.[2]

This collection of essays follows their lead, albeit from a new perspective. This volume is not so much a festschrift as it is a collection of original essays inspired by the work of Bourdeaux and the holdings of the Keston Archive. Bourdeaux's prolific scholarship appears in passing, but it is not our intent to interrogate his arguments or published works. Instead, we seek to demonstrate his significant impact on the study of religion and communism across disciplines. The contributors' varied fields—history, sociology, theology, philosophy, languages, literature—reveal the breadth and depth of his influence. Each of these essays, in its own way, memorializes and celebrates the foundation that Bourdeaux laid for future scholarship and inquiry.

Michael Bourdeaux dedicated his energy and intellect to speaking "for truth," a way of life he viewed as aligned with Soviet dissident Aleksandr Solzhenitsyn's struggle against falsehood.[3] Such an ongoing commitment to the truth meant countering the official narrative that freedom of worship was protected in the Soviet Union, even when public criticism seemed counterintuitive in the era of détente and backstairs diplomacy. It meant supporting peoples of all faiths—Christians, Jews, Muslims, Buddhists, animists, and so on—in their quest to live authentically in a system that not only discouraged religious practice but actively undermined and policed it. Unquestionably, he saw the defense of religious freedom as related to both his own understanding of the Gospel—his truth—and to the broader matter of global human rights. The violation of human rights of course outlived the Communist system in Central and Eastern Europe and continues to be a concern for many people. Events of the twenty-first century have affirmed the importance of studying religion to fully understand contemporary politics, identities, and conflicts, as scholars continue to explore "what happens to religion in modern and postmodern societies."[4]

The Cold War shaped Bourdeaux's conception of freedom of conscience, as did his assessment of late twentieth-century Christianity in an affluent and complacent Western world.[5] That global rivalry interpreted even the smallest act as political—and one might wonder how Keston's enterprise could be described otherwise—though Bourdeaux assiduously disputed that characterization. In theory, the political system under which religious persecution occurred was immaterial. In reality, Bourdeaux's focus on that persecution had a ready-made target (and audience) given the historical context. His sympathy for and indignation about the plight of believers living in Communist societies pervades his writing and the unique collection now known as the Keston Archive. The Keston collection, a "counter archive" according to Sonja Luehrmann, "assumes the same binary between religion and non-religion as Soviet state archives" but "engaged in a kind of documentary arms race . . . organized around a notion of inherent rights of religious communities."[6] Since the fall of the Soviet Union, many of those binaries so common to the Soviet system and the Cold War—us/them, good/evil, public/private, believer/Soviet, religion/ideology—have been blurred, complicated, and even rejected.[7] The archive, however, continues to provide users with unparalleled glimpses into the past through its curation of press clippings, official documents, photographs, and ephemera related to religious life during the Communist era and the preservation of *samizdat* (self-published materials), personal papers, and artifacts.[8] Keston Institute's educational mission has continued since the end of the Cold War despite its loss of funding and the relocation of the archive. It retains its strong public stance on freedom of conscience and continues to sponsor academic archival research and field research.

In geographical scope, the essays in this volume range from England to Siberia, while the chronological scope covers 1917 to the present. We choose the terms "Soviet" and "post-Soviet" to describe this temporal framing, while acknowledging the difficulties inherent in these terms. In using the term "post-Soviet" we seek to neither elide national or ethnic identities nor erase Russia's (ongoing) imperial ambitions. We find the term useful because the antireligious efforts—and the larger questions of human-rights challenges under Communist regimes—are part of the cultural and political baggage that "imperialism and oppression left behind."[9] Though such attempts to control or eliminate religious communities were not unique to the USSR or Communism in Central and Eastern Europe, Soviet influence there created conditions for religious persecution on ideological grounds and the adoption of a repressive church-state relationship in the post–World War II era.[10] The consequences of Soviet influence on religious policy and practice remain an element of postcolonial struggle.

The volume is divided into three parts. The three essays in Part I foreground the work of Michael Bourdeaux and Keston College, the institution he helmed. In chapter 1, Zoe Knox examines the innovative practices developed by Bourdeaux and Keston College personnel for soliciting, corroborating, analyzing, and organizing research materials, focusing on the significance of samizdat and its special ability to convey "truth." She argues that through these processes, collectively, Keston invented a new methodology designed to bring Communist religious persecution to the attention of human rights organizations, Western Christian communities, and Western governments, creating a collection with a remarkable afterlife.

In chapter 2, Mark Hurst challenges the reductionist view of Keston College as a "Cold Warrior," exploring the agency of its individual leaders, researchers, and supporters. While acknowledging the historical and sociopolitical context, Hurst's approach allows for a more nuanced deliberation on the history of Keston and its personnel, providing a model for any evaluation of nongovernmental organizations that functioned during the Cold War. Both essays affirm and build on Sonja Luehrmann's brilliant meditation on religion in secular archives—namely, that the character and power of archival processes matter: "We can gain a richer reading of past lives and a deeper understanding of how documentation sustains systems of power if we do not see archival documents as passive traces of actions and interests."[11] Because Knox and Hurst grapple with related methodological questions, chapters 1 and 2 are best read in tandem. Together they provide an epistemological analysis of Keston College that situates the collection within broader conversations about the production and circulation of knowledge and the place of institutions, people, and politics in that process.

In chapter 3, turning to Bourdeaux himself, theologian and philosopher Joshua Searle uses "biography as theology" to explicate the theological foundations of Bourdeaux's commitment to religious liberty. Searle illuminates key influences on Bourdeaux's life and thought, with special consideration to the integral relationship between freedom and truth in the Eastern Orthodox tradition. Considering Bourdeaux's calling, and drawing on the works of a selection of leading thinkers from East and West, the chapter offers an ecumenical perspective on his mission. Searle parses the theological and philosophical underpinnings of Bourdeaux's lifelong devotion to defending freedom of conscience. A compelling conclusion argues for the relevance of that dedication in today's world.

The four chapters in Part II focus on the Soviet Union, Bourdeaux's initial area of concern and a cornerstone of the Keston collection. Each chapter highlights different archival materials, including dissident writings, press clippings, Soviet publications, samizdat, and posters. Wallace Daniel and Barbara Martin plumb the youth religiosity of late socialism from different angles. In chapter 4, Daniel searches for the roots of the 1970s youth revival, the resurgence of interest in spiritual matters among urban intellectual youth, and locates it in the 1960s—ironically, a time when the state trumpeted its triumph over religious belief. Focusing on members of the Moscow Seminar, Daniel provides a portrait of youth uninspired by Marxist-Leninist ideology and an irrelevant, submissive Russian Orthodox Church, and on a quest for personal authenticity that led them to new questions, a new sense of community, and a new commitment to faith and free expression. In chapter 5, Martin examines the reaction of Soviet authorities to the mounting ideological challenge posed by youth religiosity in the 1970s and 1980s. The failure of atheist propaganda to win the hearts of new generations of Soviet youth born into largely nonreligious families was of great concern to authorities, who adapted their tactics to face this challenge. Martin mines the Soviet youth press, finding that propagandists sought to characterize religious fervor among youth as a threat to social cohesion, as an unserious fad unworthy of true communists, or as a West-assisted "ideological diversion" in the Cold War. Taken together, these two chapters affirm the failure of Soviet antireligious campaigns to eliminate belief in the supernatural and the "mutually constituting" relationship between state efforts and religious practice that affected personal and collective identity formation.[12] Beneath the surface of official proclamations lay a tangle of adaptation, redefinition, and reimagination practiced by Soviet citizens and authorities at the local and national levels.

In chapter 6, April French argues for the recognition and significance of the Council of Prisoners' Relatives (CPR), the longest-running human rights organization that operated in the USSR. Foreshadowing the actions of post-Helsinki human rights groups, beginning in the 1960s the evangelical women who ran the CPR published lists of political prisoners, petitioned heads of state, and directed the international community's attention to human rights violations. Through a close reading of Aleksandra Kozorezova's writing in the CPR Bulletin, French reveals the organization's development, its rights consciousness, and the gendered significance of women's leadership in the context of an evangelical subculture. French's essay joins ongoing conversations about the nature and role of samizdat—the "uncensored, grassroots system of self-publishing found in the USSR after Iosif Stalin and until perestroika . . . one of the most distinctive phenomena of the late Soviet period" and one that spread to other bloc countries.[13] Religious samizdat comprised only a fraction of the self-published material circulating during the era of late socialism; even so, CPR publications illustrate how this alternative print culture could create new communities and generate alternative versions of the truth.

Chapter 7 pivots away from the clandestine underground to state-sanctioned antireligious propaganda in posters. Julie deGraffenried surveys the unprecedented visual outpouring of anticlericalism that accompanied official efforts to diminish, if not eliminate, the role of organized religion in the Soviet Union, contextualizing these posters within a larger endeavor to create a new Soviet landscape intended to transform its inhabitants' daily habits. She analyzes the visual rhetoric of anticlericalism over time, from revolution in 1917 to reconciliation in the 1980s, comparing posters of the two major waves of antireligious ferment in light of the shifting strategies adopted by state propagandists. Building on recent scholarship about viewer reception and subjectivities, deGraffenried demonstrates the difficulties faced by the state in convincing citizens to embrace the anticlerical sentiments presented in posters. Confused messaging hindered the people's ability to comprehend the state's intended meaning, thus impeding the internalization of the revolution.[14]

Part III contains three essays that display the expansiveness of Bourdeaux's ideas and their legacies in Soviet and post-Soviet societies. Chapters 8 and 9 move beyond the USSR geographically, while chapter 10 engages Russia in the post-Soviet era. In chapter 8, linguist and literature scholar Michael Long uses an artifact of the Keston Archive to explore attempts to subvert official efforts to control knowledge production and literary expression in Czechoslovakia via book smuggling. A miniature edition of Zdeněk Mlynář's memoir might seem a curious addition to the Keston Archive, but then again, perhaps not: Bourdeaux always viewed his work on behalf of persecuted faith communities as firmly connected to the human rights movement more broadly. Long takes the tiny volume as a point of departure, then traces the development of three of the main exile publishing houses established in Western Europe by Czechoslovaks following the 1948 Communist coup and the failed Prague Spring of 1968. He describes the illegal transfer of exile literature and unofficial Czechoslovak literature to and from Czechoslovakia and the importance of the secret operation to both publishers abroad and dissidents, focusing on the motivation and activities of the "postwoman" Jiřina Šiklová. Long's chapter highlights the human relationships that made networks of knowledge production and dissemination possible.[15]

In chapter 9, writing on church-state relations under Communism—long assumed to be solely antagonistic or at best indifferent—historian Patrick Leech uncovers an episode of cooperation and partnership in Kádár's Hungary. He argues that the state showed the same ideological flexibility and pragmatism in dealing with organized religion as it did in addressing socioeconomic concerns. Leech details the causes of and alarm over rising suicide rates and related signs of social dysfunction in "the happiest barrack," then contends that the state's invitation to its churches to address such problems via social services led to a more prominent place for churches in the public square by the mid-1980s. Leech joins other recent scholars in challenging conceptual frameworks that simplify church-state relations—and the people affected by them—through juxtaposition and essentialization.[16]

In chapter 10, sociologist Sergei Filatov draws on his thirty-five years of fieldwork in Russia to provide an overview of the development of the Russian Orthodox Church after the collapse of the Soviet Union in 1991. The foremost expert on religion in Russia today and the director of the Keston Institute's ongoing *Encylopaedia* project, Filatov and his team have crisscrossed the vast country over the past several decades to document hundreds of religious communities, sites, and traditions, and to interview their adherents.[17] Having studied Russian religious life since the 1980s, Filatov reflects on the evolution of the church in its consciousness, practices, and organization, from the era of perestroika to the present, in the context of shifting religious policies in Russia. He posits the factors contributing to a "quiet evangelical evolution" in the 2000s, which transformed the church from a nearly moribund institution to one with a visible presence in public life. Despite rising criticism of the church in Russian society and the current relationship between church and state in Putin's Russia, Filatov finds in his fieldwork a slow movement toward a more democratic, relevant church now halted by the Russo-Ukrainian War. While the resurgence of religious life and institutions in the post-Soviet era surprised many, the significance of religion in political rhetoric, culture wars, conflict, ethnonational identification, and policy making is indisputable. The "power and presence of religious organizations, practice, and belief in public life in formerly socialist societies" necessitates its continued study.[18]

Throughout these essays there is a deep appreciation for Michael Bourdeaux and Keston College. Indeed, one is struck by the seeming inseparability of creator and creation. Together they posed fundamental questions about freedom of conscience in the modern world, questions that continue to provoke responses. It is not an exaggeration to say that scholarly interest in religion under Communism is a result of the tenacity of Bourdeaux and Keston College in bringing religious persecution to light. Their work revealed the daily pursuit of living truthfully, an effort that engaged a wide variety of people, from urban intellectuals in Prague to evangelical women in Siberia. Further, the organization of the Keston Archive provides a model for centering the oppressed rather than the powerful. The materials collected, particularly the unofficial samizdat, have led to wider conversations about freedom of expression, the meaning of borders, and marginalized populations. Finally, through the essays in this volume we get deeper insight into the influence of Bourdeaux and Keston College on the way the West thought about religion under Communism during the Cold War, especially as Keston staff drove home the correlation between religious liberty and human rights.

The original cause of Michael Bourdeaux and Keston College to give voice to the voiceless remains essential today. Stories of the persistence and adaptation of faith in the face of oppression continue to be told.[19] That mission of truth-speaking still exists, made richer and more imperative by our increasingly nuanced understanding of the past and those who preserve it. New directions in the study of religion and communism—on the transformation of religious practice, the negotiation of political and personal identities, the nature of antireligious campaigns and those who carried them out, the relationship of religion to empire and state-building, the entwinement of sacred and secular in everyday life, on concepts of modernity and knowledge production, and so on—build on foundations laid by Bourdeaux. It is our hope that this book brings together the past and future of the field in honor of a person whose work influenced both.

Notes

1. "Laureates: Michael Bourdeaux, Historian," Templeton Prize, https://www.templetonprize.org/laureate/michael-bourdeaux/ (accessed May 3, 2023).

2. Jane Ellis, *Georgi Vins and His Family: A Record in Letters, Poems, and Photographs* (Keston: Keston College, 1979); Jane Ellis, *The Russian Orthodox Church: A Contemporary History* (Bloomington: Indiana University Press, 1986); Jane Ellis, *The Russian Orthodox Church: Triumphalism and Defensiveness* (New York: St. Martin's Press, 1996); Michael Rowe and Michael Bourdeaux, eds., *May One Believe in Russia? Violations of Religious Liberty in the Soviet Union* (London: Darton, Longman, & Todd, 1980); Eugene B. Shirley, Jr., and Michael Rowe, eds., *Candle in the Wind: Religion in the Soviet Union* (Washington, DC: Ethics and Public Policy Center, 1989); Michael Rowe, *Russian Resurrection: Strength in Suffering: A History of Russia's Evangelical Church* (London: Marshall Pickering, 1994); Philip Walters and Jane Balengarth, eds., *Light through the Curtain: Poland, Czechoslovakia, USSR, Romania—Testaments of Faith and Courage* (Tring: Lion Publishing, 1985); Philip Walters, ed., *World Christianity: Eastern Europe* (Eastbourne: Monarch Publications, 1988); Marite Sapiets, trans.,

The Unknown Homeland (London: Mowbrays, 1978); Marite Sapiets, *True Witness: The Story of Seventh Day Adventists in the Soviet Union* (Keston: Keston College, 1990). Ellis also translated and edited several books, including Gleb Yakunin and Lev Regelson, *Letters from Moscow: Religion and Human Rights in the USSR* (San Francisco: Dakin, 1978).

3. Michael Bourdeaux, *One Word of Truth: The Cold War Memoir of Michael Bourdeaux and Keston College* (London: Darton, Longman, & Todd, 2019), ix.

4. Sonja Luehrmann, *Religion in Secular Archives: Soviet Atheism and Historical Knowledge* (Oxford: Oxford University Press, 2015), 4.

5. See, for example, "Acceptance Address by Mr. Michael Bourdeaux," May 15, 1984, Templeton Prize, https://www.templetonprize.org/laureate-sub/bourdeaux-acceptance-speech/.

6. Luehrmann, *Religion in Secular Archives*, 136, 137. Counter archives "challenge the state-centered perspective that pervades archival collections" by using collection and organizational principles that focus on groups other than the state. Luehrmann cites the work of P. Gabrielle Forman, Tony Ballantine, and Adalaine Holton for uses of the term (200n7).

7. For example, on Soviet binaries, see Victoria Smolkin-Rothrock, "The Ticket to the Soviet Soul: Science, Religion, and the Spiritual Crisis of Late Soviet Atheism," *Russian Review* 73, no. 2 (April 2014), 184; Juliane Fürst, *Stalin's Last Generation: Soviet Post-War Youth and the Emergence of Mature Socialism* (Oxford: Oxford University Press, 2012); and Frances L. Bernstein, "Envisioning Health in Revolutionary Russia: The Politics of Gender in Sexual Enlightenment Posters of the 1920s," *The Russian Review* 57, no. 2 (April 1998), 196, esp. note 26. On US binaries, see Irvin D. S. Winsboro and Michael Epple, "Religion, Culture, and the Cold War: Bishop Fulton J. Sheen and America's Anti-Communist Crusade of the 1950s," *The Historian* 71, no. 2 (2009): 209–33; and Dianne Kirby, "The Religious Cold War," in *The Oxford Handbook of the Cold War*, ed. Richard H. Immerman and Petra Goedde (Oxford: Oxford University Press, 2013), 540–64.

8. Julie deGraffenried and Zoe Knox, eds., *Voices of the Voiceless: Religion, Communism, and the Keston Archive* (Waco, TX: Baylor University Press, 2019).

9. See, for example, Paula Erizanu, "30 Years after the Collapse of the Soviet Union, Is It Time to Finally Stop Using the Term 'Post-Soviet'?," August 31, 2021, New East Digital Archive, https://www.new-east-archive.org/features/show/13044/30-years-independence-ussr-term-post-soviet-use.

10. James Kapaló and Tatiana Vagramenko, eds., *Hidden Galleries: Material Religion in the Secret Police Archives in Central and Eastern Europe* (Zürich: LIT VERLAG, 2021). In the introduction, Kapaló and Vagramenko connect the prewar attack by right-wing regimes on minority religious groups in the name of "nation" with the postwar persecution of religion by Communist regimes: "The citizens of [Romania, Hungary, the Republic of Moldova, Ukraine] shared a common experience of state repression and surveillance from the 1920s to the end of communism. Under both right-wing and left-wing dictatorships, religious difference or innovation became associated with enmity towards the state. . ." (8).

11. Luehrmann, *Religion in Secular Archives*, 36.

12. Catherine Wanner, "Introduction," in *State Secularism and Lived Religion in Soviet Russia and Ukraine*, ed. Catherine Wanner (Washington, DC: Woodrow Wilson Center Press and Oxford University Press, 2012), 2.

13. Ann Komaromi, *Soviet Samizdat: Imagining a New Society* (Ithaca, NY: Cornell University Press, 2022), 1.

14. This idea draws from Christina Kaier and Eric Naiman, eds., *Everyday Life in Early Soviet Russia: Taking the Revolution Inside* (Bloomington: Indiana University Press, 2006), 2.

15. This is a key theme of Josephine von Zitzewitz, *The Culture of Samizdat: Literature and Underground Networks in the Late Soviet Union* (London: Bloomsbury Academic, 2021).

16. On new conceptions of church-state relations, see Eren Tasar, *Soviet and Muslim: The Institutionalization of Islam in Central Asia* (Oxford: Oxford University Press, 2017). On new conceptions of believers, see Catherine Wanner, *Communities of the Converted: Ukrainians and Global Evangelism* (Ithaca, NY: Cornell University Press, 2007); and Emily B. Baran, *Dissent on the Margins: How Soviet Jehovah's Witnesses Defied Communism and Lived to Preach about It* (Oxford: Oxford University Press, 2014). On problematizing dissidence, see Barbara Martin, *Dissident Histories in the Soviet Union from De-Stalinization to Perestroika* (London: Bloomsbury Academic, 2019).

17. See "Encyclopaedia," Keston Institute, https://www.keston.org.uk/encyclopaedia, for more information and access to the five volumes of *Religiozno-obshchestvennaia zhizn' rossiiskikh regionov*.

18. Catherine Wanner and Mark D. Steinberg, "Introduction: Reclaiming the Sacred after Communism," in *Religion, Morality, and Community in Post-Soviet Societies*, ed. Wanner and Steinberg (Washington, DC: Woodrow Wilson Center Press and Indiana University Press, 2008), 2, 17.

19. Wallace Daniel, ed. and trans., *Women of the Catacombs: Memoirs of the Underground Orthodox Church in Stalin's Russia* (Ithaca, NY: Cornell University Press, 2021); Wallace Daniel, *Russia's Uncommon Prophet: Father Aleksandr Men and His Times* (DeKalb: Northern Illinois University Press, 2016); Emily B. Baran, *To Make a Village Soviet: Jehovah's Witnesses and the Transformation of a Postwar Ukrainian Borderland* (Montreal: McGill-Queen's University Press, 2022); Baran, *Dissent on the Margins*.

PART I

*Reflections on
Michael Bourdeaux
and Keston College*

Chapter 1

Keston College and Religious Samizdat

*Documenting the Persecution of Christians
in the Soviet Union*

Zoe Knox

The phenomenon of samizdat was largely unknown in the West, even to close observers of the Soviet Union, in 1969, the year Michael Bourdeaux cofounded the Centre for the Study of Religion and Communism (CSRC). *Samizdat* means "self-published" in Russian and refers to literature that was produced illegally and circulated clandestinely. Religious samizdat quickly became important to the CSRC's campaign to educate politicians and diplomats, human rights organizations, and faith groups about state-sanctioned religious persecution in the USSR and its satellite states. By the time the CSRC became Keston College in 1974, this material was central to its output.[1] Following Bourdeaux's lead, Keston personnel documented samizdat as reliable and robust testimony to the religious-rights violations committed by Communist regimes.

The imperative to document conditions for believers behind the Iron Curtain led to the collection, collation, analysis, translation, and preservation of religious samizdat, which began to reach the West in a trickle in the 1960s and soon became a flood. It was the essential research material for the experts at Keston College and for those who consulted its resources, either in person at its premises or through translations in one of its many publications. Keston's work had a worldwide audience and, through the Keston Archive, a lasting legacy.[2] The weight that

Keston researchers gave to samizdat determined the way they processed and analyzed it and continues to influence the way researchers encounter this material in the archive.[3]

Keston College was highly influential in the 1970s and 1980s.[4] Journalists from around the world contacted it for commentary on religious life under Communist regimes, and this led to press articles based on its research and radio and television interviews featuring its staff. In a dramatic example of its international profile, in April 1979 the US State Department called Bourdeaux "in the middle of the night" and summoned him to Manhattan to debrief the Russian Baptist pastor Georgii Vins.[5] The Soviet government had just expelled Vins as part of a Cold War prisoner exchange and spy swap. In 1983 British Prime Minister Margaret Thatcher handpicked Bourdeaux to participate in a meeting of Soviet specialists, leading to a "close relationship" between the two.[6] In 1984 he received worldwide acclaim when he was awarded the prestigious Templeton Prize. Keston was also well known to Soviet authorities: Bourdeaux was criticized in the Soviet press as early as 1969, Keston's publications were regularly attacked, and a Soviet double agent who defected to the West confirmed that Keston had been "near the top of the list of western organizations that the KGB had prioritized for attention."[7] It also attracted scholars from around the world. The list of staff and visitors at its first premises in London, then in the village of Keston in Kent, and finally in Oxford reads like a *Who's Who* of experts and activists in the field.[8]

The production of samizdat has long interested historians. This material was often produced under stifling constraints and risky conditions. In the absence of access to archives or the opportunity to conduct surveys and interviews, it revealed the questions and concerns, historical and contemporary, preoccupying Soviet intellectuals and dissidents. The existence of samizdat attested to the efforts of Soviet citizens to carve out a space for free expression in an environment profoundly hostile to nonconformist thought. In the 1960s, when samizdat began to reach the West, researchers focused firmly on its content. It was mined for information about life in the USSR that was hidden or obscured in official sources, which was all that was freely available. Over the next two decades, there were books analyzing the major themes in samizdat and anthologies that made this material accessible to Western audiences.[9]

The demise of the Soviet regime may have heralded the end of samizdat, but historians have continued to turn to it for insights into the past. Initially, they sought to bring underground publications into the light in order to categorize, quantify, and preserve this vast body of material.[10] This was encouraged and enabled by ambitious projects to catalogue and digitize these often-fragile texts.[11] As a result, we have a much clearer idea of the diversity of samizdat and the scale of the phenomenon. More recently, there has been a new direction in samizdat research, drawing on the literary scholar Ann Komaromi's observation that this material depended for its existence on "endorsement" by a readership, either within the USSR or abroad.[12] Josephine von Zitzewitz emphasized the need to look beyond authorship and content to analyze the readership, offering a corrective to the emphasis on the producers of samizdat rather than the consumers. The latter were of course far more numerous.[13] These scholars highlighted the importance of the informal networks underpinning samizdat and revealed the ways in which it was encountered by readers. However, thus far historians have not examined how samizdat reached Western organizations, the subsequent deliberations over what was made known and to whom, and to what end. By focusing on the role of Keston College in publicizing religious samizdat, we can start to comprehend the crucial role that such organizations played in how this material was contextualized and publicized and the function of samizdat in campaigns against the Soviet regime.

The provenance of samizdat material was often obscure and the content required explanation and analysis. Keston College played an important role in conveying its central concerns to Western audiences, expert and otherwise. Given Keston's wide reach and influence, it endorsed religious samizdat in important ways. Keston personnel passed their knowledge and interpretations along to activist organizations, research groups, and politicians and diplomats. Without its endorsement, much of this samizdat would not have come to light. Keston thus made a major contribution to how Soviet religious persecution was understood. It was instrumental in writing samizdat into the history of religion under communism, Soviet religious history, and religion and the Cold War.

This chapter will establish Michael Bourdeaux's pioneering role in using a wide range of official and unofficial material from the Soviet Union to construct informed and evidenced accounts of religious persecution. Within this broad evidential base, samizdat took center stage because it was understood by Bourdeaux to be authentic in a way that official material was not. By examining Keston College's publications, internal documents, and religious samizdat itself, this chapter will reconstruct its work. In doing so, it will demonstrate that Keston personnel marshalled evidence from samizdat for four purposes: to indict the Soviet regime for its rights violations, to expose (official) religious organizations' complicity in repression, to corroborate accounts of persecution, and to uncover stories of ordinary believers persecuted for their faith. The chapter will argue that through their approach to sources and evidence, Keston personnel were practitioners of a particular research methodology that was innovative in its use of evidence and that centered the voices of the oppressed.

Knowledge of Religious Persecution

The death of Joseph Stalin in March 1953 and the accession of Nikita Khrushchev led Soviet intellectuals to anticipate that the state would lift some constraints on free expression. While there was an initial "thaw," signaled chiefly by the mass release of prisoners from the gulag and later Khrushchev's renunciation of Stalin's cult of personality, the state ultimately retained its censorship functions, upheld an ideological monopoly, and maintained the mechanisms of repression. Michael Bourdeaux's arrival in Moscow in September 1959 as part of a year-long British Council exchange program coincided with a renewed assault on religion. The religious sphere was never part of destalinization, as Khrushchev's reforms are collectively known.[14] There was little understanding of this paradox in the West. In Bourdeaux's words, "That the situation for Christians may have been worsening after Stalin's death was never contemplated."[15]

The cycle of thaw and freeze—the expectation of greater freedom, followed by clampdowns and dashed hopes—encouraged dissent. It was spontaneous and atomized at first but became increasingly organized and coordinated, mostly by intellectuals who opposed aspects of the Communist Party's governance or, in some cases, rejected its legitimacy entirely.[16] Despite the flourishing of dissent, any overt displays of opposition to the regime were swiftly crushed and uncensored debate and discussion was forced underground. Even those participating in informal discussion groups took enormous risks in doing so. The written word therefore became a powerful tool for Soviet dissidents, so powerful that, as Komaromi observed, "Samizdat was the chief activity of Soviet dissidents."[17]

The term *samizdat* is a portmanteau derived from the Russian word *sam* ("self" or "by oneself") and *izdat* from *izdatel'stvo* ("publishing house"). Initially referring to poetry and fiction that departed from the socialist-realist cultural model imposed by the Soviet regime and copied throughout the Communist bloc, by the 1960s it was applied to a wide range of illegal material. One historian collated a long list of different types of samizdat that included everything from pornography and poetry to posters and court verdicts.[18] In its broadest usage, samizdat came to describe any text designed to evade Soviet censorship.

Bourdeaux's work was crucial to highlighting the value of samizdat to the study of Soviet society. In April 1971, for example, he participated in a roundtable discussion in London at which participants agreed that samizdat was an "important source of information and insights" that was not sufficiently recognized in the West. The title of one contemporary article that reported on the roundtable can be read as an appeal for the recognition of samizdat's value: "Samizdat: Primary Source Material in the Study of Current Soviet Affairs."[19] The event led to the foundation of the Samizdat Archive (Arkhiv Samizdata), which brought together the important material already held by Radio Free Europe.[20]

The aim of samizdat was to inform and engage like-minded individuals and later foreign audiences about conditions in the USSR, where free expression was curtailed alongside a range of other human rights. With Mikhail Gorbachev's introduction of the policy of *glasnost* ("openness, transparency"), it was no longer necessary to produce and distribute material clandestinely, thus marking the abrupt end of samizdat as a phenomenon. Underground publications were obsolete as a means of circulating information when the Kremlin next made sweeping efforts to silence dissenting voices. By the time Putin became president and especially since the antigovernment protests of 2011–13, the rise of the internet and use of mobile devices had revolutionized communications. They superseded physical publications and offered dissidents an option that had multiple advantages to printed material, chief among them immediacy and reach. In the 1960s, 1970s, and up to the mid-1980s, however, the existing technology meant that samizdat was the main source of information about religious life beyond the official churches. A significant proportion of samizdat addressed religious subjects.[21] As such, samizdat is central to the discussion of religious dissent in the late Soviet period. Much of this found its way to Keston College and into its collection.

Michael Bourdeaux's well-known encounter with two Orthodox women who had traveled to Moscow from a Ukrainian village to find a foreigner willing to smuggle out documents attesting to religious persecution, and thus to "be our voice and speak for us," marked the start of his life's mission. They appealed to Bourdeaux to make their story known in the West through firsthand accounts of their suffering. He wrote many times of this encounter, attributing it to the guiding hand of God.[22] On a more profane level, it defined his approach to reporting religious life. It was the experiences of ordinary believers that needed to be most urgently told, and in their own words.

The Paucity of the Existing Literature

Bourdeaux's curiosity about religion in the Soviet Union had been piqued during his exchange year. On his return to the United Kingdom, he looked for Western academic literature on the topic. He was frustrated to find only a handful of books published on religion since World War II and that these focused on church-state relations. For decades, the definitive text was Paul B. Anderson's *People, Church and State in Modern Russia* (1944). Intended as a study of the "interplay" between people, church, and state, there was simply no material to offer insights into the first element of that tripartite relationship—the people. Anderson drew on official church statements, Lenin's essays on religion, Stalin's party history, a little on antireligious publications such as *Bezbozhnik* (The Godless), and the *Zhurnal Moskovskoi Patriarkhii* (Journal of the Moscow Patriarchate).[23] William Stroyen's *Communist Russia and the Russian Orthodox Church, 1943–1962*, published in 1967, likewise drew on Soviet press reports, antireligious literature, and the *Zhurnal Moskovskoi Patriarkhii*. He argued that at the very same time that the Moscow Patriarchate was expanding its international profile, principally through membership in the World Council of Churches, which it joined in 1961, its domestic presence was contracting.[24] This chimed with Bourdeaux's own observations.[25]

There was one exception to the focus on church-state relations—namely, *Religion in the Soviet Union* (1961) by Walter Kolarz. In his preface, Kolarz wrote that it was written for all those "anxious to become nearer the truth."[26] In addition to the usual suite of sources, he drew on material written by believers in the West about their co-religionists in the USSR. He noted that although this material was not widely read outside of these religious communities, it brought a new dimension to the subject and was essential given the paucity of firsthand accounts. For example, his book included the first analysis of Soviet Jehovah's

Witnesses in Western scholarship. He based the discussion on two sources: an overview of the history of Witnesses and the Watch Tower Society's own material. Kolarz also drew on Baptist samizdat, which was just reaching the West when his book was published (although he did not use the term *samizdat*).[27] Kolarz thus consulted a wider range of sources than any other scholar at the time. Bourdeaux acknowledged the influence of *Religion in the Soviet Union* on his early work, writing in his memoir that it "provided a kind of framework for me in the planning and organization of my own first book."[28]

One assessment of Bourdeaux's first book, *Opium of the People: The Christian Religion in the USSR* (1965), particularly rankled him. The reviewer, Paul Oestreicher, assessed it as "*primarily* an intensely subjective book."[29] In his memoir Bourdeaux noted that it could hardly have been otherwise given how little information on Soviet religious life was available. *Opium of the People* had to draw heavily on his own experiences and observations.[30] Later in his life he told an interviewer that what he knew had been learned "not through book knowledge" but "with my own two feet."[31] During his early visits to the USSR, he learned about religious life from visiting churches and speaking to believers.

Bourdeaux realized that the impressions he gained on the ground needed to be supplemented with evidence. A chapter of his memoir titled "Seeking a Way Forward" recounted a conscious and exhaustive search for an approach or methodology to guide his own work. After despairing of the rarity of reliable, informed studies of religious life, Bourdeaux found much to admire in Nikita Struve's *Les chrétiens en URSS* (1963), published as *Christians in Contemporary Russia* in 1967.[32] Struve was based in Paris and used émigré testimony to inform his work. Alongside the usual sources, he drew on unofficial material. The footnotes refer to an "account given by eyewitness" and "confidential information." Some claims were "confirmed by Soviet citizens" and some sources were identified as "in circulation."[33] Struve's sources were not transparent or traceable, and there is no indication that he crosschecked his information, but the way he valued unofficial material and incorporated it into his scholarship laid the groundwork for Bourdeaux's approach. The chapter in Bourdeaux's memoir ends on a triumphant note: his search for how to approach the study of religious life was finally over with his discovery of Struve's work. He wrote: "Here was my model."[34]

There were a number of English-language periodicals that distributed news on religion in the Soviet Union. *Religion in Communist-Dominated*

Areas,[35] *Religious Digest*,[36] *Religion and Church in the Communist Orbit*, and *Research Materials on Religion in Eastern Europe*[37] all published translations of articles in newspapers and periodicals from the Soviet bloc. Only one of them had an explicit focus on religious institutions—namely, *Research Materials on Religion in Eastern Europe*, which was produced by the Centre de Recherches et d'Etude des Institutions Religieuses.[38] Given the sources these periodicals drew on, religious institutions were a central subject for all of them. When reporting on the Soviet Union, they relied on newspapers from across the country (e.g., *Komsomol'skaia Pravda*, *Sovetskaia Moldaviia*), official religious publications (e.g., *Journal of the Moscow Patriarchate*), and atheist periodicals (e.g., *Liudina i svit*, *Nauka i religiia*). Some of the periodicals printed complete articles or extracts from such publications with little or no commentary and others produced summaries. *Religion and Church in the Communist Orbit* featured all three. *Religious Digest* provided supplementary information about places or persons mentioned in the text and analysis that pointed to the gulf between official rhetoric and the reality.[39]

These periodicals had a very similar approach: even when there was some analysis, the scope was limited. In *Religion in Communist-Dominated Areas*, the editor Paul B. Anderson added editorial notes that contextualized the articles, commented on their tenor, or explained their significance. For instance, he wrote that the "Convincing Facts" feature in the antireligious journal *Nauka i religiia* contained "gossipy material" and pointed out the importance of a new statute on parish life in the translation of an article from the *Journal of the Moscow Patriarchate*.[40] However, in the early 1960s these periodicals mostly offered readers straightforward translations from official publications.

The limited information on Soviet religious life available in the West and the concomitant lack of insight into the experiences of ordinary believers proved a frustration for Bourdeaux. He worked for William Fletcher for some years producing summaries of Soviet press articles on religion for the Centre de Recherches. Initially, Fletcher and Bourdeaux seemed similarly committed to researching Soviet religious life. However, to the latter's dismay and discomfort, Fletcher would not consider translating samizdat.[41] Fletcher had already dismissed the importance of this material. In his 1965 book *A Study in Survival* he outlined the resources underpinning his research and wrote: "The very few relatively trustworthy materials which have been smuggled out and the small store of captured documents are not in themselves sufficient to delineate the broad picture of religion in the USSR."[42] In this sentence, he dismissed samizdat in terms of quantity and quality. Fletcher's failure to appreciate the value of religious samizdat puzzled and disappointed Bourdeaux. It had grown significantly in volume and was reaching Western researchers from an increasingly wide range of religious communities. By the time Fletcher terminated Bourdeaux's employment in 1969, the latter was convinced of the value of samizdat and determined to build his own research center to foreground its revelations.[43]

The Management of Samizdat

The centrality of samizdat to Keston College's work coupled with its growing volume necessitated careful management. Michael Bourdeaux was intent on developing a systematic approach to this material. The value of samizdat as evidence was in keeping with the view that empirical historians have of primary sources. The treatment of its content as urgent news, however, meant that Keston took a unique approach. Religious samizdat fed directly into Keston's research and advocacy and informed a range of groups that referred to its material. Keston developed a new methodology for the management of samizdat, one that shaped how researchers encountered the material during the Cold War and today.

The way in which Bourdeaux described his profession offers an insight into how he conceived of his mission and why he highlighted samizdat. He studied Russian and theology but identified himself as "a modern historian."[44] His many publications addressed developments contemporary to the time of the writing and as immediate as possible. The final chapter of *Opium of the People*, titled "New Perspectives," referred to "very recent news" and documents that had "just been released as this book goes to press."[45] It emphasized that the material was fresh from the field and it revealed what was happening on the ground in a dynamic and evolving context. The epilogue of his third book, *Patriarch and Prophets: Persecution of the Russian Orthodox Church Today*, published in 1969, presented selected samizdat documents received in 1968.[46] The final word in the book's title points to its currency. A sense of urgency meant that the firsthand accounts that reached Keston were swiftly and thoroughly mined by its personnel for any light they shed on conditions for believers in different countries, changes in religious policy, the experiences of individual believers, or developments within religious communities. Bourdeaux's memoir recounts his deliberate effort to write history even as he reported on the present.

Bourdeaux also expected Keston's staff to look for evidence of the vibrancy of religious life and the "spiritual rebirth" of the people across the region. Indeed, this was central to the mission of its academic journal, *Religion in Communist Lands*, first published in 1973 and today known as *Religion, State & Society*.[47] Evidence of a religious revival was reported in triumphalist tones and regarded as a profound and righteous challenge to the ideological monopoly of Communist regimes. The anthropologist and historian Sonja Luehrmann suggested that Keston's proclivity to highlight information that pointed to a resurgence of spiritual life may have exaggerated the degree to which Soviet citizens were turning to religion in the Brezhnev era. She stopped short of calling this a distortion but did indicate that Keston's agenda might have given a mistaken impression of a religious revival. The influence of Keston's analysis meant its interpretations had wide-ranging implications.[48]

As Keston College's profile rose in the 1970s, more and more material was sent to it from across the Soviet bloc. Keston personnel developed guidelines for members of the Research Department on how staff should read, process, and file it.[49] A 1977 document that listed which staff members had responsibility for dealing with what type of sources reveals the centrality of samizdat to Keston's work. Of the nine different types of information received from Western and Eastern European sources processed by more than a dozen researchers, samizdat was analyzed by Bourdeaux, Keston's director.[50] When samizdat documents or publications first arrived, they were passed to Jane Ellis, head of the Research Department, to check if the item was already held. If not, it was passed to a reader who recorded basic information on a "samizdat processing checklist." The readers were instructed to skim the source, paying particular attention to any "significant new information." There was one process to follow if it contained "important news which should be published at once" and another if it did not.[51] If there was new or important information, a summary was sent to Peter Reddaway, one of Keston's cofounders and an expert on Soviet dissent, and named contacts at Amnesty International, the BBC, and Radio Liberty.[52]

The same guidelines included details on the safe storage of samizdat: it was not to be removed from Keston premises and had to be locked in fireproof cabinets overnight and on weekends. If important, the source would be translated; if not, an English synopsis would be produced. Samizdat that was assessed as neither important nor urgent was to be given a reference number and sorted according to denomination, following Keston's idiosyncratic filing and archival system. The processing guidelines also contain further instructions for cross-referencing any new information with documentation that Keston already held, such as details of individuals who might be included on Keston's Christian prisoners list.[53] The document does not mention how to treat nontextual material, such as photographs and artifacts, although Keston did receive plenty of it, or unverifiable or questionable samizdat.[54] Keston gave precedence to, and assumed the authenticity of, written sources.

It was Keston's aim to circulate knowledge as widely as possible. The guidelines recorded who was alerted to new information gleaned from incoming sources and through what media. The samizdat destined for urgent publication was analyzed and reproduced in Keston publications. One of the main outlets was *Religion in Communist Lands*. The other regular publications included *Keston News Service* (*KNS*), a fortnightly newsletter that aimed to publish "up-to-the-minute information" for the benefit of the press, journalists, the BBC, and international press agencies.[55] It was akin to a compilation of press releases. Historian Mark Hurst observed that the hasty production and amateur aesthetics of *KNS* mimicked the look and feel of samizdat.[56] Bourdeaux himself made the comparison; in his editorial in the first issue he wrote: "To be quick and topical, this must be a *samizdat* enterprise."[57] This was an effort to get across the urgent and honest nature of the accounts therein; in other words, an effort to convey truthfulness. Keston produced two periodicals designed for a more general readership, *The Right to Believe* and *Frontier*. In addition, it supported the publication of books by Keston's personnel and associates. These books highlighted the experiences of particular Christian churches (e.g., *True Witness: The Story of Seventh Day Adventists in the Soviet Union*), nations (e.g., *Land of Crosses: Struggle for Religious Freedom in Lithuania, 1939–78*), or individual cases (e.g., *Aida of Leningrad: The Story of Aida Skripnikova*), discussed below.[58] The authors largely based their analysis on the samizdat obtained by Keston.

Samizdat that did not contain new and important information still had a range of "targets," to use the terminology in the processing guidance. The targets were the press, missions, radio stations, churches and councils of churches, human rights organizations, "the east,"[59] the general public, supporters, and academics. Although Bourdeaux was consistently disappointed by the level of coverage that Keston's work was given by the Western media, its experts and evidence did underpin a great deal of reporting on religious life in the region, in the United Kingdom especially but also across Western Europe. Alyona Kojevnikov, an information officer at Keston, reflected on the success of Keston's efforts to portray itself as impartial, balanced, and evidence-based. In 2019 she wrote: "It was accepted in media circles that 'if it comes from Keston College, it can be used without further checking'—a true accolade from the hard-bitten journalists of Reuters, United Press International, Associated Press and so on."[60] The presentation of samizdat as fundamentally truthful had repercussions beyond the interpretation and analysis presented in Keston's own publications.

Historians have underestimated how Keston's approach to samizdat was crucial to the knowledge that news agencies, academic experts, policy makers, and others accessed about religious life under communism. An examination of Keston's uses of samizdat material demonstrates how this methodology influenced Western understandings of the Soviet regime in the late stages of the Cold War.

The Uses of Religious Samizdat

Keston College utilized samizdat in its campaign against religious persecution in four main ways. First, it used samizdat to indict the Soviet regime for violations of freedom of conscience. Keston personnel combed through material for evidence that Communist authorities persecuted, harassed, and discriminated against religious leaders, faith communities, and individual believers. The aim was to provide as much detail as possible on where and when this took place, who was targeted, and on what pretext. For example, the booklet *Religious Prisoners in the USSR: A Study by Keston College* (1985) was one in a series of prisoner lists. It provided profiles of inmates from a range of faith groups, from the Armenian Apostolic Church and Jews to Tolstoyans and Hare Krishnas. It outlined the alleged crimes for which believers were most commonly arrested and provided profiles of prisoners, listing their year of birth, date of arrest, the criminal code under which they were convicted, sentence, place of incarceration, and so on. The booklet also revealed the conditions endured by the prisoners by reproducing their testimonies. It included lengthy extracts from inmates' letters to family members and other firsthand accounts of their treatment and conveyed their appreciation of Western attention to their plight.[61] The details in the prisoner profiles were collated from a wide range of sources, official and unofficial. Taken together, this disparate material offered a convincing case of the regime's systematic persecution of religious believers of all stripes.

A recurring theme in Keston's publications was that the Soviet regime failed to comply with its own constitutional guarantees of freedom of conscience. This legal argument was a common one in the broader dissident movement. The socialist dissident Roy Medvedev acknowledged this when he described one of the four main groups of dissidents as "legalists" who objected to the regime on the basis of law.[62] An exemplar of this approach was the samizdat periodical *Chronicle of Current Events*, which first appeared in 1968. Every issue began with Article 19 of the 1948 Universal Declaration of Human Rights, which upholds the right to freedom of opinion and expression. The *Chronicle* documented cases in which the Soviet state violated that right. These legal arguments gained greater traction with the signing of the Helsinki Accords in 1975, which obliged the Soviet Union to uphold international human rights norms.

The influence of legalist arguments was evident in Bourdeaux's work. He meticulously documented the gulf between the Soviet regime's guarantees of freedom of conscience and the reality on the ground, drawing on Soviet law and on samizdat. *Patriarch and Prophets*, for example, opened by outlining the legal restrictions on believers.[63] The remainder of the book examined the various ways that the state violated the basic rights of Orthodox clergy, monks and nuns, and laity. A chapter titled "The Legal Dimension" reproduced the famous *Declaration (Zaiavlenie)* sent by two Orthodox priests, Nikolai Eshliman and Gleb Yakunin, to the Chairman of the Supreme Soviet, N. V. Podgorny, in December 1965. The *Declaration* detailed the illegality of the measures enforced by the Council for the Affairs of the Russian Orthodox Church (CAROC),[64] the government agency that oversaw religious life. Eshliman and Yakunin observed: "These actions have flagrantly violated the principle of socialist law and the basic legislative requirements of the Soviet government determining the relations of the Soviet state to the church . . ." Far from the mediatory body it was intended to be, CAROC had become "an organ of unofficial and illegal control over the Moscow Patriarchate." They outlined the ways in which CAROC interfered in the internal life of the Orthodox Church, rendering its leadership thoroughly submissive to the atheist state.[65] Although the *Declaration* was reproduced in *Patriarch and Prophets* without commentary, in the footnotes, Bourdeaux pointed the reader to other documents that supported the priests' charges, cross-referencing them with other samizdat materials for corroboration and verification.[66]

By basing their protest on legal arguments, Eshliman, Yakunin, and other Soviet dissidents employed the regime's own terms of reference and thus repeated and respected the language of the oppressor. More-over, by addressing the *Declaration* to Podgorny, the authors appealed to the state itself. In an insightful article, anthropologist Serguei Oushakine analyzes the futility of any protest that proceeds within the constraints of the regime's discursive framework. In the samizdat they produced, "the dissidents' resistance expressed itself in amplification of the discourse of the dominant, rather than in reversal of it."[67] The "terrifying mimicry of samizdat"—the adoption of the regime's own language—cast the dissidents into obscurity once the language that upheld that system became redundant. This, Oushakine explained, is why Soviet dissidents had no presence in post-Soviet public discourse.[68] This argument might be applied to Keston College to explain the drop in its profile after the demise of Soviet-style communism. By fore-grounding the value, and the "truth," of religious samizdat centered on socialist legality, Keston operated within the framework of the oppressive system. Like dissidents whose case rested on Soviet law, Keston had limited relevance once the USSR collapsed.

Second, Keston College used samizdat to expose the collaboration of the leaders of registered (and therefore officially recognized) religious institutions with the Soviet regime. This was evident in official statements issued by such collaborating institutions or published in the Soviet press, which confirmed what the regime permitted religious leaders to do and say and (by omission) revealed what it did not permit. Bourdeaux acknowledged the possibility that individuals in the Moscow Patriarchate may have negotiated "behind the scenes" on behalf of Orthodox believers but the documentation was too scanty to draw any firm conclusions.[69] Unofficial religious groups were either denied registration by the state or refused to apply for official recognition on the grounds that this would acknowledge and uphold the authority of the atheist regime to determine the contours of religious life. By turning to unofficial sources, Keston allowed the voices of those who were forced to operate underground to be amplified.

The case of Soviet Baptists illustrated this most starkly. The official Soviet Protestant organization was the All-Union Council of Evangelical Christians-Baptists (AUCECB), which incorporated four different denominations: Baptists, Pentecostals, Evangelical Christians, and Mennonites. The Soviet government merged them under one administrative umbrella in 1945, ostensibly for administrative purposes. The AUCECB was dogged by schism from its inception, but in August 1961 a significant split emerged that divided Soviet Baptists into two factions, registered and unregistered. Georgii Vins was one of the leaders of the latter faction. It comprised Baptist communities that rejected the concessions and compromises required for registration with the state.[70] Some of the dissenters became known as the *initsiativniki*, so called because they initiated demands that their right to freedom of conscience be respected. They established an underground periodical, *Bratskii Listok* (Fraternal Leaflet), the answer to the official *Bratskii Vestnik* (Fraternal Chronicle). On its pages they expressed opposition to the AUCECB, calling its leaders traitors and apostates for cooperating with the regime and accepting constraints on religious life. They also recounted the persecution of Soviet Baptists. In response, the AUCECB condemned the *initsiativniki* as politically motivated. AUCECB leaders pointed to a flourishing Evangelical Baptist religious life within the USSR and Soviet Baptist connections with the global ecumenical community to counter these claims. AUCECB leaders were particularly concerned that their defense of Soviet religious policy reached an international audience.[71]

The emergence of this coordinated opposition was the central theme of Bourdeaux's second book, *Religious Ferment in Russia: Protestant Opposition to Soviet Religious Policy* (1968). The Baptists started systematically sending material to Keston College. Bourdeaux reproduced these documents in translation, accompanied by commentary that connected this textual material to the broader context. Keston also reproduced material from the unregistered Baptists in its periodicals, giving the campaign against the collaboration of the AUCECB with the Soviet regime widespread publicity.

Bourdeaux identified the publications by unofficial Baptists as the earliest organized religious opposition to the regime (see chapter 6). It certainly circulated the best-produced samizdat, printed at a time when most of it was handwritten or typewritten.[72] The Baptists had their own printing presses, hidden in subterranean spaces and secret rooms, and while they were not the only religious community in the USSR to have sophisticated mechanisms for production, wide distribution networks, and a high degree of coordination, as research on Jehovah's Witnesses has shown,[73] they were the best known. This is partly because they established the channels to smuggle literature out of the country and partly because their co-religionists in the West publicized their struggles. Western Protestant groups like Underground Evangelism and the Billy Graham Evangelistic Association lobbied on behalf of Soviet Protestants, using a wide range of methods. Unlike Keston, their campaigns were often characterized by anticommunist rhetoric, which wedded them to Cold War political postures. In contrast, Keston was always careful to portray its work as balanced and nonpartisan, even apolitical. Bourdeaux attributed the obscuration of the facts of religious life in the USSR to political agendas, both anti- and pro-communist.[74] He even went so far as to avoid the word "dissidents," preferring "democrats."[75] Keston criticized the Soviet regime not for its ideological foundations but for the restrictions, legal and extralegal, that it imposed on religious life. By amplifying the voices of believers from unregistered groups, as expressed in samizdat, Keston wanted the evidence to speak for itself.

Third, Keston used samizdat to supplement official accounts of Soviet religious life. Michael Bourdeaux's frustration with William Fletcher arose from his conviction that religious samizdat was revealing in its own right but became especially valuable when the information therein was cross-referenced with other types of sources.[76] Samizdat fleshed out instances of religious persecution about which Keston could obtain only scanty details through other channels.

It is worth recalling how little Western observers knew before samizdat started to trickle out of the USSR. This can be gauged from Walter Kolarz's discussion of a report published by the Moscow Patriarchate on the "Conference in Defense of Peace of All Churches and Religious Associations in the USSR," held in May 1952 in the Trinity-Sergius Lavra, Russia's most famous monastery. The report listed the conference delegates. Kolarz observed that the list did not include "all" churches and religious organizations. The fact that the report "greatly enhanced our knowledge" of the recognized religious organizations speaks to the limited information that Western observers could obtain. Kolarz wrote that the report also "showed the limits of Soviet religious tolerance." He could extrapolate from it which groups had local but not central representation and which ones were forced into a clandestine existence because they could not or would not register.[77] These included the Jewish Communities of Moscow and Kiev, for example, but not other official Jewish groups. Until the 1960s, when samizdat began to regularly reach the West, scholars like Kolarz had to glean much from little. Bourdeaux could see the potential of cross-checking religious samizdat with material produced by the official churches, information from state agencies, press reports, and antireligious propaganda—the sources on which scholars had previously almost exclusively relied.[78]

The samizdat periodical *Chronicle of the Catholic Church of Lithuania*, which first appeared in 1972, largely informed Keston's reporting on the situation for Lithuanian Catholics. Bourdeaux found much to admire in the *Chronicle*'s methodology, comparing it favorably to two samizdat periodicals, one secular and the other religious, that were much better known to Western observers: "One notable feature of the Soviet *samizdat* journals on human rights and religious liberty is their faithfulness to the facts. A church newspaper published in Britain or America would find it hard to vie with the record consistently achieved by the *Chronicle of Current Events* or the *Bulletin* of the Council of Baptist Prisoners' Relatives. The achievement of the *Chronicle of the Lithuanian Catholic Church* is on this level. For this there must be careful coordination with a network of informants and [the] tightest editorial control."[79] The names of the editors of the *Chronicle of the Catholic Church* had to be obscured for their own safety, making the circulation of regular, reliable, and detailed information about Lithuanian Catholic life even more impressive.

The information provided in the *Chronicle* was supplemented by material from various quarters, including an extraordinary samizdat artifact that reached Keston College in 1972: the "Memorandum of the Lithuanian Catholic Church." The Memorandum was in fact a petition to Leonid Brezhnev from "the Catholics of Lithuania" written in December 1971. The petition noted that although there was a widespread desire for peace after World War II, this was not possible since "the foundation of lasting peace is justice and respect for human rights. And so, we, the Catholics of Lithuania, are deeply disturbed by the violation of these rights, since the believers of our nation are still deprived of freedom of conscience, and the Church is subject to persecution." It outlined the state's control over religious life, the discrimination against ordinary Catholics, and the exile of bishops and incarceration of priests.[80] Petitioners signed their names below the typewritten text. There were more than one hundred copies of the Memorandum in circulation, bearing over 17,000 signatures, which the Keston researcher Xenia Dennen estimated was only a quarter of the number that were originally circulated. The others had been seized by the KGB.[81] The copies in Keston's possession were originally taken by a Lithuanian religious activist to Moscow to present to Brezhnev. The carrier's chance encounter with a British diplomat led to the Memorandum's journey out of the USSR in a diplomatic bag, a remarkably conventional way of moving sensitive material from east to west given other methods of samizdat transmission. The details of the petition were widely circulated by Keston. It was evidence of the vibrancy of Roman Catholicism and the defiance of Catholics in the face of longstanding efforts by Soviet authorities to subdue and contain the church within the Lithuanian Catholic enclave. These very different samizdat—the *Chronicle* and the petition—were used to publicize the challenges posed to Lithuanian Catholic life by Communist authorities despite assurances of religious freedom.

Fourth, Keston used samizdat to tell the stories of individual believers. In the Soviet context, even seemingly innocuous acts like reading children a bible story could be construed by the state as a challenge to its authority. Keston's focus on ordinary believers overturned the narrative that dissent in the Soviet Union was part of an enduring conflict between those in power and the Russian intelligentsia.[82] The majority of religious samizdat was written by laypeople. They were forced into dissent by a party-state apparatus that insisted that activities that in other contexts might be regarded as no more than ordinary religious practices were deviant, marginal, and in some cases criminal.

Samizdat was important for piecing together why particular believers were targeted, the sentence, where they were confined, and their treatment. This information allowed Keston to identify patterns or shifts in the state's approach to certain communities or in particular regions. The proportion of persecuted believers Keston was aware of will never be known. It is clear that at a time when there was very little information available in the West about the experiences of ordinary Soviet citizens, Keston highlighted cases about which it obtained robust, expansive, or striking evidence. It publicized these through the lists of prisoners of conscience published fortnightly in *KNS* and in publications such as *Religious Prisoners in the USSR*. It also produced more extended examinations of individual cases. The diverse evidence base underpinning Keston's files on individual prisoners of conscience led Sonja Luehrmann to liken them to Soviet police files on suspects.[83]

The case of Aida Skripnikova, a young Baptist woman, was well known to Western Christians following her first trial in 1961 that led to her incarceration in a psychiatric hospital. Skripnikova's crime was distributing postcards with religious themes on Nevsky Prospekt, Leningrad's major thoroughfare. The details of Skripnikova's second trial, which took place from July 11 to 15, 1968, might have been largely unknown were it not for eleven strips of fabric that eventually reached Michael Bourdeaux. These recorded in remarkable detail the courtroom exchanges between judge, procurator, lawyer, character witnesses, and Aida herself. Someone present at the trial clandestinely transcribed the proceedings onto a cut up bedsheet. A sympathizer later wrapped the strips around their torso and smuggled them over the border into Finland. Bourdeaux eventually received them in 1969.[84] The source is unusual not only because of its physical form but also in the level of detail it offered on the court proceedings.

Keston College publicized Skripnikova's trial immediately. Bourdeaux and Xenia Howard-Johnston (later Dennen) coedited the short book *Aida of Leningrad*, published in 1972. It featured a translation of the transcript in toto alongside essays on the broader context against which Skripnikova's trial had taken place and her biography, beliefs, and activism.[85] The effort to make individual cases widely known was successful in Skripnikova's case, possibly because as a young, single woman, she was perceived as especially vulnerable. Keston's efforts led to a grassroots letter-writing campaign among British Christians. In letters to Members of Parliament and the Prime Minister, they highlighted Skripnikova's plight and asked that her treatment, and that of Soviet believers more broadly, be raised with their Soviet counterparts.[86] The concrete effect of this specific campaign is difficult to pinpoint, but overall, Keston's use of samizdat was impactful because it highlighted the severe challenges encountered by ordinary believers, underground religious communities, and dissenting religious leaders when exercising basic religious rights and offered evidence that supplemented (and often countered) the official narrative, which was often all that was otherwise available. Keston College was a small research center that had a big impact on the West's knowledge and understanding of religious life under Soviet regimes, secured through its emphasis on the rich evidential base provided by samizdat.

Michael Bourdeaux and his Keston College colleagues developed a particular research methodology in their campaign to highlight religious persecution under Communist regimes. Sonja Luehrmann described Keston as "an important switchboard through which knowledge about Soviet religion travelled westward during the Cold War."[87] In his memoir, Peter Reddaway wrote that it "simply gathered, digested, and circulated the facts to anyone interested."[88] Keston had greater import than merely as a conduit for the transmission of information, as in Luehrmann's interpretation, or as a clearinghouse for "the facts," as Reddaway recalled. The scholarship on samizdat has underestimated the significance of Keston's role in placing this material at the center of research into life under communism. In its pioneering use of religious samizdat, Keston shaped the way this material was encountered, approached, contextualized, and ultimately understood by Western analysts of religion and observers of the USSR.

By drawing on a range of material in the Keston Archive, Keston's own books and periodicals, and contemporaneous publications on religion under communism, this chapter has shown that Keston's researchers foregrounded samizdat. Their use of samizdat material reveals an idealization, even romanticization, of its perceived basic essence—namely, that it was truthful.[89] The notion of "truth" was central to Bourdeaux's work and a quality he valued above all else. Despite the fact that production, distribution, and consumption networks were often opaque or even obscured, samizdat was regarded as authentic in a way that documents emanating from the official religious organizations, Soviet authorities, and antireligious and atheist experts were not.[90] Although these sources of information could be illuminating, it was by corroborating and cross-checking with samizdat that they became usable. Until Bourdeaux began making a case for it, Western Sovietologists had largely ignored the grassroots accounts of religious life that were breaching the Cold War divide. Bourdeaux insisted on their uses even before that trickle became a flood. As a result of this emphasis, Keston was able to tell the stories of ordinary believers. This generated increased interest in samizdat as a source until it became a mainstay of research on religious life under Communist regimes.

This essay has argued that Keston utilized samizdat for four main purposes. First, it was used to indict Soviet authorities on legal grounds. Even before the Helsinki Accords of 1975 enshrined human rights in international law, Bourdeaux and Keston personnel emphasized the disjuncture between the regime's commitment to human rights and fundamental freedoms and its treatment of religious institutions, faith communities, and individual believers. In 1968, Bourdeaux wrote that letters by the Orthodox priests Eshliman and Yakunin were "undoubtedly the most significant texts on church-state relations to come out of the Soviet Union since the Revolution."[91] Their letters, along with innumerable other samizdat accounts, illustrated the stark divide between the state's legal provisions and the reality for believers. Second, samizdat was used to expose the collaboration between officially recognized religious institutions and the Communist regime. This was perhaps the most controversial aspect of Keston's work, since many defended these religious leaders' efforts to ensure the survival of their institutions.[92] Without compromise, many more churches would have been forced underground—a particular challenge for sacramental faiths like Russian Orthodoxy. Third, samizdat was cross-referenced with other sources to highlight cases of religious persecution, giving it an evidential value beyond its immediate content and concerns. It could provide additional detail on cases in which very little was otherwise known. Finally, samizdat was used to uncover and document cases that might otherwise have been overlooked or may have vanished completely. The aim was to highlight physical and spiritual suffering and, for those incarcerated in labor camps, prisons, or psychiatric institutions, to generate support from Western politicians, diplomats, and the public for their release. In some cases it worked, as the expulsion of Vins demonstrated.

To return to Komaromi's insight, if samizdat was not endorsed—in other words, valued enough to be passed on, recommended, smuggled out of the country, or translated—it largely sank without trace.[93] By endorsing religious samizdat, Keston College ensured that this material was known in the West. Without its endorsement, much of it would have disappeared.

Bourdeaux's memoir records his disappointment and frustration that his research and Keston's broader output did not receive greater attention. It is perhaps the afterlife of Keston's work that will prove most significant, an irony given that Bourdeaux put great store in its immediate relevance. Keston preserved samizdat that even its authors feared might never see the light of day. Bourdeaux describes Georgii Vins's emotion upon visiting Keston and viewing the material: "He physically shed tears when [he] saw his own original signature and those of his trusted friends on some of the documents in our possession. He had seen them many years before, between his two periods of imprisonment, but he thought all copies had been confiscated by the KGB. Now here they were again and he could hold them in his hands."[94] The preservation of parts of the Lithuanian Catholic Memorandum was another example, although scholars visiting the Keston Archive can only access a facsimile: the originals were returned to the Lithuanian Church and are held by the Martynas Mažvydas National Library of Lithuania. Bourdeaux and his colleagues' emphasis on collecting and utilizing unofficial accounts and amplifying the voices of believers has led to a unique collection of samizdat. Although it has been suggested that the journal *Religion, State & Society* was "perhaps one of Keston's greatest academic legacies,"[95] this honor should surely be reserved for the Keston Archive, now located at Baylor University. The samizdat holdings—which make up the majority of the collection—need to be considered by researchers with Keston's pioneering approach to samizdat in mind.

Notes

The author is grateful to Larisa Seago for help with accessing a wide range of sources in the Keston Archive at Baylor University in Waco, Texas. The essay has benefited from comments and questions from audiences at presentations at The Association for Slavic, East European, and Eurasian Studies 2022 convention in Chicago and the British Association for Slavonic and East European Studies 2023 annual conference in Glasgow, as well as expert feedback from the editors of this volume and from Mark Hurst.

1. For the sake of simplicity, the CSRC will be referred to as "Keston" or "Keston College" throughout.

2. In addition to other holdings, the archive has more than four thousand samizdat items from Communist countries. It is the world's largest collection of religion-related samizdat. See Kathy Hillman and Larisa Seago, "Alive and Available," *Christian Librarian*, no. 64 (2014), 40.

3. Sonja Luehrmann, *Religion in Secular Archives: Soviet Atheism and Historical Knowledge* (Oxford: Oxford University Press, 2014), 134–61.

4. Bourdeaux wrote that it was the only organization in the Anglophone world "to study and document all aspects of religious life (both Christian and non-Christian) in those countries which are governed by Communist or Marxist regimes." Michael Bourdeaux, *Land of Crosses: Struggle for Religious Freedom in Lithuania, 1939–78* (Chulmleigh: Augustine, 1979), xv.

5. Michael Bourdeaux, *One Word of Truth: The Cold War Memoir of Michael Bourdeaux and Keston College* (London: Darton, Longman and Todd, 2019), 205–6.

6. Bourdeaux, *One Word of Truth*, 162.

7. Quote taken from Knox interview. Bourdeaux, *One Word of Truth*, 118–19; Bourdeaux, "Soviet Attacks on CSRC," *Keston College News Service*, no. 1 (trial number), May 17, 1974, 8–9; Zoe Knox, "An Interview with Philip Walters for *Religion, State & Society*," *Religion, State & Society* 50, no. 1 (2022), 124. See also Xenia Dennen, "The KGB's 'Bête Noire'," London, Gresham College Lecture, May 23, 2013, https://www.gresham.ac.uk/lectures-and-events/the-kgbs-bte-noire.

8. See, for example, the recollections of an American researcher who spent a month at Keston in 1983: Mark R. Elliott, "In Lieu of a Review: Reminiscences on Reading *One Word of Truth: The Cold War Memoir of Michael Bourdeaux and Keston College*," *Occasional Papers on Religion in Eastern Europe* 41, no. 3 (2021), 50–51.

9. For two examples, see Ludmilla Alexeyeva, *Soviet Dissent: Contemporary Movements for National, Religious, and Human Rights*, trans. Carol Pearce and John Glad (Middletown, CT: Wesleyan University Press, 1985); and Michael

Meerson-Aksenov and Boris Shragin, eds., *The Political, Social and Religious Thought of Russian Samizdat: An Anthology* (Belmont, MA: Nordland Publishing, 1977).

10. Hyung-Min Joo, "Voices of Freedom: *Samizdat*," *Europe-Asia Studies* 56, no. 4 (June 2004): 571–94; Gordon Johnston, "What Is the History of Samizdat?," *Social History* 24, no. 2 (May 1999): 115–33.

11. Most notably the database Soviet Samizdat Periodicals: Uncensored Texts of the Late Soviet Era, https://samizdat.library.utoronto.ca/.

12. Ann Komaromi, "Samizdat and Soviet Dissident Publics," *Slavic Review* 71, no. 1 (2012), 75.

13. Josephine von Zitzewitz, *The Culture of Samizdat: Literature and Underground Networks in the Late Soviet Union* (London: Bloomsbury Academic, 2020).

14. For an overview, see Zoe Knox, "Russian Religious Life in the Soviet Era," in *Oxford Handbook of Russian Religious Thought*, ed. R. Poole, G. Patterson, and C. Emerson (Oxford: Oxford University Press, 2020), 60–75.

15. Michael Bourdeaux, "Persecution, Collusion, and Liberation: The Russian Orthodox Church, from Stalin to Gorbachev," in *The Dangerous God: Christianity and the Soviet Experiment*, ed. Dominic Erdozain (DeKalb: Northern Illinois University Press, 2017), 55.

16. Alexeyeva, *Soviet Dissent*.

17. Komaromi, "Samizdat and Soviet Dissident Publics," 70.

18. Johnston, "What Is the History of Samizdat?," 126–28.

19. Albert Boiter, "Samizdat: Primary Source Material in the Study of Current Soviet Affairs," *The Russian Review* 31, no. 3 (July 1972), 282.

20. Boiter, "Samizdat," 282–85. Open Society Archive, Central European University, Budapest, Hungary. Arkhiv Samizdata (Radio Free Europe, Munich).

21. A content analysis of the major themes in the Samizdat Archive found that 1,047, or 20 percent, of its total of 6,607 samizdat items were religious in focus. Joo, "Voices of Freedom."

22. See, for example, Bourdeaux, *One Word of Truth*, 87.

23. To illustrate the paucity of research materials in the 1960s, Bourdeaux noted in his memoirs that Anderson's book was still cited as an authoritative text twenty years after publication. Anderson acknowledged that "documentation is exceedingly limited." Paul B. Anderson, *People, Church and State in Modern Russia* (London: Student Christian Movement Press, Ltd., 1944), 8.

24. William Stroyen, *Communist Russia and the Russian Orthodox Church, 1943–1962* (Washington, DC: Catholic University of America Press, 1967), 113. Stroyen argues that the Moscow Patriarchate was thoroughly dependent on its support of state objectives for its survival.

25. Michael Bourdeaux, "Russia's Young Christians," *The Observer*, January 29, 1961, 5.

26. Kolarz continues: "I believe it is an essential part of this truth that religious believers form the new oppressed class of the communist regime." Walter Kolarz, *Religion in the Soviet Union* (London: Macmillan, 1961), v.

27. For reasons that are unclear, Kolarz did not quote from Soviet material that was "not available for export." This effectively ruled out any publications that had not been approved by the censors.

28. Bourdeaux, *One Word of Truth*, 82.

29. Cited in Bourdeaux, *One Word of Truth*, 102, emphasis in the original.

30. Bourdeaux, *One Word of Truth*, 101–3.

31. From a 2010 interview with Bourdeaux cited in Mark Hurst, *British Human Rights Organizations and Soviet Dissent, 1965–1985* (London: Bloomsbury, 2016), 117.

32. Nikita Struve, *Les chrétiens en URSS* (Paris: Seuil, 1963). Nikita Struve, *Christians in Contemporary Russia*, trans. Lancelot Sheppard and A. Manson (London: Harvill Press, 1967). The English edition is a translation of the revised and expanded second edition published in French in 1964.

33. Struve, *Christians in Contemporary Russia*, 451n55; 455nn161, 163.

34. Bourdeaux, *One Word of Truth*, 83.

35. Published by the National Council of Churches.

36. *Religious Digest* also covered China.

37. Called *Translations* until 1957.

38. Known simply as Centre de Recherches, or CRE, this was a research organization founded by William Fletcher and based in Geneva. See *Research Materials on Religion in Eastern Europe* 1, no. 1 (March 1967), 1.

39. See, for example, the reference to "communist double-talk" in *Religious Digest*, no. 87 (January 3, 1959), 2.

40. See *Religion in Communist Dominated Areas* 1, no. 2 (April 16, 1962), 3; and 1, no. 3 (April 30, 1962), 1.

41. Bourdeaux, *One Word of Truth*, 108.

42. William C. Fletcher, *A Study in Survival: The Church in Russia 1927–1943* (London: SPCK Publishing, 1965), 10.

43. Bourdeaux, *One Word of Truth*, 120.

44. Bourdeaux, *One Word of Truth*, 283. His description as a past awardee is simply "historian" on the Templeton Prize website. "Laureates," *Templeton Prize*, https://www.templetonprize.org/templeton-prize-winners-2/.

45. Michael Bourdeaux, *Opium of the People: The Christian Religion in the USSR*, 2nd ed. (London: Mowbrays, 1977), 209, 220. These passages are unchanged from the first edition, published in 1965.

46. Michael Bourdeaux, *Patriarch and Prophets: Persecution of the Russian Orthodox Church Today* (New York: Macmillan, 1969), 330–44.

47. Michael Bourdeaux, "News from the Centre," *Religion in Communist Lands* 1, no. 1 (1973), 3. For the reflections of a former editor on the journal's evolution, see the published exchange in Knox, "An Interview with Philip Walters," and the audio interview "Religious Freedom: The Soviet Union and Russia Today," *Religion, State & Society Podcast* (November 2022), https://open.spotify.com/episode/5zmVtrPsfB6owhMtpslU08.

48. Luehrmann, *Religion in Secular Archives*, 151, 161.

49. "Reading and Processing of Samizdat Documents and Publications (March 1977)," KC Materials / 64 / 2, Keston Center for Religion, Politics and Society, Baylor University. In this copy of the document, the title has two insertions written by hand: "Soviet" between the words "of" and "samizdat" and "all" before the word "publications."

50. A chart in the 1977 document showing sources and targets is analyzed in Mark Hurst, "Information Flow at Keston," in *Voices of the Voiceless: Religion, Communism, and the Keston Archive*, ed. Julie deGraffenried and Zoe Knox (Waco, TX: Baylor University Press, 2019), 61–63.

51. "Reading and Processing of Samizdat Documents and Publications (March 1977)," 1.

52. Samizdat should then be sent to whomever it was addressed to, if this was specified.

53. "Reading and Processing of Samizdat Documents and Publications (March 1977)."

54. The wide range of material (textual, visual, artifacts) received by Keston is discussed in deGraffenried and Knox, *Voices of the Voiceless*, which showcases the diversity of the Keston Archive.

55. Michael Bourdeaux, "Editorial," *Keston College News Service*, no. 1 (trial number), May 17, 1974, 2.

56. Hurst, *British Human Rights Organizations*, 127.

57. Bourdeaux, "Editorial," 2. The word "samizdat" is underscored rather than italicized in the original. Note that the title was later shortened to *Keston News Service*.

58. Marite Sapiets, *True Witness: The Story of Seventh Day Adventists in the Soviet Union* (Kent: Keston College, 1990); Bourdeaux, *Land of Crosses*; Xenia Howard-Johnston and Michael Bourdeaux, eds., *Aida of Leningrad: The Story of Aida Skripnikova* (London: Mowbrays, 1972).

59. A hand-drawn line on the document suggests that this relates to information broadcast by US-funded Radio Liberty into the Soviet bloc from its Munich base.

60. Alyona Kojevnikov, "Memories of a Keston Information Officer," in deGraffenried and Knox, *Voices of the Voiceless*, 50.

61. Keston College, *Religious Prisoners in the USSR: A Study by Keston College* (Kent: Keston College, 1985). This was an expanded version of *Christian Prisoners in the USSR*, first published in 1979, which included other religions. Struve's book perhaps provided a model for Keston's prisoner list. Appendix 3 was a list of Russian Orthodox bishops who were "martyrs for their faith." In Struve, *Christians in Contemporary Russia*, 393–98. A list of imprisoned unregistered Baptists supplied by the Baptists themselves appeared as an appendix in Michael Bourdeaux, *Religious Ferment in Russia: Protestant Opposition to Soviet Religious Policy* (New York: Macmillan and St. Martin's Press, 1968), 211–29. Bourdeaux passed the list on to Amnesty International, and it became its first list of Soviet prisoners of conscience. Bourdeaux, *One Word of Truth*, 113.

62. Roy Medvedev, *On Soviet Dissent* (New York: Columbia University Press, 1979).

63. Bourdeaux, *Patriarch and Prophets*, 17–20.

64. In 1965 the Council for Russian Orthodox Affairs merged with the Council for Religious Cults to become the Council for Religious Affairs, or CRA.

65. Nikolai Eshliman and Gleb Yakunin, *Zaiavlenie*, December 15, 1965. A copy is in the Soviet Union Orthodox Subject Files, box 49, folder 10, Keston Center for Religion, Politics, and Society.

66. Bourdeaux, *Patriarch and Prophets*, 189–94. At the same time, the authors sent an open letter to Patriarch Alexi. The open letter also appeared in *Patriarch and Prophets*, 194–223.

67. Serguei Alex. Oushakine, "The Terrifying Mimicry of Samizdat," *Public Culture* 13, no. 2 (Spring 2001), 203.

68. Oushakine, "The Terrifying Mimicry of Samizdat," 191–214. Komaromi also downplayed the dissident legacy, writing that dissidents "had little or no demonstrated impact on the Soviet regime, during Mikhail Gorbachev's perestroika, during the fall of the Soviet regime, or in helping to shape a more democratic and just government after the end of the Soviet Union." Komaromi, "Samizdat and Soviet Dissident Publics," 71.

69. Bourdeaux, *Patriarch and Prophets*, 12.

70. Bourdeaux memorably summed up the essential difference thus: "The registered Baptists allowed their children to wear the red neckerchief of the atheistic young pioneers; the unregistered did not." Bourdeaux, *One Word of Truth*, 203.

71. A. Bychkov, I. Orlov, A. Stoyan, and V. Kulikov, "Russian Baptist Response," in "Nairobi: A Door Opened," *Religion in Communist Lands* 4, no.1 (1976), 16–17.

72. The early issues of *Bratskii Listok* were handwritten but mechanically copied. *Bratskii Listok*, no. 1 (January 1965). Soviet Union Unregistered Baptists Subject Files, box 19, folder 18, Keston Center for Religion, Politics, and Society.

73. Emily B. Baran, *Dissent on the Margins: How Soviet Jehovah's Witnesses Defied Communism and Lived to Preach about It* (New York: Oxford University Press, 2014); Zoe Knox, "Preaching the Kingdom Message: Jehovah's Witnesses and Soviet Secularization," in *State Secularism and Lived Religion in Soviet Russia and Ukraine*, ed. Catherine Wanner (Oxford: Oxford University Press, 2012), 244–71; Tatiana Vagramenko, "Bunker Printing Press," in *Hidden Galleries: Material Religion in the Secret Police Archives in Central and Eastern Europe*, ed. James Kapaló and Tatiana Vagramenko (Zürich: LIT Verlag, 2020), 19.

74. Bourdeaux, *Opium of the People*, 202. This did not prevent Keston's critics from claiming it was politically motivated. Gerd Stricker and Walter Sawatsky, "Postscript—Keston Institute in Transition," *Occasional Papers on Religion in Eastern Europe* 23, no. 3, art. 6 (2003), 2–3. Amnesty International also struggled to portray its work as apolitical in the Cold War context. Christie Miedema, *Not a Movement of Dissidents: Amnesty International beyond the Iron Curtain* (Göttingen: Wallstein Verlag, 2019).

75. Bourdeaux, *One Word of Truth*, 113, 236. Ann Komaromi acknowledged that the term "dissidents" was "loaded with political freight in the Cold War," in Komaromi, "Samizdat and Soviet Dissident Publics," 72.

76. Most clearly stated here: "*Samizdat* and the Soviet press were, after all, different aspects of the same topic, and press articles could be used as

cross-references to the *samizdat*, and even prove its authenticity," Bourdeaux, *One Word of Truth*, 108.

77. Kolarz, *Religion in the Soviet Union*, 34–35.

78. As already acknowledged, Struve's use of émigré testimony marked his approach. For an example of how a range of sources informed his estimates of the number of reform Baptists, see the deliberation in Michael Bourdeaux, "The Background," in Howard-Johnston and Bourdeaux, *Aida of Leningrad*, 19–20.

79. Bourdeaux, *Land of Crosses*, 255. On the *Chronicle of Current Events*, see Peter Reddaway's account of translating and editing this periodical in *The Dissidents: A Memoir of Working with the Resistance in Russia, 1960–1990* (Washington, DC: Brookings Institution Press, 2020), 120–31.

80. "Memorandum," in Bourdeaux, *Land of Crosses*, 126–28.

81. Xenia Dennen, "The Lithuanian Memorandum," in deGraffenried and Knox, *Voices of the Voiceless*, 57–60.

82. Oushakine, "The Terrifying Mimicry of Samizdat," 191–214.

83. Luehrmann, *Religion in Secular Archives*, 145.

84. Michael Bourdeaux, "The Trial of Aida Skripnikova," in deGraffenried and Knox, *Voices of the Voiceless*, 32–36.

85. Howard-Johnston and Bourdeaux, *Aida of Leningrad*.

86. "Aida and the British Public," *Protestant Communities in the USSR*, https://www.dhi.ac.uk/Protestantism/section/?section=aida.

87. Luehrmann, *Religion in Secular Archives*, 134.

88. Reddaway, *The Dissidents*, 197.

89. The concepts of truth, integrity, and honesty as they relate to firsthand accounts of life under communism come up countless times in Bourdeaux's memoir *One Word of Truth*. He foregrounds truth in the title, which draws on the Russian dissident Aleksandr Solzhenitsyn's Nobel Prize in Literature lecture in 1970. Solzhenitsyn called for writers and artists to be outspoken and defiant in the face of attempts to silence and repress them, whatever the cost. Bourdeaux, *One Word of Truth*, ix. See also "Acceptance Address by Mr. Michael Bourdeaux," May 15, 1984, https://www.templetonprize.org/laureate-sub/bourdeaux-acceptance-speech/. I am grateful to Mark Hurst for bringing this address to my attention.

90. Peter Reddaway goes even further, linking the questioning of the credibility of samizdat with challenging the integrity of dissidents. Reddaway, *The Dissidents*, 150, 156.

91. Bourdeaux, *Religious Ferment in Russia*, 183.

92. The two different paths that churches in the Communist bloc could follow were summarized in the title of a book that Bourdeaux contributed to: *Discretion and Valour: Religious Conditions in Russia and Eastern Europe*, ed. Trevor Beeson (Glasgow: Collins, Fontana Books, 1974). For Bourdeaux's reflections on this predicament, see *One Word of Truth*, 186.

93. Komaromi, "Samizdat and Soviet Dissident Publics," 75.

94. Bourdeaux, *One Word of Truth*, 206.

95. Hurst, *British Human Rights Organizations*, 145.

CHAPTER 2

"Beyond the 'Bête Noire'?" Keston College and the Cold War

Mark Hurst

The efforts of Keston College to document the position of religious belief in Communist lands were by their very nature intertwined with the ebbs and flows of the Cold War. The persecution of believers in the Soviet bloc was driven by both ideological and pragmatic concerns of the Communist superpower. Religion offered the space to foment alternative thought that could challenge the ideological dogma the Soviet authorities were constructing to consolidate and maintain their rule. The desire to push back against official policy and support those who were persecuted for their beliefs can be caught up in this ideological space. As a result, it is all too easy to put those who were active in supporting religious believers in the same bracket as outright Cold Warriors, individuals who sought to use a variety of cultural, economic, and political means to fight the ideological war against the Soviet Union.[1]

From their position in Britain, those affiliated with Keston College, an organization founded to document the position of religious belief in the Soviet bloc, could be portrayed as taking part in the broader conflict of the Cold War. Efforts to collate information about human rights violations against religious believers in the Soviet bloc through the collection of samizdat and other material made Keston a recognized authority on this issue. The information collected at Keston filtered through to the numerous publications produced by the organization, ranging from the *Keston News Service*, its academic journal *Religion in Communist Lands*, and a wide-ranging series of books.[2] Through these outputs, it obtained a reputation of expertise on religious issues in both the Soviet Union and the Communist countries of East and Central Europe. This in turn led to some of its researchers becoming prominent commentators on these issues, perhaps most notably the Anglican clergyman Michael Bourdeaux, the leading figure of the organization from its foundation. Bourdeaux's expertise helped to inform government policy toward the Soviet Union. For example, he was invited by British Prime Minister Margaret Thatcher to attend an event in 1983 at Chequers designed to inform her about life in the Soviet Union at a pivotal point in the Cold War, echoing her "close interest in all human rights matters" in the region.[3]

Keston's reputation was noted on both sides of the Iron Curtain. As well as holding a position of influence among policymakers in the West, Keston was also a thorn in the side of the Soviet authorities. In a Gresham College lecture in 2013, Xenia Dennen, then Chairman of the Keston Institute, described Keston as "the KGB's bête noire," owing to its position "near the top of the KGB's list of the most dangerous Western organizations."[4] While Keston's collection and dissemination of information that highlighted human rights violations behind the Iron Curtain was doubtless threatening to the Soviet authorities, describing Keston in such terms raises a number of interesting historiographical issues. Dennen's comments were made in a public lecture where some license can be given for the use of strong terminology to convey a position and reduce complex themes into more readily digestible phrases for a public audience. In this case, that Keston played an important role in the Cold War, and that its efforts were met with frustration by the KGB perhaps played into Cold War binaries.

Dennen's comments are not unique in this framing. The title of Michael Bourdeaux's 2019 memoir, *One Word of Truth: The Cold War Memoir of Michael Bourdeaux and Keston College,* strongly indicates the centrality of the international conflict to his life, and that it was perhaps the lens through which he reflected on his life's work. Cold War binaries have been highlighted by critical friends of Keston. In commenting on Keston's approach to the Soviet Union, Paul Oestreicher, a human rights campaigner and Anglican priest, noted in a slightly cryptic letter to Bourdeaux that he (Bourdeaux) was "blind in one eye," signing the letter, "Your friend, partially sighted—in both eyes."[5] In this letter,

Oestreicher identified what he saw as Bourdeaux's inability to see the positive aspects of the Soviet system, while highlighting his own inability to fully "see" either superpower. This, again, positions Bourdeaux's efforts squarely in the context of the Cold War. Defenders of Keston's efforts in this period also drew on the Cold War context to highlight its ideologically neutral aims as a defense mechanism against these accusations. Peter Reddaway, a founding member of Keston and an academic with research expertise in Soviet dissent, noted in his memoirs that Keston was "an apolitical research and educational group which simply gathered, digested, and circulated the facts to anyone interested."[6] While this may have been the case, claiming to be truly apolitical in the context of the Cold War was remarkably challenging, and a position that other human rights organizations such as Amnesty International also sought to take, often without success.[7] Even the claim that Keston stood aside from the ideological tensions of the day makes a direct reference to the Cold War framework, reiterating its centrality to understanding this organization.

The parallels between Keston's development and the ebbs and flows of international relations in this period are striking. However, drawing too close a parallel risks removing the agency of those affiliated with Keston, rendering them as Cold Warriors caught up in an ideological conflict. This approach undervalues the myriad of reasons that individuals chose to support organizations like Keston, often devoting their lives and huge amounts of personal effort to its cause. These reasons may include altruistic concern for the persecuted, religious and spiritual motivations, and broader interests in Slavic culture and traditions, among others.

Cold War historians are aware of the need to expand their understanding of the conflict and the way in which it permeates a broad remit of historiographical areas.[8] In the case of Keston, can we go further and step beyond the immediate context of the Cold War? What benefits might this offer? What motivated these individuals beyond the confines of the Cold War, and what would it tell us about Keston and its work? Matthew Connelly's call for historians to remove the "Cold War lens" from their work highlights the way in which scholars can unwittingly fall into patterns of thought that unconsciously shape our understanding of this period.[9] By unconsciously positioning Keston's history as intertwined with the Cold War, the criteria by which to assess and consider its activity is often set in binary terms for or against the Soviet Union. Not only does this limit a critical assessment of the organization, but it is also reductive in understanding Keston's work. Attempting to remove this lens opens the space to give agency to Keston as an organization and to those who have been affiliated with it. Given that an understanding of religion in the Soviet bloc is entwined with the broader developments of the Cold War, to remove this lens entirely risks dismissing a significant issue in Keston's history. This would also be a practical impossibility given the impact that the Cold War had on various aspects of Keston's work. Nevertheless, by acknowledging the wide-ranging impact that the specter of the Cold War has on how we understand organizations like Keston, and by attempting to think beyond this framework, this approach promises significant rewards—both for a historical understanding of Keston and for other transnational advocacy groups in this period.

The Evolution of Keston

Keston itself has undergone a process of reidentification in recent years. After the collapse of the Soviet Union, Keston's raison d'être has shifted from documenting religious life in Communist lands to the preservation of its archive and library, which include samizdat collections and other materials relating to religion in the Soviet bloc. These holdings moved from Keston, a small village in Kent, to Oxford, and finally to its current location at Baylor University, in Waco, Texas, where a Keston research center was established in 2007. Keston recently celebrated its fiftieth anniversary and marked the location of its former premises in Keston with a blue plaque—mimicking English Heritage's blue plaques placed on buildings of historic importance.[10] These events dovetailed with the publication of memoirs by Michael Bourdeaux and Peter Reddaway, two of Keston's founding members, and of books exploring the value of Keston's archive and highlighting the richness of material that it holds for historical research.[11] As an organization, Keston is more acutely aware of its history than ever before. It could even be argued that despite recent initiatives, such as an encyclopedia project to document the contemporary situation of religious believers in the Russian Federation, its institutional concerns have shifted from the present to the past. The vast bulk of its work, including efforts to promote and preserve its archive and the funding of scholars working on issues relating to religion in the former Soviet bloc, looks backward, more so than at any time in its history.

It is a pertinent time to address how Keston's history is understood. The bellicose rhetoric from contemporary Russian authorities, the brutal persecution of political opponents such as Vladimir Kara-Murza, Boris Nemtsov, and Alexei Navalny, and the military action in Ukraine have led many commentators to assert that the Cold War has returned.[12] The previous persecution of the Russian Orthodox Church has now been replaced by its significant political importance in the Russian Federation (see chapter 10).[13] This was notable in the persecution of Pussy Riot after their 2012 "Punk Prayer." While the response to their protest occurred in a political context different than that of the Soviet antireligious campaigns, two members of the group were sentenced to time in a penal colony for "hooliganism motivated by religious hatred," something that captured international attention.[14] In the current context, understanding the role of religion in the former Soviet bloc is arguably more important than ever given its political importance. Historical perspectives on this issue, which are likely to draw heavily on Keston's archives, will undoubtedly be valuable in assessing these contemporary issues in historical context. This is especially so given the relative paucity of scholarship on religion in the Soviet bloc during the Cold War, an aspect of international relations that deserves closer attention by scholars.[15]

Despite playing an important role in documenting religious belief and persecution in the Soviet bloc, Keston has been relatively unexplored by historians. Jenny Robertson's *Be Our Voice* (1984) sympathetically explores Keston's activities, perhaps unsurprisingly given that it was published as part of Keston's book series and with a proportion of its royalties going to Keston College.[16] In recent years Keston has been explored in the context of its position within the broader network of activists concerned with human rights in the Soviet Union, and by scholars focusing on a brief assessment of its efforts in the post–Cold War period.[17] It is clear, however, that there is more to be done on this topic. In the history of Soviet human rights issues, the importance of the international network of activists who gathered to put pressure on the Soviet authorities is often overlooked. The predominant focus to date has understandably been on the persecuted and their efforts in this struggle.[18] Human rights activists themselves have garnered increased scholarly attention in recent years, and assessing their role has become increasingly important in understanding the transnational nature of human rights activism in the twentieth century.[19]

Three Motivators

In the context of these issues, a critical reassessment of Keston's relationship to the Cold War is timely. This chapter will consider three major motivators for those affiliated with Keston that are divorced from the central ideological drive of the Cold War and instead involve personal motivation, morality, and religious faith. This approach allows an original focus beyond the "bête noire," which will in turn open up a more nuanced perspective on Keston's history. The aim of this approach is not to fundamentally rewrite Keston's history, nor to overlook the importance of the Cold War, but instead to highlight the value of thinking about the organization beyond the Cold War framework and to assess what this can reveal about the organization's history.

To begin, this chapter will consider the personal motivations of individuals affiliated with Keston, seeking to offer agency to those who supported its efforts. Focusing on the individual offers a more personal engagement with Keston's activism, an engagement that was often concerned with a myriad of issues beyond the superpower conflict. Given the nature of this collection, this chapter will predominantly focus on Michael Bourdeaux, drawing on his writings and archival materials. This is not to suggest that the history of Keston should be restricted solely to an assessment of Bourdeaux, as there is clearly scope for this analysis to be expanded to cover a wide variety of individuals affiliated with the organization. Instead, given the historiographical complexity of the issue at hand, and the restrictions of space, focusing on Bourdeaux offers a workable, and fitting, approach for this collection.

This chapter will then focus on the impact of broader moral concerns about human rights, a concept that has undergone extensive historiographical reinterpretation in recent years.[20] While now widely understood as an influential force in contemporary international relations, Keston's history is intertwined with the so-called breakthrough moment for human rights in the 1970s when it transitioned from a fringe political concern to occupying a central position in international politics. The way in which human rights as a concept was understood also changed for prisoners of conscience in the Soviet bloc, shifting from relative obscurity to becoming a core ideal for many dissidents.[21]

Finally, this chapter will consider religious faith and its impact on Keston. While this might seem like an obvious motivation for those affiliated with Keston, given the number of its patrons that were or are prominent religious figures, this factor is often overlooked.[22] Taken together, these three motivations demonstrate the substantial historiographical potential of going "beyond the bête noire" and the need to exercise caution when considering transnational organizations in the context of the Cold War.

Personal Motivations

One liberating aspect of assessing Keston beyond the Cold War lens is the opportunity to consider the personal agency of those who supported its efforts. While many of those affiliated with Keston were clearly appalled by the ideologically motivated actions of the Soviet authorities in suppressing religious belief and persecuting believers, ideology was not necessarily a primary motivation for their efforts. If this were the case, other organizations with a more explicitly anticommunist ethos would have offered a more natural home. Attempts to interrogate the decision-making process of an individual open the space to engage with history on a personal level, focusing on the agency of individual actors to make active and informed decisions. Understanding the individual motivation of historical figures, however, is a challenging task for the historian.[23] These benefits need to be set against the inherent historiographical complexities of assessing individual agency. By its nature, historical research necessitates a temporal distance from those it studies. As a result, assessing the rationale behind stakeholders' actions is limited by the inherent limitations of empirical source material in assessing a past reality, let alone a past way of thinking.[24] Given this limitation, offering an accurate and reliable assessment of the motivation behind someone's decision to either support Keston or more formally work for the organization is remarkably challenging. Oral history interviews may offer a way around this. However, given the cultural, social, and political predominance of the Cold War, it is also highly likely that regardless of the initial motivation itself, memories of these motivations will be shaped by a "cultural circuit" following the dominant narratives of the day.[25] For example, although Bourdeaux has described his memoir as being one of the Cold War, it is all but impossible to know the extent to which he felt his life was part of the Cold War at the time of his actions, or if this is a retrospective label applied to understand the period from a post–Cold War perspective, where the superpower conflict may loom more prominently. Understanding individual agency is a complex task, with an intellectual lineage going back to the Enlightenment and intricacies that go far beyond the scope of this chapter.[26] Being aware of the methodological challenges in ascribing, assessing, and analyzing the agency of an individual can be very historiographically challenging, as it forces historians to critically engage with their own role in constructing the past—a space that can be intellectually disarming. This is especially the case for contemporary historians, who often develop personal relationships with their subjects, further complicating issues of agency.[27]

Those affiliated with Keston were drawn to its work for a variety of reasons that are all but impossible to capture in an essay of this length. In the case of Bourdeaux, Keston was established to formalize the work that he and his supporters had been engaging in since the early 1960s. Much of this developed seemingly organically from Bourdeaux's personal interactions with the Soviet Union, which often came about through chance. For example, Bourdeaux's initial plan to train as a German interpreter while on National Service were derailed by toothache, which caused him to miss the required entrance examinations for the course. After discussing this with a senior officer, he was instead placed in the Russian interpreters' course. The rationale for these courses was doubtless due to the Cold War and the strategic benefits of having a body of trained Russian speakers in the British military. However, Bourdeaux's personal commitment to his new language clearly went beyond this rationale. After completing his National Service, he changed his career plans and decided to study Russian and French at Oxford University, rather than French and German.[28] Similarly, after later returning to university to study theology, he successfully applied for a scholarship to study at a Serbian Orthodox seminary in Belgrade, but on seeing a note on the noticeboard of the Taylorian Institute at Oxford, as Bourdeaux put it, "God judged differently." This note advertised a call from the British Council for Russian graduates to take part in a fully funded cultural exchange in the Soviet Union, which Bourdeaux also successfully applied for "with a mixture of regret and excitement" at having to give up the Serbian opportunity.[29] The purpose of this exchange was to build connections, something that had potential strategic and propaganda value for states on both sides of the Iron Curtain, but in Bourdeaux's case the appeal of spending time in the Soviet Union was doubtless driven by a personal interest.

Whether these events would have occurred without broader Cold War issues is debatable, but the same could be said about fate intervening through Bourdeaux's dental problem or his chance passing by a noticeboard. What is notable in both instances is that for them to have such an impact, they required significant personal investment, and it is debatable whether this would have been sustained by ideological reasons alone. The chance nature of some of these events, alongside Bourdeaux's clear love for Slavic cultures and languages, are important to consider when assessing the motivations for his later work. In many ways, these easily overlooked factors may in fact have been more influential in Bourdeaux's personal history than the more immediate context of the Cold War, albeit more challenging to account for.

This can be seen in Bourdeaux's first major work on the persecution of religious belief. His 1965 book, *Opium of the People*, is very much a personal account of his experiences in the Soviet Union, drawn from his year in Moscow as an exchange student in 1959 and a subsequent shorter trip in 1964 accompanying a group of teachers.[30] Given the content of this book, and its title drawn from Karl Marx's infamous and often misunderstood quote on the role of religion in society, it is easy to see it on face value as an anti-Soviet book written in the context of Cold War tensions. However, beneath this veneer is Bourdeaux's clear personal frustration with the events he experienced. This was echoed in Bourdeaux's recollections of both the publication and reception of the book in Britain. He was frank about his frustrations in finding a publisher, having approached many different companies with an increasingly worn manuscript before Faber and Faber agreed to publish it after substantial revision. Despite receiving positive comments in the popular and academic press, including a serialization of extracts from the book in the *Church Times*, a prominent Anglican weekly newspaper, Bourdeaux recalled that the publication of the book was met with "an outcry of horror."[31] The reason for this recollection may have been due to the relative lack of impact that his book had on public perceptions of religious belief in the Soviet Union, rather than a vocal attack on its contents. In this period, concerns for Soviet human rights violations were relatively low in the West in comparison with later decades, likely due to public attention being focused on other international issues such as concerns about nuclear warfare after the Cuban Missile Crisis, the impact of decolonization on regional security in Africa and Southeast Asia, and the potential weaponization of the space race. Nevertheless, the personal frustrations here are easy to recognize.

Many of the concerns raised in *Opium of the People* only came to be major issues in international relations during later decades, so a sense of being overlooked in 1965 may have also contributed to Bourdeaux's recollection of its reception. *Opium of the People* was not just an academic text about "far away" lands, but in many ways a personal account of Bourdeaux's experiences. Not getting the expected positive reaction likely cut Bourdeaux deeply. Again, this personal dimension is easy for historians to overlook in comparison with the Cold War context, especially in the decades following McCarthyism and the "Red Scare."[32] This is not to suggest that Bourdeaux was not critical of the Soviet authorities in this book, but instead to highlight that this book, like his others, was motivated by a multitude of issues, not just Cold War politics. Indeed, while his memoir focuses explicitly on the Cold War, something alluded to in its subtitle, clearly there is more to Bourdeaux's life than this focus alone. He recognizes this in the memoir itself, noting his regret in its afterword that "there are aspects of my life which could have been greatly expanded in these memoirs, but I had to concentrate on the history of Keston, beginning with an explanation of how, without my knowing it at the time, I was led towards this goal."[33]Whether the history of Keston is as intertwined with the Cold War as this statement might subtly suggest is debatable. An attempt to see the space beyond this will, like aspects of Bourdeaux's personal history, benefit from expansion too.

Human Rights

The Cold War was not the only major issue in international relations in the latter years of the twentieth century. This period also saw the increased recognition and support for human rights in a fashion that was markedly different from previous generations. The foreign policy of some nations was no longer openly driven by pragmatic state desire alone, but also by what was considered morally right and ethically justifiable. The Cold War casts a long shadow over the history of human rights, to the extent that it is difficult to see the development of human rights as we understand it today without the superpower conflict. While it is easy to point toward longstanding traditions of rights throughout human history, contemporary perspectives on human rights were doubtless shaped by events directly related to the Cold War.[34] The 1948 Universal Declaration of Human Rights (UDHR) has become a foundational document for many in understanding the entrenchment of human rights in the modern world. That it was written in a period when superpower relations were beginning to rapidly chill is not coincidental. The Jackson-Vanik Amendment of 1974, which sought to link trade between the superpowers to the Soviet treatment of the *refuseniks*, was a moment where United States foreign policy became intertwined with potential economic sanctions in response to human rights violations.[35] This is important in contemporary international affairs, as economic and cultural sanctions are increasingly used as the main weapon against states that abuse human rights.[36] The fallout from the Vietnam War also led to a reevaluation of international relations, which can be clearly seen in Jimmy Carter's positioning of human rights ideals as the centerpiece of his administration's foreign policy.[37] This arguably still has a prominent legacy today, where actions in foreign affairs are often discussed or justified within the framework of human rights.

In their assessment of the later years of the Cold War, historians have pointed to human rights activism as a significant factor leading to the collapse of the Soviet Union.[38] Much of this has come from a critical reassessment of the history of human rights by scholars such as Stefan-Ludwig Hoffman, Lynn Hunt, and Samuel Moyn. This reassessment has focused on a critique of the often-assumed *longue durée* of the history of human rights.[39] Challenging this narrative and recasting the history of human rights as a much shorter phenomenon than previously considered, they argue that the concept of "human rights" gained political salience only well into the twentieth century. While the exact timing of this "breakthrough" moment for human rights is disputed, with suggestions ranging from the 1970s to the 1990s and beyond, it is clear that Keston came to the fore during a period when human rights were undergoing a transformation in public consciousness.

The impact of the "breakthrough" moment for human rights was not limited to campaigners in the West. Some dissidents in the Soviet bloc also became more aware of human rights discourses in this period. This was especially the case after the signing of the Helsinki Accords in 1975, which framed human rights as an important domestic issue in the Soviet Union. Not only did this broad understanding of human rights offer the wide-ranging and often diffuse dissident movement common space to engage with the concept, but the principles of human rights as enshrined in the UDHR and the Helsinki Accords were appealing in the struggle against an oppressive regime that restricted these rights.[40] It is perhaps of little surprise that the *Chronicle of Current Events*, one of the most important samizdat publications coming out of the Soviet Union, prominently displayed on each of its editions Article 19 of the UDHR, which sets out the right to freedom of opinion and expression.[41]

In his memoir, Bourdeaux recognized the increased awareness of Soviet persecution of religious believers as a "human rights issue," highlighting his early interactions with Amnesty International and how he supplied the organization with "its first-ever list of Soviet prisoners of conscience."[42] Whether Bourdeaux understood this as a human rights issue at the time is debatable. The entrenchment of human rights discourses after the "breakthrough" period of the 1970s presented the language through which to describe these events, which had not been widely available earlier. Nevertheless, the use of human rights terminology in his memoir highlights how these efforts were later understood by Bourdeaux, who saw them as driven by a moral concern rather than an outright Cold War campaign.

While Keston's work clearly engaged with human rights issues, it is not necessarily the case that it should be explicitly defined as a human rights organization.[43] Keston affiliates have frequently stressed that the organization's institutional ethos was to document religious life in Communist lands, not to report the violation of human rights—a subtle but important difference. An editorial in the first edition of its academic journal *Religion in Communist Lands* notes: "The Centre [for the Study of Religion and Communism][44] hopes that *Religion in Communist Lands* will be of educative value and will become a forum for the presentation and discussion of *all* aspects of the religious situation in Communist societies—both the positive and the negative aspects—for the Centre is a research organization, not concerned with presenting a particular viewpoint; it is non-political and independent of denominational affiliation."[45] As a result of this desire to find a politically neutral but morally concerned position, Keston was both close to and far apart from human rights issues. Walking this political tightrope may have been influenced by the ideological tensions of the Cold War and an implicit desire to step aside from this conflict in order to focus on the lives of religious believers. However, the draw of the morality of human rights and the desire to protect freedom of belief and conscience were undoubtedly important to Keston's work.

Religious Faith

Given Keston's central desire to document religious life in the Soviet bloc, it is perhaps unsurprising that religious faith motivated many individuals associated with it. The story of Keston's origins and the way in which they have been recounted by its leading figures offers insights into the impact of religion on the organization. Bourdeaux was asked to "be the voice" of persecuted Soviet believers after a chance meeting with two Ukrainians during a trip to Moscow in 1964. Bourdeaux described this meeting as "the way of the hand of God" and a divine moment when "God wrenched the steering wheel out of my grasp," setting him on the path to dedicate his life to be the voice of these individuals.[46] This moment had clear importance for Bourdeaux, Keston, and the memory of what justified their efforts. It features prominently on the cover of Bourdeaux's memoir and is directly referenced in several obituaries of Bourdeaux following his death in 2021.[47] The theme of divine intervention is also echoed in Bourdeaux's written work. In the first sentence of *Risen Indeed* (1983), in a section titled "A Few Pages of Autobiography," Bourdeaux notes that "God's signature is on the small events of this world just as indelibly as on the large."[48] *One Word of Truth* put this even more explicitly: "It is obvious that divine intervention was never far away and, at times, directly controlled a series of events which led me to found Keston College and sometimes reassured me and pointed the way forward."[49]

In his lecture to commemorate Keston's fiftieth anniversary, Rowan Williams engaged with this issue in a slightly different manner, describing Keston's work as a celebration of "the endurance of those who show us what faith might actually mean when things get serious."[50] This, timed with Williams's discussion of the so-called death cell philosophy, may appear relatively morbid at face value, especially in a public lecture at a celebratory event. However, his words cut to the core of the efforts made by those affiliated with Keston, which were often made in challenging circumstances that dealt with the nadir of humanity. What drove individuals to keep going in the face of ever-depressing reports about human rights violations in the Soviet bloc? This is an issue that concerns a myriad of organizations. In his assessment of Amnesty International, Stephen Hopgood has argued that the organization has become in many ways a "secular religion," something that has given it an almost impenetrably strong institutional ethos. Hopgood highlights the language used by Amnesty's supporters in defending their cause and the personal sacrifice of many of its researchers as "potent evidence for a kind of secular religiosity born of collective action, sacrifice, and suffering."[51] This "secular" religiosity has protected Amnesty's reputation amid scandal and controversy and demonstrates the power of a strong institutional ethos.[52]

In this context, Keston's relationship with religion is much more apparent—its raison d'être is to document religious life, its patrons are prominent religious figures from a variety of faiths, and many of its supporters are members of the clergy. As a result, personal religious faith undoubtedly played an important role in motivating and directing Keston's efforts. This can also be clearly seen in its publications. *Frontier*, a glossy magazine produced by Keston, was clear in its religious intent with recommendations of topics and individuals to pray for alongside religious imagery.[53] This can also be seen in its more academic publications too, albeit more subtly. Issues of *Religion in Communist Lands* contain "prayer-pointers," suggestions for persons or causes to pray for, and Bourdeaux notes in one of his regular "News from the Centre" sections that additional suggestions could be provided on request.[54] Editions of the *Keston News Service* sometimes contained religious imagery, such as the cover of the April 24, 1981 issue, which carried the phrase "Christ is Risen" in various languages.[55] In these examples, the specter of the Cold War fades into the background while concerns for the promotion and protection of religious faith clearly comes to the fore.

Owing to this engagement in religious life, Keston's interactions with religious institutions offer another space to consider its history beyond the Cold War. Bourdeaux's receipt of the 1984 Templeton Prize recognized the work that he and Keston accomplished in documenting religious belief in the Soviet bloc and offered him a platform on which to engage with a wide audience. While his acceptance speech for this prize deals with Cold War issues, it was primarily a measured call for compassion and support for believers. This was done using religious language, including: "The Christian, too—as Russian believers teach us—must love the Communist, while retaining his right to oppose much of what Communism stands for. Yet, in an equally real sense, every Christian of principle has to be 'anti-Soviet', [*sic*] if the term 'Soviet' stands, as it certainly does, for the imposition of state atheism."[56] Bourdeaux was clearly critical of the Soviet authorities and their persecution of religious believers but framed his criticisms in moral terms rather than ideological. His later assertion that Christians should be opposed to Soviet authorities because of their atheist policies confuses this slightly, but again he emphasized religious faith, not ideology. The explicit issue here was the Soviet policy of state atheism, rather than communism itself—a subtle but important distinction. The focus of this criticism was on the persecution of religious belief and not on the Soviet government per se. These criticisms might have equally been leveled at any antireligious regime. This nuance can also be seen in the way in which Bourdeaux addressed his critics in this acceptance speech: "We finally come sharply face to face with the question Keston College is often asked: Doesn't your work damage East-West relations and make détente recede even further over the horizon? To which I reply with a phrase I've both used and, I hope, applied over the last 20 years: 'We need reconciliation, but we can never build reconciliation on anything other than the truth'."[57]

Bourdeaux's insistence on truth and reconciliation follows the rhetoric of Alexander Solzhenitsyn, incidentally the 1983 recipient of the Templeton Prize, and the broader Christian rhetoric of compassion. The Cold War lens means that it is easy to see this statement as driven by pragmatism motivated by ideological concerns, whereas the reality is likely more rooted in religious belief. Indeed, the appeal of Solzhenitsyn's call for morally based resistance against the Soviet authorities— "One word of truth shall outweigh the whole world"—clearly resonated with Bourdeaux, who used part of this phrase for the title of his memoir *One Word of Truth*.[58] This idea of morally based resistance was also evident in Bourdeaux's public challenge to the World Council of Churches (WCC). In a Chatham House lecture in October 1984 that was later republished in *Religion in Communist Lands*, Bourdeaux stated in forthright terms that the WCC's policy toward the Soviet Union had failed and called for the organization to reevaluate its approach to focus on "aid for the persecuted 'morally, materially and politically'."[59] Much of his frustration was borne out of a perceived lack of action by the WCC in comparison with the World Psychiatric Association, whose members had been more active in their efforts against the political abuse of psychiatry in the Soviet Union, something that resulted in the Soviet withdrawal from the Association in 1983 due to international pressure.[60] In this 1984 lecture, Bourdeaux could have easily drawn on Cold War rhetoric to make his case, following the example of Ronald Reagan, who asserted that the Soviet Union was an "evil empire" that needed to be challenged. Instead, by focusing on the moral case for action, Bourdeaux's position was doubtless more strongly justified and followed Keston's broader aim to be apolitical, no matter how problematic this was in the context of that time. The concerns that underpinned his position clearly reveal his predominant focus on the plight of religious believers rather than playing Cold War politics.

A close reading of Bourdeaux's memoir offers an intriguing insight into the way in which historians have understood how the Cold War has shaped his life and the broader history of Keston. In the first lines of the memoir, Bourdeaux notes: "It was 1989 and the world was changing. During my life I have been eyewitness to several extraordinary events, into which I was propelled by the unseen hand of God."[61] These opening sentences highlight an interesting tension in the way in which Bourdeaux, and arguably by extension Keston, can be understood historically. In the first sentence, the Cold War context is front and center, while in the second, religious belief takes center stage. This tension is subtle, but it potentially underpins how we understand Bourdeaux's life. It also extends more broadly into how Keston's history is understood, as Dennen's "bête noire" comments suggest. While Keston's efforts were doubtless met with anger by the Soviet authorities playing into the ideological Cold War arena, its efforts were also likely motivated by a myriad of personal and institutional concerns beyond this Cold War framework. This is a compelling yet complex historiographical space for further exploration.

In Bourdeaux's case, religious faith, altruistic concern for fellow believers, and a concern for religious life were clear motivators for his life's work. To reduce his contributions to nothing more than those of a Cold Warrior is damaging to his legacy and historically inaccurate. This is neither to suggest that the Cold War had no impact on Bourdeaux nor that he and Keston could apolitically step aside from the conflict to offer a neutral perspective. In the context of the Cold War, this desire for neutrality can be seen as a political move in itself, one that makes this issue all the more complex. Bourdeaux's comments, such as "Whenever I met the Protestants in the Soviet Union I would have the feeling, 'Communism can't win here'," further complicate matters.[62] Was this statement born out of a committed and ideologically driven anti-Soviet stance or more out of frustration at how the Soviet authorities persecuted religious believers? It is impossible to be definitive, owing to the historiographical complexities outlined in this chapter. Nevertheless, if we are unaware of our potential biases toward favoring the Cold War context in assessing this issue, we may miss some of the complexities driving his efforts. This issue is relevant to a wide variety of individuals involved with Keston and, more broadly, with nongovernmental organizations active in campaigning against human rights violations in the Soviet bloc in the second half of the twentieth century, whose efforts can also be stripped of necessary nuance by the Cold War lens.

There are moments in Keston's history that are clearly intertwined with the Cold War, such as the blacklisting of many of its members, preventing them from obtaining Soviet visas, propaganda attacks against Keston led by Soviet writers, and the dramatic impact that the collapse of the Soviet Union had on the direction of the organization.[63] Ultimately, it is clear that without the ideological conflict between the superpowers and the myriad of tensions that this caused, the history of those affiliated with Keston would have been vastly different. Had the persecution of religious believers occurred in an alternative Soviet bloc that existed without an international Cold War, the response to these abuses would have doubtless been very different, given that they would have come from nations less concerned about ideological victories. Nevertheless, there are aspects of both Keston's work and Bourdeaux's personal motivations that go beyond the Cold War framework.

Keston clearly did not exist in an ideological vacuum, and its supporters had agency. The challenge for historians is to recognize this despite the looming specter of the Cold War over Keston's work, going beyond "the bête noire" narrative to offer a more nuanced and critical understanding of the organization's history. Although it is clearly impossible to consider Keston outside the context of the Cold War, thinking outside of this often-reductive framework opens a significant space to think more critically about the agency, motivations, and actions of those affiliated with Keston. This is becoming more important in an era when contemporary Russian foreign policy and its treatment of political dissidents increasingly mimics that of the Soviet state and the common tropes and clichés of the Cold War become all too easy to adopt.[64] While these challenges are often intellectually insurmountable, in addressing them head on, historians can breathe new life into our understanding of political dissent, improving the quality of their research and offering increased agency to the individuals who are assessed.

Notes

I would like to thank a number of colleagues for their incisive, critical, and supportive comments about this chapter during both its conceptualization and writing. I owe particular thanks to Xenia Dennen, Michael Hughes, Zoe Knox, Corinna Peniston-Bird, and the British Association for Slavonic and East European Studies Study Group on Religion and Spirituality in Russia and Eastern Europe, to whom an early version of this chapter was presented in April 2022.

1. Frances Stonor Saunders, *Who Paid the Piper? The CIA and the Cultural Cold War* (London: Granta Books, 1999).

2. Mark Hurst, *British Human Rights Organizations and Soviet Dissent, 1965–1985* (London: Bloomsbury, 2016), 122–35.

3. Hurst, *British Human Rights Organizations and Soviet* Dissent, 138. Quote from David Grealy, *David Owen, Human Rights and the Remaking of British Foreign Policy* (London: Bloomsbury, 2023), 124.

4. Xenia Dennen, "The KGB's 'Bête Noire'," Gresham College Lecture, May 23, 2013, http://gresham.overthrowmothership.co.uk/lectures-and-events/the-kgbs-bte-noire.

5. Michael Bourdeaux, *One Word of Truth: The Cold War Memoir of Michael Bourdeaux and Keston College* (London: Darton, Longman and Todd, 2019), 165.

6. Peter Reddaway, *The Dissidents: A Memoir of Working with the Resistance in Russia, 1960–1990* (Washington, DC: Brookings Institution Press, 2020), 197.

7. For example, see Hurst, *British Human Rights Organizations and Soviet Dissent*, especially chapter 5, "Attempting Impartiality"; and Christie Miedema, "Impartial in the Cold War? The Challenges of Détente, Dissidence, and Eastern European Membership to Amnesty International's Policy of Impartiality," *Humanity* 10, no. 2 (2019): 179–205.

8. Federico Romero, "Cold War Historiography at the Crossroads," *Cold War History* 14, no. 4 (2014): 685–703.

9. Matthew Connelly, "Taking off the Cold War Lens: Visions of North-South Conflict during the Algerian War of Independence," *The American Historical Review* 105, no. 3 (2000): 739–69.

10. Michael Bourdeaux, "Keston College—The Plaque 1972–1992," *Keston Newsletter*, no. 30 (2019): 3–6.

11. Bourdeaux, *One Word of Truth*; Julie deGraffenried and Zoe Knox, eds., *Voices of the Voiceless: Religion, Communism, and the Keston Archive* (Waco, TX: Baylor University Press, 2019); and Reddaway, *The Dissidents*.

12. Edward Lucas, *The New Cold War: How the Kremlin Menaces Both Russia and the West* (London: Bloomsbury, 2008); Simon Tisdall, "The New Cold War: Are We Going Back to the Bad Old Days?" *The Guardian*, November 19, 2014, https://www.theguardian.com/world/2014/nov/19/new-cold-war-back-to-bad-old-days-russia-west-putin-ukraine; and Jon Henley, "Most Europeans Believe US in New Cold War with China and Russia," *The Guardian*, September 22, 2021, https://www.theguardian.com/world/2021/sep/22/most-europeans-believe-us-in-new-cold-war-with-china-and-russia-poll.

13. John Garrard and Carol Garrard, *Russian Orthodoxy Resurgent: Faith and Power in the New Russia* (Princeton, NJ: Princeton University Press, 2008).

14. For more, see Masha Gessen, *Words Will Break Cement: The Passion of Pussy Riot* (London: Granta Books, 2014).

15. For example, see Dianne Kirby, ed., *Religion and the Cold War* (Basingstoke: Palgrave Macmillan, 2003); and James C. Wallace, "A Religious War? The Cold War and Religion," *Journal of Cold War Studies* 15, no. 3 (Summer 2013): 162–80.

16. Jenny Robertson, *Be Our Voice: The Story of Michael Bourdeaux and Keston College* (London: Darton, Longman and Todd, 1984).

17. Hurst, *British Human Rights Organizations and Soviet Dissent*; Davorin Peterlin, "An Analysis of the Publishing Activity of Keston Institute in the Context of Its Last Three Years of Operation in Oxford (2003–2006)," *Occasional Papers on Religion in Eastern Europe* 30, no. 1 (February 2010): 1–17; and Gerd Stricker and Walter Sawatsky, "Postscript–Keston Institute in transition," *Occasional Papers on Religion in Eastern Europe* 23, no. 3 (2003): 1–8.

18. For example, see Philip Boobbyer, *Conscience, Dissent and Reform in Soviet Russia* (London: Routledge, 2005); Robert Hornsby, *Protest, Reform and Repression in Khrushchev's Soviet Union* (Cambridge: Cambridge University Press, 2013); and Robert Horvath, *The Legacy of Soviet Dissent, Dissidents, Democratisation and Radical Nationalism in Russia* (London: Routledge, 2005).

19. Tom Buchanan, *Amnesty International and Human Rights Activism in Postwar Britain, 1945–1977* (Cambridge: Cambridge University Press, 2020); Tom Buchanan, "Human Rights Campaigns in Modern Britain," in *NGOs in Contemporary Britain: Non-State Actors in Society and Politics since 1945*, ed. Nicholas Crowson, Matthew Hilton, and James McKay (Houndmills: Palgrave Macmillan, 2009); Ron Dudai, "The Long View: Human Rights Activism, Past and Present," *Journal of Human Rights* 7, no. 3 (2008): 299–309; Margaret Keck and Katherine Sikkink, *Activists beyond Borders: Advocacy Networks in International Politics* (Ithaca, NY: Cornell University Press, 1998); Barbara Keys, "The Telephone and Its Uses in 1980s U.S. Activism," *Journal of Interdisciplinary History* 48, no. 4 (2018): 485–509; Robin Redhead and Nick Turnbull, "Towards a Study of Human Rights Practitioners," *Human Rights Review* 12 (2011): 173–89.

20. For examples of this voluminous literature, see Kenneth Cmiel, "The Recent History of Human Rights," *The American Historical Review* 109, no. 1 (February 2004): 117–35; Jan Eckel and Samuel Moyn, eds., *The Breakthrough: Human Rights in the 1970s* (Philadelphia: University of Pennsylvania Press, 2013); Barbara Keys, *Reclaiming American Virtue: The Human Rights Revolution of the 1970s* (Cambridge, MA: Harvard University Press, 2014); Stefan-Ludwig Hoffman, ed., *Human Rights in the Twentieth Century* (Cambridge: Cambridge University Press, 2011); and Samuel Moyn, *The Last Utopia: Human Rights in History* (Cambridge, MA: Belknap Press, 2010).

21. Benjamin Nathans, "The Disenchantment of Socialism: Soviet Dissidents, Human Rights, and the New Global Morality," in Eckel and Moyn, *The Breakthrough*, 33–48.

22. See "Patrons and Members of the Council," Keston Institute, https://www.keston.org.uk/officers.

23. For more on this, see David D'Avray, *Rationalities in History: A Weberian Essay in Comparison* (Cambridge: Cambridge University Press, 2010).

24. For more on this, see Roland Barthes, "The Death of the Author" in *Image-Music-Text* (London: HarperCollins, 1977).

25. For an example of this effect in a different context, see Corinna Peniston-Bird, "'I Wondered Who'd Be the First to Spot That': Dad's Army at War, in the Media, and in Memory," *Media History* 13, no. 2 (2007): 183–202.

26. Mustafa Emirbayer and Ann Mische, "What Is Agency?" *American Journal of Sociology* 103, no. 4 (1998): 962–1023.

27. For example, see Walter Johnson, "On Agency," *Journal of Social History* 37, no. 1 (2003): 113–24.

28. Hurst, *British Human Rights Organizations and Soviet Dissent*, 115–16.

29. Bourdeaux, *One Word of Truth*, 50–52.

30. Michael Bourdeaux, *Opium of the People: The Christian Religion in the USSR* (London: Faber and Faber, 1965).

31. Hurst, *British Human Rights Organizations and Soviet Dissent*, 119–21.

32. Kyle Cuordileone, "The Torment of Secrecy: Reckoning with American Communism and Anticommunism after Venona," *Diplomatic History* 35, no. 4 (2011): 615–42.

33. Bourdeaux, *One Word of Truth*, 294.

34. Micheline Ishay, *The History of Human Rights: From Ancient Times to the Globalization Era* (Oakland: University of California Press, 2008); and Paul Lauren, *The Evolution of International Human Rights: Visions Seen* (Philadelphia: University of Pennsylvania Press, 2011).

35. Geoffrey Levin, "Before Soviet Jewry's Happy Ending: The Cold War and America's Long Debate over Jackson-Vanik, 1976–1989," *Shofar* 33, no. 3 (2015): 63–85.

36. See "What are the sanctions on Russia and are they hurting its economy?" BBC News, May 25, 2023, https://www.bbc.co.uk/news/world-europe-60125659.

37. Keys, *Reclaiming American Virtue*.

38. Sarah Snyder, *Human Rights Activism and the End of the Cold War: A Transnational History of the Helsinki Network* (Cambridge: Cambridge University Press, 2011); Daniel Thomas, "Human Rights Ideas, the Demise of Communism and the End of the Cold War," *Journal of Cold War Studies* 7, no. 2 (2005): 110–41.

39. For an especially engaging discussion of this issue, see Stefan-Ludwig Hoffman, "Human Rights and History," *Past and Present* 232, no. 1 (2016): 279–310; Lynn Hunt, "The Long and the Short of the History of Human Rights," *Past and Present* 232, no. 1 (2016): 323–31; and Samuel Moyn, "End of Human Rights History," *Past and Present* 232, no. 1 (2016): 307–22.

40. Benjamin Nathans, "Soviet Rights-Talk in the Post-Stalin Era," in Hoffman, *Human Rights in the Twentieth Century*, 166–90; and Nathans, "The Disenchantment of Socialism."

41. Peter Reddaway, *Uncensored Russia: The Human Rights Movement in the Soviet Union* (London: Jonathan Cape, 1972).

42. Bourdeaux, *One Word of Truth*, 113.

43. Mark Hurst, "The Birth of the Last Utopia: Is Keston Really a 'Human Rights' Group?" *Keston Newsletter*, no. 21 (2015): 17–25.

44. Before its move to the village of Keston, Keston College was known as "The Centre for the Study of Religion and Communism."

45. Xenia Howard-Johnston, "Editorial," *Religion in Communist Lands* 1, no. 1 (1973), 6.

46. Hurst, *British Human Rights Organizations and Soviet Dissent*, 118–19.

47. Bourdeaux, *One Word of Truth*, rear cover; Xenia Dennen, "Michael Bourdeaux Obituary," *The Guardian*, April 16, 2021, https://www.theguardian.com/world/2021/apr/16/michael-bourdeaux-obituary; "The Rev Canon Michael Bourdeaux Obituary," *The Times*, May 1, 2021, https://www.thetimes.co.uk/article/the-rev-canon-michael-bourdeaux-obituary-wfsh-chbth; and "Obituary: Michael Bourdeaux," *Church Times*, April 16, 2021, https://www.churchtimes.co.uk/articles/2021/16-april/gazette/obituaries/obituary-canon-michael-bourdeaux.

48. Michael Bourdeaux, *Risen Indeed: Lessons in Faith from the USSR* (London: Darton, Longman and Todd, 1983), 1.

49. Bourdeaux, *One Word of Truth*, 293.

50. Rowan Williams, "Why Religious Liberty Matters," *Keston Newsletter*, no. 31 (2020), 3.

51. Stephen Hopgood, *Keepers of the Flame: Understanding Amnesty International* (Ithaca, NY: Cornell University Press, 2006), 18–21, 216.

52. Tom Buchanan, "'The Truth Will Set You Free': The Making of Amnesty International," *Journal of Contemporary History* 37, no. 4 (2002): 575–97; Mark Hurst, "What Oxfam Can Learn from Charities That Survived Scandals," *The Conversation*, February 23, 2018, https://theconversation.com/what-oxfam-can-learn-from-charities-that-survived-scandals-92197.

53. For example, see "Prayer and Praise," *Frontier* (July–August 1992), back cover.

54. Michael Bourdeaux, "News from the Centre," *Religion in Communist Lands* 1, no. 2 (1973), 3. *Religion in Communist Lands* is now published as *Religion, State and Society* and has undergone an evolution in purpose and direction since the end of the Cold War. For more on this, see Zoe Knox, "An Interview with Philip Walters for *Religion, State and Society*," *Religion, State and Society* 50, no. 1 (2022): 118–29.

55. *Keston News Service*, no. 122 (April 24, 1981), front cover.

56. "Acceptance Address by Mr. Michael Bourdeaux," May 15, 1984, https://www.templetonprize.org/laureate-sub/bourdeaux-acceptance-speech/.

57. "Acceptance Address."

58. Alexander Solzhenitsyn, "Nobel Lecture," https://www.nobelprize.org/prizes/literature/1970/solzhenitsyn/lecture/.

59. Michael Bourdeaux, "The Russian Church, Religious Liberty and the World Council of Churches," *Religion in Communist Lands* 13, no. 1 (1985), 26.

60. For more on this, see Hurst, *British Human Rights Organizations and Soviet Dissent*, especially chapter 2.

61. Bourdeaux, *One Word of Truth*, xiii.

62. Bourdeaux, *One Word of Truth*, 72.

63. For an example of a propaganda attack in which Bourdeaux was accused of "willy-nilly" confusing the position of Baptists in the Soviet Union, see Yuri Alexandrov, "Baptists in Russia," *The Times*, December 2, 1966, 5.

64. Marc Bennetts, *Kicking the Kremlin: Russia's New Dissidents and the Battle to Topple Putin* (London: Oneworld, 2014); Masha Gessen, *The Future Is History: How Totalitarianism Reclaimed Russia* (London: Granta Books, 2018); Mark Hurst, "Crossing the Curtain: British Activists and the Echoes of Soviet Dissent in Contemporary Russian Human Rights Activism," *Cambridge Review of International Affairs* 36, no. 4 (2023): 513–31; and Peter Pomerantsev, *Nothing Is True and Everything Is Possible: Adventures in Modern Russia* (London: Faber and Faber, 2015).

CHAPTER 3

The Truth Will Set You Free

The Theological Foundations of Michael Bourdeaux's Commitment to Religious Liberty

Joshua T. Searle

Prophets, both ancient and modern, have hailed from diverse social and economic backgrounds. They are sometimes, like the Prophet Ezekiel, descended from a distinguished lineage of priests. Others, such as the Prophet Isaiah, were courtiers of the ruling elite. But prophets are often of humble origin, as was the case with the Prophet Amos, who worked as a shepherd and farmer of sycamore figs. Given the wide range of people throughout history who have answered the call to become a prophet, it should be no surprise that in more recent times the prophetic summons came not to an established prelate in London or Canterbury but to the son of a baker living in the small Cornish village of Praze-An-Beeble. It is something of a cliché to say that "God moves in mysterious ways," but one does not necessarily need to believe in divine providence to appreciate the sense of vocation that summoned Michael Bourdeaux, this Cornish baker's son, to become one of the most formidable advocates for human rights and religious freedom of his generation. In order to see Bourdeaux's achievements in their proper perspective, it is essential to understand the sense of prophetic vocation, arising from his deeply held religious commitment to freedom and truth, that sustained him throughout his life of advocacy on behalf of persecuted believers suffering under totalitarian regimes. This chapter is thus directed toward the elucidation of the theological significance of freedom and truth—the values to which Bourdeaux devoted his long and fruitful life.

It should be acknowledged that, notwithstanding his extraordinary erudition, broad mind, and piercing intellect, Bourdeaux never thought of himself as a theologian or philosopher of the academic caste. From his memoirs it can be inferred that he considered himself to be primarily a historian or journalist and campaigner rather than a scholar.[1] His numerous published works exhibit a greater concern for the accuracy of his factual reporting than for the development of a sophisticated system of abstract ideas. Nevertheless, his commitment to practical action on behalf of persecuted believers was undergirded by his deep Christian convictions concerning the sanctity of truth and freedom. He was motivated to campaign for religious liberty not simply out of vague humanitarian sentiment or even out of an abstract sense of moral duty but rather because he regarded freedom and truth as the twin imperatives of the Gospel of Christ to which, from an early age, he devoted his life. Beneath all the various engagements and diverse achievements of Bourdeaux's long career there lay certain changeless principles and convictions that arose out of his Christian faith. Therefore, while it is important to focus on Bourdeaux's practical achievements as an internationally acclaimed champion of religious liberty, it is equally necessary to situate his accomplishments within their theological context. Only then, I will argue, can we undertake a comprehensive and judicious assessment of Bourdeaux's lasting legacy and the ongoing relevance of Keston into the twenty-first century.

The main aim of this chapter is thus to elucidate the religious foundations of freedom and truth in order to offer a theological understanding of Bourdeaux's contributions to religious liberty. Toward this end, this chapter explores the integral relation of freedom and truth within the Christian tradition. This was a prominent theme in Russian Orthodox theology, including the works of theologians whom Bourdeaux acknowledged as key influences on his life and thought. These ideas offer new perspectives on Bourdeaux's prophetic vocation to present a faith-filled, Gospel-centered alternative to the stifling dogmatism of officially endorsed Soviet atheism. This chapter begins with an account of Bourdeaux's religious convictions before proceeding to a discussion concerning the meaning of Christian freedom, drawing particularly on Eastern Orthodox ideas. Taking Bourdeaux's life and witness as my point of departure, my aim is to offer a theological perspective on Bourdeaux's lifelong commitment to the cause of religious freedom. The chapter concludes with an assessment of the ongoing relevance of Bourdeaux's work and the lessons he continues to teach us about how to defend freedom and truth in today's world, which is witnessing a revival of new forms of political extremism and a resurgence of ideologies that are hostile to human freedom and dignity.

"The Chief Fact with Regard to Him": Bourdeaux's Vocation as a Christian Prophet

"It is well said, in every sense," remarked Thomas Carlyle, "that a man's religion is the chief fact with regard to him."[2] This observation is especially applicable to the life of Bourdeaux, for whom religion was a matter of utmost concern. Although Bourdeaux was a lifelong Anglican churchman and had served as a parish priest, his religious commitments involved far more than the mere profession of a creed or self-identification with a particular denomination. Religion, to borrow again from Carlyle, was a matter "concerning his vital relations to this mysterious Universe and his duty and destiny there."[3] Had it not been for his religious commitments, Bourdeaux's contributions to religious liberty would have been not merely incomprehensible but also impossible. His Christian faith is what made him such an indomitable advocate for liberty and truth. In the words of one of his early mentors at Oxford, Nicolas Zernov,[4] Bourdeaux regarded Christianity as "the most dynamic and challenging force in the history of mankind" and "the main hope of men's liberation from . . . the despotism of their deified rulers."[5] Bourdeaux's Christian upbringing, nurtured and enriched by his broadness of outlook and wide reading, equipped him with a set of deep religious convictions that sustained and inspired him throughout his long life of service and sacrifice on behalf of freedom. His life serves as a vivid illustration of R. G. Collingwood's observation that religion at its best can serve as "the giver of freedom and salvation, because it liberates the soul from the life of imagination, of semblance and unreality, and leads from the things that are seen and temporal to the things that are unseen and eternal."[6]

In an age of widespread skepticism in which religious faith is customarily ridiculed or vilified by its contemporary cultural despisers, Bourdeaux's life testifies to the life-giving and life-enhancing qualities of a religious worldview that enables believers to lift their gaze above the seeming hopelessness of present circumstances to a future hope that is anticipated in faith. This ability to rise above the semblance of reality was to prove essential in Bourdeaux's lifelong struggle against the falsehoods and propaganda of both Soviet Communism and, later, post-Soviet authoritarianism. With the gift of prophetic perception, Bourdeaux believed that by advancing the cause of religious freedom he was responding to the call of the Gospel. His memoirs make it clear that he interpreted his work as part of a prophetic calling from God to become a "voice for the voiceless."[7] He believed that it was "God's choice for my life that I should arrive in Moscow during the very month in which the growing anti-religious campaign acquired a public profile."[8] Friedrich Nietzsche averred that "everyone carries within himself a productive uniqueness at the core of his being; and when he discovers it, a peculiar radiance appears around him that indicates the singularity" of his life's purpose.[9] Imbued with an ardent sense of prophetic vocation and fortified by his momentous encounters with persecuted believers, Bourdeaux was able to discover his life's purpose, which he pursued with resolute faith and courage.

The reference to Bourdeaux's "prophetic calling" is not incidental. It was clear that not only did Bourdeaux (reluctantly) acknowledge his role as a prophet, but also that his prophetic calling was recognized and affirmed by others, including his close friends.[10] In the Christian tradition, a prophet is someone who is called and equipped by God to become an ambassador of God to the people and a mediator of God's message. The prophet becomes a mouthpiece that God uses to communicate a word of truth to the people. Bourdeaux was endowed with many gifts of intellect, empathy, and charisma, which he dedicated to his calling. A prophet is not the same as a priest, although these two vocations can be complementary: a priest represents the people before God, whereas a prophet is someone who represents God before the people.

In seeking thus to represent God to the people, Bourdeaux realized early on that neither the force of his personality nor his persuasive rhetoric was the decisive factor in his prophetic ministry. He believed that he had a duty simply to tell the truth about the state of religion and the plight of believers behind the Iron Curtain. He did not allow emotional judgments to obtrude into his reporting on the facts. "My task," he wrote, "was not to give my own interpretation: I simply had to speak as a medium for the voice which I had heard so decisively and which I must find ways of continuing to hear."[11] When he was asked by the persecuted Christians to "be our voice," Bourdeaux emphasized the word *our*; what mattered was not his own personal interpretation, but the truth of *their* voice concerning *their* plight as persecuted believers under Soviet Communism. Rather than attempting to spin stories or embellish narratives in order to heighten the emotional resonance of his advocacy, Bourdeaux sought to "stick strictly to the realm of provable fact" without "invoking the miraculous."[12] In fact, Bourdeaux could be rather scathing of other advocates of religious freedom who relied more on personal charisma and extravagant rhetoric than simple appeals to corroborated eyewitness accounts and verified facts to garner sympathy for persecuted believers.[13]

The reason why Bourdeaux was mainly content to "let the facts speak for themselves" was because he believed in the inherent power of truth to accomplish the purposes of God in the world. It is likely that Bourdeaux learned this vital lesson from Aleksandr Solzhenitsyn, after whose famous dictum "One word of truth shall outweigh the whole world" Bourdeaux titled his memoirs. As Bourdeaux once remarked, "the very act of publishing the truth is a defense of those people who are caught up in unpleasant situations for religious reasons in Russia and elsewhere."[14] This commitment to factual accuracy was to characterize Keston's work during Bourdeaux's tenure to the extent that Keston acquired an enduring reputation for providing "completely reliable information for those who want to know what is going on in modern Russia."[15]

Bourdeaux understood, like many prophets before him, that this commitment to telling the truth would come at a great cost. After his encounter in 1964 with two Ukrainian believers, Feodosia and Efrosinia, outside the ruins of a recently demolished church in Moscow, he realized that "from that moment the direction of my life was set" and that he "had to find some way of serving the persecuted Church full time."[16] Since there were no organizations that could financially support him and his young family in pursuit of this vocation, he understood that to fulfill the calling "would mean giving up personal security and branching out on my own."[17] He would need to set aside comfort, security, and regular employment in order to pursue his singular calling. Reflecting on his decision years later, Bourdeaux noted that a "hard struggle would lie ahead, with many years of further preparation before I could properly begin."[18] Bourdeaux's memoirs recount several moments of great danger and severe hardships that he faced throughout the years of advocacy on behalf of persecuted believers.

Yet, as a committed Christian, Bourdeaux understood that, as he put it, "the path to resurrection leads through the door of Calvary."[19]

Imbued with this sense of vocation, he viewed even his hardships and struggles through the optic of hope. He lived with a sense of expectation that God was working his purposes out in the world. In the tradition of the great prophets of church history, Bourdeaux was attentive to the ways in which God realizes his purposes for the world and establishes his kingdom in it. It was his firm conviction that "God's signature is on the small events of this world just as indelibly as on the large."[20] This overriding sense of God's hand over the events of world history nurtured in him the conviction, which he noted in his diary when he was still a young exchange student in Moscow, that "Communism can't win here."[21] This conviction arose not simply from intuition, but from his awareness of the ways in which divine providence was working its purpose out in the course of world events. As Bourdeaux put it in 1971, "The Spirit is moving in very strange and wonderful ways in Russia, and it seems to me that the days of communism are unquestionably numbered."[22] In the darkest days of religious persecution, Bourdeaux held high the hope that it was not the dehumanizing ideology of Soviet Communism that would have the last word, but the truth of Christ and the power of the Gospel. This hope enabled him to envision a brighter future in which freedom and truth would triumph over oppression and falsehood.

In this respect, Christianity was the overriding reality that served as a fixed point of reference around which Bourdeaux oriented his life and work. For him, Christianity was preeminently a religion of freedom. The pathos of freedom could be described as the vivifying theme of his prophetic calling. Like the biblical prophets who declared God's plan to "break the yoke of slavery" and "set the captives free," freedom was at the center of Bourdeaux's understanding of his prophetic role and responsibility to serve God's purposes in the world.[23] By championing the cause of freedom, he believed he was helping to bring the Kingdom of God to earth. It is, accordingly, to an examination of the central theme of Christian freedom that this chapter now turns.

A Blessing or a Curse? Orthodox Perspectives on the Meaning of Freedom

Throughout his writings, Bourdeaux displays a keen interest in Orthodox spirituality as well as a deep knowledge of Orthodox theology. Toward the end of his life, he remarked that he had been "profoundly influenced by the experience of Russian Orthodox believers over six decades."[24] As a young Anglican ordinand in Oxford in the 1950s, Bourdeaux was disposed to hold charitable opinions of Eastern Orthodoxy.[25] Under the aegis of Nicolas Zernov, Bourdeaux became a supporter of the Fellowship of St. Alban and St. Sergius, a religious community based in Oxford that promotes unity and fellowship between Anglican and Orthodox Christians.[26] He believed that Eastern Orthodoxy "encloses spiritual treasures which can inspire the world."[27] Many of the outstanding defenders of freedom who recur throughout his writings, such as Gleb Yakunin and Aleksandr Men, were Orthodox priests.[28] In his early work, *Opium for the People,* Bourdeaux refers favorably to the "new lights of Christianity."[29] These leading figures, who had converted to Orthodox Christianity from Marxist atheism (via idealism), included Nikolai Berdiaev, Sergei Bulgakov, Semyon Frank, and Piotr Struve, who were all persecuted and banished by the Soviet authorities.

Although Bourdeaux was familiar with the writings of leading Orthodox thinkers who had given lucid expression to the meaning and significance of religious freedom, he refrained from offering a focused or sustained account of freedom in his own writings. In piecing together the ways in which he refers to freedom throughout his writings, it can be inferred that Bourdeaux's implicit understanding corresponded to the standard formulation of freedom as the ability to believe and express one's religious convictions in public without external constraint, as well as the freedom to persuade others of the truth of these convictions.[30] For Bourdeaux, freedom of conscience was one of the points on which his religious—that is, Christian—beliefs converged entirely with his political—that is, liberal—convictions. The view of freedom as the absence of external restraint has become axiomatic within Western liberal democracies. Individual citizens of a free society should be permitted to pursue their own interests according to their inclinations, on condition that they do not infringe on the liberty and well-being of other individuals.[31] The liberal tradition formed the basis of many of the political liberties and civil rights, including the freedom of religion, that are taken as axiomatic in many parts of the Western world today.[32]

The Eastern Orthodox tradition, in contrast to the Western liberal tradition, has tended to view freedom not simply as the absence of external restraint or coercion but as something with a positive meaning and content. Freedom is viewed not as mere arbitrariness but has a purpose and direction. A key figure in this regard was the philosopher Georg Wilhelm Friedrich Hegel, whose philosophy of freedom influenced not only the thinking of Russian Socialists such as Bakunin, Belinsky, and Lenin, but also the theology of leading Orthodox Christians such as Sergei Bulgakov and Nikolai Berdiaev.[33] Hegel defined freedom as rational "self-determination" (*Selbstbestimmung*).[34] Licentious pursuit of one's sensory pleasures resulted not in freedom but in a condition of spiritual self-enslavement, whereas true liberty, according to Hegel and his followers—most notably, Karl Marx—consisted in the power to bring self-determined goals into effect by framing purposes through the application of reason. When this view is supplemented by a theological viewpoint, this positive condition of freedom is achieved not solely through the application of human reason but by the infusion of God's grace into the human spirit, which empowers a person to live according to the truth of the Gospel of Christ and to set self-determined goals in pursuit of this ultimate end.[35] Freedom, from this perspective, is thus regarded as the liberty to follow Christ without help or hindrance from any outside power, such as church or state, on the path of obedience toward newness of life in the Holy Spirit.

Nowadays, the question concerning religious freedom tends to be confined to the political sphere and is understood in a formal sense as a basic right of individuals either to believe or not to believe. Freedom of religion is customarily regarded as a citizen's formal, abstract entitlement in a free society. Since Isaiah Berlin wrote his famous essay on *Two Concepts of Liberty*, the version of "negative liberty" that he advocated has become the ideological mainstay of liberal democracy in the West.[36] Critics, however, have claimed that the problem with negative liberty is that it attempts to base a theory of ethics on an existential abyss of absolute freedom.[37] Freedom is analogous to nothingness; it exists only as a logical abstraction in relation to real essences.[38] A theological conception of freedom posits that freedom only becomes substantive and transformative to the extent that it is able to connect with something that does have ontological substance, such as truth, beauty, or love. Therefore, from a theological perspective, freedom of religion should be viewed not simply in its a negative or formal aspect but seen more as a duty and obligation to live according to the truth, as revealed in the Person of Christ.

In his foreword to *A Future and a Hope*, which I coauthored with Mykhailo Cherenkov, Bourdeaux drew attention to "one of the most telling passages of the book," referring to a section in which I had offered a brief commentary on the "Parable of the Grand Inquisitor" from Fyodor Dostoevsky's great novel *The Brothers Karamazov*.[39] When

I spoke to Bourdeaux, at the time *Future and a Hope* was published in 2014, he shared with me that as he read this section of the book he was struck by the idea that people living under the Soviet system were inclined to view freedom not as a source of happiness but as a crushing burden that they were glad to relinquish. He was both intrigued and perturbed by the idea that freedom could be regarded not merely as a blessing or a gift but as an onerous liability. Berdiaev, also referring to the Grand Inquisitor, once remarked, "freedom is a burden rather than a right, a source of tragedy and untold pain,"[40] and claimed that it is identified by most human beings not as a blessing but as a curse that condemns them to perdition: "Freedom is a fatal gift that leads people to ruin."[41] Dostoevsky's Grand Inquisitor thus refers to the "great anxiety and terrible agony" that people must endure when they are called on to make an authentically free decision for themselves.[42] Addressing Christ, who has returned to Seville at the height of the Spanish Inquisition, Dostoevsky's Grand Inquisitor remarks, "I tell thee that man is tormented by no greater anxiety than to find someone quickly to whom he can hand over that gift of freedom with which the ill-fated creature is born."[43]

The idea of freedom, not simply as a gracious gift but as a burdensome task, occupies an important place not only in Russian literature but also in Eastern Orthodox theology. As one Russian Orthodox theologian put it, "A free rational being is obliged to bear the burden of freedom and is not entitled to revoke this obligation."[44] Freedom is an endowment of humanity in a condition of grace, which enables the believer to "partake of the divine nature" (2 Peter 1:4) in a process known as *theosis*.[45] Ever since Gregory of Nyssa (born c. 335), Eastern Orthodoxy has regarded freedom as the "main component of the understanding of the divine image in humanity."[46] The affirmation of human freedom is bound up with the recognition of the inherent worth and dignity of human persons as beings who bear the divine image, or *imago Dei*.[47] Freedom is an attribute of the human likeness to God.[48]

One group that drew inspiration from this idea of freedom was a dissident faction that emerged in Moscow in 1974, known as the Christian Seminar (see chapter 4).[49] These mainly young and largely self-educated Orthodox dissidents drew on the resources of Christian theology in search of a new "set of values"[50] that would confer "a life-giving sense of purpose, a pivot around which existence can organize itself."[51] The activities and ideas of the Christian Seminar feature prominently in several of Bourdeaux's writings and he clearly sympathized with their plight, especially after Soviet authorities began to clamp down on the group and imprison its leaders.[52] In a statement issued by the Christian Seminar, these dissidents maintained that "the right of religious freedom is based in the unique dignity of the human person, as well as in the image and likeness of God. The sacred freedom of the Church was won by Christ and cleansed by his blood on Golgotha."[53] According to Orthodox theology, freedom is an "expression of God's way of being." God is "free in the sense that He always is that which He wills to be and always acts in accordance with His will."[54] Drawing from these established themes and ideas of Orthodox theology, dissident groups such as the Christian Seminar insisted that freedom, as an inherent attribute of divinized humanity, was an essential component of human dignity. The Christian Seminar's members believed that by taking a stand for freedom, they were protecting and enhancing the divine image of redeemed humanity: "By standing up for the freedom of the church, we are standing up for our right to live according to the commandments of the Christian faith." For the members of the Christian Seminar, freedom denoted not merely the absence of external constraints, but was rather "the greatest gift of God and a sign of the divine presence in the human person . . . This freedom governs human consciousness, and the Lord God Himself reveals it even in the most powerless form."[55]

Within the dogmatic tradition of Eastern Orthodoxy, human freedom is based on the teaching concerning human participation in the life of the Holy Trinity (*theosis*): "For Orthodox Christians, divine freedom supports human freedom, and human freedom is called to cooperate with divine freedom."[56] Although the divine image and likeness of human beings has been tarnished by sin, the spiritual qualities of freedom, love, and creativity remain part of human nature, even after the fall.[57] Since "freedom is an intrinsic characteristic of every being made in God's image and likeness," every human being has the ability to pursue either good or evil according to the extent to which his or her conscience is attuned to the promptings of the Holy Spirit.[58] Pavel Evdokimov expressed this traditional view of Russian Orthodox theology in these terms: "A human being is free because s/he is the image of divine freedom; hence s/he has the opportunity to choose."[59]

Although it is impossible for a human being, in a fallen state, to attain to the perfect freedom that God intends for humanity, God reestablishes the divine image through the incarnation of His Son in order to show the way to "the synergistic path of redemption."[60] Only when this synergy has been established is a person able to experience true freedom.[61] God sends His Son into the world in order to show people that spiritual freedom is attained only through the merging of the person of the human being with the person of the God-Human (Christ, the incarnate *Logos*) in a process of divinization (or *theosis*). The Orthodox idea of *theosis* thus involves the process through which the liberating grace of the divine life gradually subdues the enslaving whimsical impulses of fallen human nature. The life of the flesh is supplanted by life in the Spirit, which denotes the condition of true freedom in Christ. As the great Russian mystic Vladimir Solovyev expressed it, the goal of the Christian life is to change "the centre of man's life from his nature as given to the absolute transcendent world" of the spirit, in which true freedom is to be found.[62] The essence of Christian spiritual formation can thus be seen as a growth in the spiritual freedom of the believer.

Lessons from Michael Bourdeaux concerning Freedom and Dignity in a New Authoritarian Age

Although Bourdeaux held Orthodox theology in high esteem, he had deep misgivings about the political and cultural expressions of Russian Orthodoxy. He maintained that his high opinion of Orthodoxy related to "Orthodox Christianity rather than Orthodoxy as a purely historico-cultural phenomenon"[63] and deplored the ways that Orthodox Christianity had been misappropriated to promote authoritarian politics and national chauvinism under the guise of religious zeal.[64] Bourdeaux's detailed knowledge of Russian history alerted him to the dangers of any attempt by the Russian Orthodox Church-State to unite political and religious institutions into the totality of a single authority. This Orthodox belief in the *symfonia* of spiritual and temporal power was a dominant theme in the history of imperial Russia from Ivan the Terrible to Nicholas II.[65] Bourdeaux was unequivocal in his censure of this notion: "*symfonia*, I assert, is a betrayal of the basic Christian—and democratic—belief in freedom of conscience."[66] He was particularly concerned that "since the collapse of communism in 1991, the *symfonia* has resounded with ever more glaring political orchestration."[67] As well as his outspoken criticism of the *symfonia*, Bourdeaux was deeply suspicious of Orthodox theologians and church leaders who promoted the virtues of the supposed vitality of Russian spirituality over and against the apparent decadence and immorality of the "liberal" West. In the post-Soviet era Bourdeaux highlighted the hypocrisy of post-Soviet Orthodox clerics who denounced homosexuality and the apparent decay of "traditional Christian values" in the West while turning a blind eye to the sins of rampant corruption, authoritarianism, and the murder of journalists and other opponents of the Russian oligarchic regime. Bourdeaux saw through the attempts by Russian propagandists to portray Russia as a pristine source of Christian values that was opposed to the "gay," "soulless," and "decadent" West.

Bourdeaux lived to witness the transition of Russia from the dark days of Soviet despotism into a new kind of kleptocratic authoritarianism, which has been euphemistically labeled "managed democracy."[68] The naive optimism that Russia would embrace Western ideals of freedom and become a thriving democracy was shattered by the chaotic and turbulent decade of the 1990s. As a result, writes the Yale historian Timothy Snyder, a "politics of radical hope gave way to a politics of bottomless fear," thus paving the way for an authoritarian figure like Vladimir Putin to become the de facto dictator of the post-Soviet Russian state in the early 2000s. Snyder uses the term "unfreedom" to describe a condition that results from the disillusion of the mass population with political structures and the abandonment of hope for a better future.[69] Unfreedom is an ideological destination at which people arrive by way of post-truth cynicism concerning the validity of the foundational social virtues of truth, equality, liberty, and justice that are the lifeblood of civil society and democratic government.[70] The rise of antidemocratic politics in post-Soviet Russia has created a new climate of hostility between Russia and the West. In the illiberal authoritarian regime of Vladimir Putin, policy has been displaced by propaganda. This process of displacement has occurred alongside broader cultural shifts that have created a hospitable environment for authoritarian despotism.

While the Soviet Union began to disintegrate in the late 1980s following the reforms of glasnost and perestroika, Bourdeaux reflected on the challenge that confronted Western civilization: "Never has it been more important for the West . . . to understand the nature of this challenge and to involve themselves morally in the processes which are unfolding."[71] Thanks to the heroic witness of countless Christian dissidents during the Soviet era, Christianity managed to survive the onslaught of antireligious propaganda and Communist social engineering. Today the challenges for both Christianity and Western civilization are quite different. The enemies of liberty nowadays tend to attack or discriminate not only against the truth claims of particular religions or their freedom to worship.[72] The assault is directed, rather, against truth and freedom themselves. Sometimes the enemies of freedom even use religion as a hammer to shatter people's belief in the existence of truth and freedom. Toward the end of his life Bourdeaux grew increasingly concerned at the ways in which authoritarian politicians throughout the world were using Christianity as a weapon in their assault on liberal democracy. He lamented the naivety of Christians who had been persuaded to support authoritarian politicians, such as Donald Trump, Vladimir Putin, and Viktor Orban, because they pursue their dehumanizing agendas under the banner of the promotion of "traditional Christian values."[73]

Despite the attacks on democracy by its Christian enemies, Bourdeaux believed throughout his life that Christianity and democratic freedoms are not only compatible but essentially coexistent. Although this chapter has focused on the theological formulation of the meaning of freedom, this account does not negate the validity of more commonplace notions of freedom associated with liberal democracy. The two approaches to liberty, the political and the theological, can be viewed as distinct but related phenomena that are both necessary to a full account of human freedom in the contemporary world. Therefore, we may reasonably make the following claim—namely, that freedom proceeds from two main sources: first, from secular democratic values and principles; and second, from faith-based values of human dignity, self-determination, and human rights.

One of the most important theological lessons that I have learned from Bourdeaux's life and work is that these two aspects of freedom are mutually reinforcing. Although modern understandings of political and religious freedom are based on the Judeo-Christian tradition, liberty is not merely a religious value but also the foundation of Western democracy. Therefore, one need not necessarily be a fundamentalist Christian to believe that freedom is a basic human right and a precondition of human dignity; likewise, one need not necessarily be a dogmatic secularist to acknowledge the democratic legitimacy of liberal values and principles. Those who care about religious freedom today must avoid the danger, identified by the Orthodox theologian Leonid Kishkovsky, of setting one view of freedom (religious) against the other (political). "Sometimes," notes Kishkovsky, "those who critique Western culture for its wrong understanding of freedom can become apologists for the denial of freedom."[74] An ideology built entirely on a dogmatic theological view of positive freedom could result, in the worst case, in a form of theocratic despotism, such as that promoted by the Russian fascist theorist Alexander Dugin, and by other supporters of Eurasian-ism. On the other hand, an ideology built exclusively on a secular view of negative freedom could result in a shallow bureaucratic state that becomes prey to the enemies of the open society. A healthy and stable society should be able to accommodate both kinds of freedom. As Lord Acton remarked, "Freedom protects us from being controlled by others. Thus, it demands that we control ourselves."[75]

Bourdeaux deplored Soviet Communism, precisely because of its hostility to freedom. He lamented "the totality with which commu-nism in practice rejected every proven human and religious value, stripping men and women of trust in each other, excising any sense of individual responsibility for the destiny of society, robbing people of their future, just as the rewriting of history had robbed them of their past."[76] Bourdeaux believed that, at its best, Christianity could furnish humanity with the virtues that communism had stripped away: the virtues of interpersonal trust and the sense of individual responsibil-ity for oneself and one's neighbors that comes from having a sense of hope for the future. Bourdeaux hoped that Soviet ideology would be replaced neither by an Orthodox theocracy nor a secular bureaucracy but by a generous vision of what Aleksandr Men called "the tradition of open Christianity."[77] Therefore, in the same way that Christianity offered "the most visible ideological alternative to communism" under the Soviet regime, so today, I would agree with Bourdeaux that Chris-tianity, at its best, offers the most credible ideological alternative to authoritarian populism of the post-Soviet era.[78]

It is lamentable, however, to observe how, throughout the post-Christian West, Christianity has lost its vivacity and creative dynamism. Far from being an ideological alternative to authoritarianism, Christi-anity has too often been an ideological crutch, helping to prop up cor-rupt regimes from Putin's Russia to Trump's America. Christianity has become inert, compromised, and conformist. Christian leaders from both East and West have yielded to the temptation to build a separate relationship with the state or have been lured by promises of patronage, preferential treatment, favorable legislation, and state discrimination against the perceived "enemies" of traditional Christian values, such as homosexuals and religious minorities.[79] In return for these dubi-ous "benefits" of political power and patronage, Christian churches are expected to show their loyalty to the state and to collaborate with its authoritarian institutions. Therefore, as Bourdeaux himself would cau-tion us, Christianity must be understood not as a religion of domina-tion that provides an ideological fig leaf to cover the naked corruption of totalitarian regimes, but as a religion of freedom and truth that promotes the dignity of the human person. Christianity should be understood not as a national political institution, but as a global movement of spiritual emancipation that infuses the public space with Gospel values of compassion, justice, and truth. Above all, this true vision of Christianity must have as its foundation the person and work of the Messiah who declared, "Ye shall know the truth and the truth shall set you free."

In the final years of his life, as he reflected on what had inspired him to found Keston College, Bourdeaux mentioned that "I had then a vision of a new Europe: one in which religious liberty was universal; one in which Russia would be able to contribute its full complement to new ideals, to new democracy."[80] Now that Bourdeaux, sadly, is no longer with us, the responsibility of his successors is to help to bring this vision into reality. As people of good will from all faiths (and none) seek to live according to the values of dignity and freedom, it is imperative that they learn from Bourdeaux and other prophets of liberty that freedom is not an automatic entitlement but a precious and fragile gift that must be cherished and defended. In this new age of authoritarianism, as threats to open society emerge throughout the world, we must be prepared morally and intellectually for an enduring struggle in defense of freedom. The life and legacy of Bourdeaux are exemplary as we contemplate the formidable challenges ahead and gather the resources that we will need to confront them. As the world emerges from the shock and disruption of the Covid-19 pandemic, the universal impression is that humanity is experiencing a time of momentous change and social upheaval. The need for prophets like Michael Bourdeaux, who are prepared to take a stand for freedom and truth, has never been greater.

Notes

1. See, for example, Bourdeaux's remark that he was writing "more as a journalist than a researcher." Michael Bourdeaux, *One Word of Truth: The Cold War Memoir of Michael Bourdeaux and Keston College* (London: Darton, Longman and Todd, 2019), 253.

2. Thomas Carlyle, *Heroes, Hero-Worship and the Heroic in History* (London: Chapman and Hall, 1840), 4.

3. Carlyle, *Heroes*, 5.

4. As Bourdeaux acknowledges, Zernov played a key role in encouraging him to take up the cause of religious freedom on behalf of persecuted believers in the USSR. See Bourdeaux, *One Word of Truth*, 79.

5. Nicholas Zernov, *The Russian Religious Renaissance of the Twentieth Century* (New York: Harper and Row, 1963), 298.

6. Robin G. Collingwood, *Speculum Mentis or The Map of Knowledge* (Oxford: Oxford University Press, 1924), 153.

7. Bourdeaux, *One Word of Truth*, 87.

8. Bourdeaux, *One Word of Truth*, 64.

9. Friedrich Nietzsche, *Unzeitgemässe Betrachtungen. Drittes Stück: Schopenhauer als Erzieher* (Chemnitz: Ernst Schmeitzner, 1874), 30.

10. See, for instance, the recognition of Bourdeaux's prophetic calling in the obituaries to him written by Hugh Wybrew and Mark E. Elliott in *Keston Newsletter* 34 (2021): 4–13.

11. Bourdeaux, *One Word of Truth*, 87.

12. Michael Bourdeaux and Lorna Bourdeaux, *Ten Growing Soviet Churches* (Bromley: MARC Europe, 1987), 19.

13. An example of this is Bourdeaux's critique of the flamboyant Romanian Evangelical Lutheran priest Richard Wurmbrand, who according to Bourdeaux sometimes "held his audiences worldwide with a torrent of rhetoric which, sadly, sometimes went beyond the evidence of the known facts." Bourdeaux, *One Word of Truth*, 218.

14. Michael Bourdeaux, et al., *The Clash between Christianity and Communism* (Witney: Gateway Fellowship, 1971), 18.

15. Donald Coggan, "Foreword," in Michael Bourdeaux, *Risen Indeed: Lessons in Faith from the USSR* (London: Darnton, Longman and Todd, 1983).

16. Bourdeaux, *One Word of Truth*, 85.

17. Bourdeaux, *Risen Indeed*, 9.

18. Bourdeaux, *One Word of Truth*, 87.

19. This quotation is taken from Bourdeaux's acceptance address of the Templeton Prize in 1984. Full text available from www.templetonprize.org/laureate-sub/bourdeaux-acceptance-speech (accessed January 29, 2022).

20. Bourdeaux, *Risen Indeed*, 1.

21. Bourdeaux, *One Word of Truth*, 72.

22. Bourdeaux, *Clash between Christianity*, 8.

23. Throughout the Old Testament there are numerous examples of prophetic declarations announcing God's intention to free his people from slavery and oppression. See, for example, Isaiah 42:7, 61:1; Jeremiah 30:8; Ezekiel 13:20, 30:18; Nahum 1:13; Hosea 11:4; Zechariah 9:11.

24. Michael Bourdeaux, "The Russian World and Its Challenge: Concept, Ideology and Religion," in *Solidarity, Freedom and Compassion: Proceedings from the London Consultation on Ukraine at Lambeth Palace*, ed. Joshua T. Searle (Chicago: BMS World Mission/Mission Eurasia, 2015), 16–17.

25. I am grateful to Mark E. Elliott, who pointed this out to me in our correspondence.

26. Bourdeaux noted in his memoirs that he served for a period as a member of the council of the Fellowship of St. Alban and St. Sergius. See Bourdeaux, *One Word of Truth*, 79.

27. Michael Bourdeaux, *The Gospel's Triumph over Communism* (Minneapolis, MN: Bethany House, 1991), 107.

28. Bourdeaux, *One Word of Truth*, 236–40; Bourdeaux, *Gospel's Triumph*, 88–89 and 94–97; Michael Bourdeaux, *Religious Ferment in Russia: Protestant Opposition to Soviet Religious Policy* (London: Macmillan, 1968), 183–89.

29. Michael Bourdeaux, *Opium for the People: The Christian Religion in the USSR* (Oxford: Mowbrays, 1977), 49.

30. This conviction has been central to the Western tradition of political liberalism, to which influential thinkers such as John Locke, David Hume, Voltaire, Adam Smith, and John Stuart Mill gave eloquent expression.

31. This view is associated primarily with John Stuart Mill's famous treatise of 1859. Mill argued "the only purpose for which power can be rightfully exercised over any member of a civilized community, against his will, is to prevent harm to others. His own good, either physical or moral, is not a sufficient warrant." John Stuart Mill, *On Liberty* (London: John W. Parker and Son, 1859), 22.

32. Freedom of religion is enshrined in Article 18 of the Universal Declaration of Human Rights, issued by the United Nations in 1948: "Everyone has the right to freedom of thought, conscience and religion; this right includes freedom to change his religion or belief, and freedom, either alone or in community with others and in public or private, to manifest his religion or belief in teaching, practice, worship and observance." See Edward Lawson, *Encyclopedia of Human Rights* (London: Taylor & Francis, 1996), 552.

33. The constraints of time and space do not permit here a detailed discussion of the influence of Hegel on social thought during the imperial and Soviet eras of Russian history. For more details, see Frederick Copleston, *A History of Philosophy: Volume 10: Russian Philosophy* (London: Continuum, 2003), 48, 79–84.

34. Tommaso Pierini, *Theorie der Freiheit: Der Begriff des Zwecks in Hegels Wissenschaft der Logik* (Paderborn: Fink Wilhelm, 2006), 49.

35. See, for example, Sergei Bulgakov's definition of freedom as "the expanding of potential for the manifestation and self-affirmation of the human spirit," in Sergii Bulgakov, *Towards a Russian Political Theology*, ed. Rowan Williams (Edinburgh: T&T Clark, 1999), 44.

36. Isaiah Berlin, *Two Concepts of Liberty* (Oxford: Clarendon Press, 1958).

37. Elsewhere I have attempted to apply this insight toward the interpretation of the chaotic events that followed the disintegration of the Soviet Union in the early 1990s when the abyss of negative freedom in Boris Yeltsin's "free" Russia created an economic and moral vacuum in which anarchy thrived and nihilism flourished. The chimera of "absolute freedom" generated a void of chaos into which post-Soviet society ignominiously collapsed with disastrous consequences that are still being felt to the present day. See Joshua T. Searle and Mykhailo N. Cherenkov, *A Future and a Hope: Mission, Theological Education and the Transformation of Post-Soviet Society* (Eugene, OR: Wipf and Stock, 2014), 63.

38. John Macquarrie, *Stubborn Theological Questions* (London: SCM, 2003), 68–69.

39. Michael Bourdeaux, "Foreword," in Searle and Cherenkov, *Future and a Hope*, ix.

40. Nicolas A. Berdyaev, *Dream and Reality: An Essay in Autobiography*, trans. K. Lampert (London: Geoffrey Bles, 1950), 177.

41. Nikolai A. Berdiaev, *O naznachenii cheloveka* (Moskva: Respublika, 1993), 62. All translations from Russian, Ukrainian, and German sources in this article are my own.

42. Dostoevsky, quoted in Peter Wake, *Tragedy in Hegel's Early Theological Writings* (Bloomington: Indiana University Press, 2014), 17.

43. Fyodor Dostoevsky, *The Brothers Karamazov*, trans. Constance Garnett (Ware: Wordsworth Classics, 2007), 230.

44. Andrei Tret'iakov, "Religiozno-filosofskaia traditsiia vostochnogo khristianstva v uchenii o svobode," in *Smysl i granitsy svoboda cheloveka* (Vienna: Bialystok 2007), 13, see also 13–20.

45. The term *theosis* is commonly regarded as the foundation of Eastern Orthodox theology and spirituality. The term refers to the process of the assimilation of human nature with the divine nature and the full restoration of the *imago Dei*. As a result of *theosis*, human nature becomes "so clear and polished that it perfectly reflects its divine source of Light." See Michael J. Christensen, "The Promise, Process, and Problem of Theosis," in *Partakers of the Divine Nature: The History and Development of Deification in the Christian Traditions*, ed. Michael J. Christensen and Jeffrey A. Wittung (Grand Rapids, MI: Baker, 2007), 23–31.

46. Sergej A. Čursanov, "Freiheit (orthodox)," in *Handwörterbuch Theologische Anthropologie: Römisch-Katholisch/Russisch-Orthodox*, ed. Bertram Stubenrauch and Andrej Lorgus (Freiburg: Herder, 2013), 256.

47. Marina Shishova, "Spiritual and Political Dimensions in the Conception of the Russian Orthodox Church Concerning Dignity, Freedom and Human Rights," in *Orthodox Christianity and Human Rights*, ed. Alfons Brüning and Evert van der Zweerde (Leuven: Peeters, 2012), 351–64.

48. Michael Prokurat, Michael D. Peterson, and Alexander Golitzin, *The A to Z of the Orthodox Church* (Plymouth: Rowman & Littlefield, 1996), 197–98.

49. For more on the aims and activities of this group, see Jane Ellis, "USSR: The Christian Seminar," *Religion in Communist Lands* 8, no. 2 (1980): 92–101.

50. The Christian Seminar even used Nietzsche's term "the transvaluation of values" (*Umwertung aller Werte*) in its literature.

51. Tatyana Goricheva, "The Religious Significance of Unofficial Soviet Culture," *37*, no. 19 (September–December 1979). The name of the journal was *37*.

52. Michael Bourdeaux and Katharine Murray, *Young Christians in Russia* (London: Lakeland, 1976); Bourdeaux, *Risen Indeed*, 30–37.

53. Christian Seminar, "Deklaration der Prinzipien des Moskauer Jugendseminars," in *Russische Jugend im Aufbruch*, ed. Eugen Voss (Zollikon: G2W-Verlag, 1982), 35.

54. Tret'iakov, "Religiozno-filosofskaia traditsiia," 14–15.

55. Christian Seminar, "Deklaration der Prinzipien," 39.

56. Nonna Verna Harrison, "The Human Person and the Image and Likeness of God," in *The Cambridge Companion to Orthodox Christian Theology*, ed. Mary B. Cunningham and Elizabeth Theokritoff (Cambridge: Cambridge University Press, 2008), 82, see also 78–92.

57. Ruth Coates, *Deification in Russian Religious Thought: Between the Revolutions, 1905–1917* (Oxford: Oxford University Press, 2019), 32.

58. Tret'iakov, "Religiozno-filosofskaia traditisiia," 14.

59. Pavel Evdokimov, *Zhenshchina i spasenie mira* (Minsk: Luchi Sofii, 1999), 48.

60. Georges V. Florovsky, cited in Donald Fairbairn, *Eastern Orthodoxy through Western Eyes* (Louisville, KY: Westminster John Knox, 2002), 91.

61. Fairbairn, *Eastern Orthodoxy*, 90-91.

62. Solovyev, quoted in Frederick C. Copleston, *Philosophy in Russia: From Herzen to Lenin and Berdyaev* (Wellwood: Search, 1986), 215.

63. Bourdeaux, *Gospel's Triumph*, 108.

64. See Bourdeaux, "Putin and the Patriarch," *Keston Newsletter* 5 (2008), in which the author expresses his concern that Putin and the then-newly installed Moscow Patriarch were attempting to revive the Byzantine-Moscow concept of *symphonia*.

65. According to John P. Burgess, the Byzantine notion of *symphonia* continues to influence the relationship between church and state in the authoritarian regime of Vladimir Putin. See Burgess, *Holy Rus': The Rebirth of Orthodoxy in the New Russia* (New Haven, CT: Yale University Press, 2017), 10, 38, 203.

66. Bourdeaux, "The Russian World," 17.

67. Bourdeaux, "Foreword," x.

68. Timothy Snyder, *The Road to Unfreedom: Russia, Europe, America* (London: Bodley Head, 2018), 45.

69. Quote from Snyder, *Road to Unfreedom*, 40.

70. Joshua T. Searle, "A Theological Case for Ukraine's European Integration: Deconstructing the Myth of 'Holy Russia' versus 'Decadent Europe'," *International Journal of Public Theology* 16, no. 3 (2022), 301-3.

71. Bourdeaux, *Gospel's Triumph*, 211.

72. This is not to deny the deplorable cases of state persecution targeting specific religious minorities, such as Uyghur Muslims in Xinjiang, China, or dissident Protestant Christians in Russia, which unfortunately continues to the present day.

73. Joshua T. Searle, *Theology after Christendom: Forming Prophets for a Post-Christian World* (Eugene, OR: Cascade, 2018), 57.

74. Leonid Kishkovsky, "Russian Theology after Totalitarianism," in *The Cambridge Companion to Orthodox Christian Theology*, ed. Mary B. Cunningham and Elizabeth Theokritoff (Cambridge: Cambridge University Press, 2008), 270.

75. John Dalberg-Acton, cited in Maciej Zieba, *The Surprising Pope: Understanding the Thought of John Paul II* (Lanham, MD: Lexington Books, 2000), 86.

76. Bourdeaux, *Gospel's Triumph*, 3.

77. Maikl Bordo and Sergei Borisovich Filatov, *Atlas sovremennoi religioznoi zhizni Rossii*, vol. 3 (Sankt Peterburg: Letnii sad, 2005), 259. See also Vladimir Il'ich Iliushenko, *Otets Aleksandr Men': Zhizn' i smert' vo Khriste* (Moskva: Pik, 2000), 170-71.

78. Quote from Walter Kolarz, *Religion in the Soviet Union* (London: Macmillan, 1961), 1. Bourdeaux acknowledged that "Kolarz's work provided a kind

of framework for me in the planning and organization of my own first book [*Opium of the People*]." See Bourdeaux, *One Word of Truth*, 82.

79. For an insightful description and judicious critique of these antidemocratic trends within evangelical Christianity, see David P. Gushee, *Defending Democracy from Its Christian Enemies* (Grand Rapids, MI: Eerdmans, 2023).

80. Bourdeaux, "The Russian World," 17.

PART II

New Perspectives on Religion in the Soviet Union

CHAPTER 4

The Awakening of Soviet Youth

The Quest for Authenticity in the 1960s and 1970s

Wallace L. Daniel

In coming to power in Russia, the Bolshevik Party claimed to be riding a deeply rooted historical trend in which religion would soon die out. Religion, Bolshevik leaders believed, belonged to the past, had served as an instrument of exploitation by the ruling class, and had originated in superstition and mythology. An industrial, scientific, and rational public order promised to kill off naturally what remained of a backward-looking set of beliefs. In 1922, elaborating the new Soviet ideology, Lenin called Christianity a naive faith whose extirpation "was essential for our struggle against the governing religious obscurantists."[1] Michael Bourdeaux, British scholar and church leader, devoted his academic career to exploring the efficacy of Lenin's statement in the lives of religious believers in the Soviet Union and their struggles to maintain their integrity and fundamental convictions. The Keston Archive contains a wealth of information on lived religion in the many decades following Lenin's pledge.

In the late 1960s and 1970s, the Soviet official press boasted a nearly complete victory over this vestige of the past. In May 1976, lecturing about the status of religion in the Soviet Union, the deputy chair of the Council for Religious Affairs, Vasilii Grigor'evich Furov, reported that religion was rapidly disappearing. In the last five years, he stated, about 700 religious establishments had closed and about 1,000 Orthodox churches once registered as active congregations were no longer in use. Surveying the country as a whole, Furov painted an even larger picture of religion's decline during the years of Soviet power. Presently, the Soviet Union had ten times fewer Orthodox churches than existed in prerevolutionary Russia: they had declined from 77,676 to 7,500. Catholic churches, which once numbered 4,200 in the Baltic region, had now shrunk to 1,000. In regions where Islam had flourished, only 1,000 mosques remained out of the former 24,000; the number of synagogues had decreased from 5,000 to 200, only 92 of which were registered, and fifty rabbis were all that remained.[2]

In his lecture, Furov characterized the present relationship between church and state as "normalized," a condition evidenced by formerly recalcitrant priests having reformed and allied themselves with the government. Most of them, he said, supported government policies and were staunch advocates of Soviet patriotism. Harmony and goodwill described the bond that existed between the remaining churches and the Soviet government. He attributed this peaceful condition to the "modernist, reforming tendencies" that "were penetrating ever deeper into parish life, actively supporting the domestic and foreign policy of the USSR."[3] Furov did not gloss over certain obstacles—namely, individuals, vestiges of the past, who expressed "anti-Soviet" views. On the whole, however, he considered these aberrations. Then, in a concluding statement filled with irony, he spoke of the possibility of state support for the church while the state continued to wage ideological war against the church.

Writing at the end of the same decade as Furov's public assessment, the Orthodox priest Fr. Gleb Yakunin expressed a much different view of the Russian Orthodox Church's present condition. Instead of speaking about "modernizing trends," he strongly criticized the government's unlawful interference in religious affairs, which, he believed, had significantly weakened the Orthodox Church's presence in Russian life. At every level, from the patriarch to the parish, government policies had undermined and corrupted the Orthodox Church's capacity to carry out its responsibilities.

Most important, in contrast to the figures Furov employed, Yakunin did not see religion as dying out in the Soviet Union. "In Russia, at the present time," Yakunin wrote, "an awakening of religious consciousness is taking place. Those who are reaching out for religion, who are coming to it, only yesterday were atheists."[4] He spoke of this growing consciousness as a springtime after many years of hibernation. Neither the Orthodox Church nor the state understood the significance of this awakening, he asserted. The state's ideological commitments had left it blind to present realities, particularly the thirst for new ways of thinking among the young.

The contentions that Yakunin advanced presented several questions about the death or rebirth of religious consciousness. Did a religious awakening actually exist, and if so, what evidence supported the reality of its existence? How widespread was this "awakening" and why? What other questions did this awakening raise and with what significance? In the late 1960s and 1970s, the emergence of this so-called awakening served as a key element in Gleb Yakunin's and other participants' evolution as religious activists.

In response to these questions, this chapter will first seek to place the awakening of Soviet youth in context, describing the social and intellectual conditions that fostered the quest for new identities and purposes. It then moves to the creation of the religious-philosophical Moscow Seminar, the individuals who spearheaded the Seminar, the threats it posed to the Soviet regime, and the readings the members explored. How members of the Moscow Seminar approached the readings opened up a whole new way of thinking about the past, present, and future of religion in the Soviet Union that continued to germinate long after the Seminar passed from existence.

Fresh Directions

In the mid- to late 1960s, the ideological beliefs and commitments that had so inflamed earlier generations of Soviet citizens had begun to lose their power. Nikita Khrushchev's speech to a closed session at the Twentieth Party Congress in February 1956, denouncing his predecessor Joseph Stalin as a cruel, despotic, and irrational leader, opened a Pandora's box of questions about the Stalinist system and the ideology that supported it. Following the long Stalinist winter, a period known as "the Thaw" launched a large series of disputes that ranged across Russian literature, the arts, and Russian history. Ultimately, questions about history led to a growing interest in the contributions of the church to the development of the Russian state.

"In the sixties," said Tatiana Goricheva, a participant in this revival of interest, "when the breakdown of the myth of Stalin and the ideals of communism began, we saw that culture served as a point of departure . . . Cultural values helped us come out of the underground towards the light."[5] As they began their search for new ways of interpreting Russian history and culture, the generation of the 1960s lacked an immediate bridge connecting them to the past. The bridge had to be discovered. Because prerevolutionary Russian religious history received little attention in schools and individuals had no solid body of facts on which to build, the process of discovery was often trial-and-error, leading to many misconceptions and sometimes to extreme views. Yet the hunger for discovery attracted increasing numbers of people who aspired to know more about certain subjects, particularly religion, that the school system had forbidden them to explore.

The revived interest in religion took multiple forms. It especially fascinated young intellectuals who wanted a deeper understanding of the Russian past and how Russian traditions might offer a pathway to building the future. They desired honest answers, not the textbook responses they heard repeatedly voiced by official spokespersons and the media. They valued multiple perspectives on issues they confronted in their own lives—problems concerning meaning and faith and the development of a vibrant community. These were religious issues, and normally their discussion took place within the framework of the Church. In the late 1960s and 1970s, their exploration evolved outside the boundaries of that institution.

The rejuvenated interest, as the theologian Fr. Michael Aksenov-Meerson has pointed out, did not signify the first time such a movement had occurred in the Soviet Union. During and immediately after World War II, the Orthodox Church enjoyed a brief period in which a large number of churches were reopened and religious life quickly revived.[6] Despite the wave of violence directed against the church in the prewar decade, it had not dampened the desire of the Russian people to restore places of worship. But, as Aksenov-Meerson noted, the revival in the late 1960s differed significantly from its predecessor. The earlier resurrection originated from people who had grown up in the church and were already religious believers. The young generation who led the late 1960s revival grew up as atheists, were educated to consider religion as superstition, and had no experience with church life. In addition, unlike their predecessors who remained committed to the regime, the young generation had no such allegiance.[7] They questioned everything. They especially revolted against the government's intolerance of dissent, its reluctance to admit multiple points of view, and its restrictions on free expression.

By the late 1960s, disillusionment with the Soviet state and its sup-portive ideology had made deep inroads into Soviet youth, mostly in the age range of eighteen to thirty years. They had become disenchanted with what life under the present regime had to offer, and the state's promised road to the future held little attraction. In their dissatisfac-tion with the established order and in the revolutionary spirit that had animated their predecessors, they resembled similar groups of young people during the same period in France, Great Britain, and the United States. Like them, Soviet youth searched for a deeper and more authen-tic meaning of life than their predecessors offered. Unlike their counter-parts elsewhere, however, Soviet youth were not in rebellion against the capitalist social and economic system. They rebelled against a political order that pushed them into narrowly defined social categories, limited their freedom of choice, and tried to restrict their imagination. In short, they disdained the state's attempt to control the mind and the spirit.

This refusal to conform to the established order is what drew Aksenov-Meerson, a future Orthodox priest, into open rebellion. A bril-liant student of history at Moscow State University in the early 1960s, Aksenov-Meerson became a dissident at the end of his first year, which resulted in his expulsion. During that year, he had decided that he could no longer accept the ideological straitjacket that forced the interpreta-tion of history into a prescribed framework. After leaving the univer-sity, he entered a period of uncertainty and confusion about his future course. "I would have become a terrorist," he said to me, "if at that time, on a whim, I had not traveled out to the parish of Fr. Aleksandr Men," a remarkable Orthodox priest whose parish outside Moscow attracted similar young members of the Russian intelligentsia.[8]

Men's reputation as one of a small number of unusually gifted Orthodox priests had rapidly spread in the late 1960s in the Russian capital and other nearby cities. His parish in the small town of Taraso-vka, where he served from 1962 to 1970, lay on the railroad line from Moscow to Zagorsk, now Sergiev Posad, the traditional seat of Russian Orthodox theology. An increasing number of Russian youth journeyed to Tarasovka each Sunday morning to attend services and to engage in conversation with the well-read, open-minded Fr. Aleksandr.[9] Their numbers expanded in the 1970s following his move to Novaia Derev-nia, near the town of Pushkino. A master conversationalist, a staunch believer in the importance of dialogue, Men was a rare example of a priest who expressed openness to the world.[10] During a time when many young people searched for new directions in their lives and questioned everything, Men opened up for them a fresh, often compelling look at Orthodox Christianity, which heretofore they had been taught to denigrate.

The seeds Men planted about freedom, faith, and human purpose germinated still further in the writings of Anatolii Levitin-Krasnov. In his early career, Levitin-Krasnov had taught Russian literature in a Leningrad elementary school. There, encouraging his students to read the Symbolist poets, he raised questions about the influence of Orthodox Christianity on the poetry of this creative group of writers, and he discovered that his students had a keen interest in spiritual topics. "I can see before me now those 30 children, pale, disheveled little boys and urchin-like girls with pigtails, all of them with their eyes fixed on me. And I, only 23 years of age, wearing the same cheap jacket as they, leaning on the ink-stained teacher's desk and reading . . . making no secret of my religious beliefs."[11] His faith in the promise of Russian youth never wavered. By the 1970s, Levitin-Krasnov wrote that Russian youth had begun to set out on a long journey. Everywhere in society, one felt the silence, but also the expectation: "The night is over. The sleepers are waking up. Life is beginning to stir. What will the day be like?"[12]

The dialogue that Levitin-Krasnov advanced in his writings received a considerable boost in the early 1970s from an Orthodox priest who changed the entire structure of his church services. Fr. Dmitrii Dudko possessed an affinity for people struggling to survive and build their own community.[13] A short, broad-shouldered, gray-headed ebullient priest with an omnipresent smile, Dudko had a dynamic preaching style and welcoming approach to newcomers who entered the several churches he served in Moscow and neighboring towns in the late 1960s and early 1970s. He especially attracted young people and families, who found this lively, easygoing priest much different from the stodgy, ill-prepared, and coarse-mannered churchmen they had previously encountered. Dudko was not a deep thinker. His theology often seemed hastily conceived and superficial. But these intellectual deficiencies did not impede his significance. Although he did not set out to challenge authority or to remake the political establishment, the methods Dudko employed threatened the hierarchy's top-down approach to knowledge and to truth at its core. His sermons, but especially his Saturday evening sessions that welcomed dialogue, provided an education to the five hundred to six hundred people in attendance, giving them facts and perspectives they had not heard in their schooling. The discussions continued for nine sessions, until the tenth when Dudko announced that they were suspended upon orders from Patriarch Pimen.[14] But the sermons had opened doors to questions about certain topics that could not easily be closed.

To Gleb Yakunin, such priests provided clear testimony of what was possible when energetic, outward-looking priests engaged the Russian people in issues related to their lives. These examples he saw in sharp contrast to the otherworldly predispositions of the great majority of Orthodox priests who did little more than offer praises to God, praises he considered useless: They believe their "goal is divine service—simply to glorify God—but God, having glory in abundance, does not need glorification by human beings. The Moscow Patriarchate is incapable of understanding its primary goal is missionary work, of following the supreme mandate that Christ gave to the Church."[15] Given the present condition of the Orthodox Church, Yakunin did not see much opportunity for it to relate effectively to the young or to individuals searching for new meaning in their lives.

Instead, the impetus for continuing this quest came from a different direction. In the mid-1970s, informal seminars among the youth sprang up in Moscow, Leningrad, and several other cities.

The Participants

Ideas in history do not always move in a straight line, as the English historian J. H. Hexter wrote many years ago, but take a zigzag course, advancing, retreating, and then often reappearing in different forms.[16] One cannot trace a direct line between Dudko's evening sessions and the student seminars that sprang forth a year later. But the questions raised in the earlier discussions about freedom, community, and culture were not transitory issues that disappeared, to be forgotten as time moved on. They reemerged and began to be explored more deeply and expansively than before.

In September 1974, a little more than a year after the patriarch suspended Dudko's Saturday evening sessions, a religious-philosophical seminar was formed in Moscow. The Moscow Seminar invited young people interested in learning more about religious issues to attend. It was the brainchild of twenty-four-year-old Aleksandr Ogorodnikov, a former student of the All-Union State Cinematography Institute in Moscow, who had already rejected the philosophical principles underlying Soviet ideology.[17]

In early 1974, the plan to organize a special seminar emerged gradually in Ogorodnikov's mind. In the previous year, he had met Fr. Aleksandr Men, had traveled to his parish multiple times, and the two of them had become friends. He shared his idea with Men, who encouraged him and offered advice on the seminar's organization.[18] Ogorodnikov had also attended Dudko's Saturday evening gatherings, where Dudko's openness inspired him. He considered Dudko his spiritual father. When he initiated his seminar, Ogorodnikov established three main reasons for its existence: to enhance the participants' theological understanding, "which we could not obtain by any other means," to create a Christian community based on mutual love, and to engage in missionary work.[19]

The Moscow Seminar attracted some outstanding personalities who remained with Ogorodnikov during most of its activities. There were several prominent leaders, including Tatiana Shchipkova, a teacher from Smolensk; Vladimir Poresh, her former student; and Lev Regelson, a mathematician and physicist who, before his conversion to Russian Orthodoxy, had worked at the Moscow Planetarium. A brief description of their personal evolution offers a view of their attraction to the Moscow Seminar and the quest for a more authentic life.

In 1974, aged fifty, Tatiana Shchipkova was a rare exception to the young age of nearly all the seminar's participants, one of them her own son and two others who resided in Smolensk.[20] A lecturer in the Pedagogical Institute in Smolensk, where she had taught for more than a decade, Shchipkova specialized in classical languages—Latin, Old French, and Old Romanian—and classical cultures and history. In her Latin class, while remaining close to the prescribed order of things, she often managed to integrate several sessions on the rise of Christianity in the ancient world:

> I had a usual class on first-year Latin. For thirteen or fourteen years, it had been my practice to teach the students about the culture and history of ancient Rome, as well as elementary Latin grammar. A week before I gave the first-year students preparatory lessons on the rise of Christianity, on the personhood of Christ, on His parables, and the significance of Christianity in the subsequent fate of Rome, Europe, and humankind.[21]

In 1977 Shchipkova went further, deciding to be open and honest in her teaching:

On June 7, I continued my lectures on Christianity and explained to the students that the Christian religion was still alive (the first time that a teacher had told the students of such a thing). I explained to them that, in our time, it is attracting more and more educated people in the Soviet Union as well as in other countries and that I am a believer myself . . . We were not in the habit of telling the truth about ourselves, and so the students were unaccustomed to hearing it. They were stunned by what I said, listened in total silence, and did not ask a single question. Judging by everything, no one ran off to report me.[22]

Word of Shchipkova's confession, however, did reach the administration. In mid-June, she was summoned before the faculty and accused of disseminating religious propaganda. She maintained that she "was not guilty of propagating anything that would risk my work and position." "My goal," she said, "was to give my students a representation of this huge world and its cultural phenomena."[23] Shchipkova recounted that no one in the faculty meeting at which she was charged rose up to defend her, although she remained convinced that some had sympathetic views. For what the faculty called spreading lies, the school administration dismissed Shchipkova from her teaching position.

A second seminar participant, Vladimir Poresh, had grown up in Smolensk, where he had studied under Shchipkova. She recalled him as an extremely talented and sensitive student with an inquiring mind that questioned everything.[24] Poresh often remained after class to question her about various points in her lecture, Shchipkova said, and sometimes offered a carefully constructed counterargument. She recalled her sadness to see him leave when he moved away to enter Leningrad State University.[25]

The next times Shchipkova saw Poresh, in late 1969 and again in 1970, he had changed. After the Soviet invasion of Czechoslovakia in 1968, he had entered a period of depression. Convinced of "his own spiritual enslavement and that of everyone around him," he had contemplated suicide. But he worked his way through this and, when she next saw him, sometime in 1973, he expressed joy and expectation. "I have begun a new phase of my life," he told Shchipkova: "I've got to know someone called Sasha Ogorodnikov. We have decided to create a culture within a culture."[26] He said that he had begun to read Russian religious philosophy and, although he found it difficult, he saw in it the spiritual foundation for which he had searched for a long time.

As a close friend and collaborator of Ogorodnikov, Poresh provided a link between the Moscow Seminar and a similar student seminar that Ogorodnikov helped to organize in Leningrad.[27]

A third leading participant in the Moscow Seminar, Lev Regelson, came from a distinguished Moscow family. Born in 1929, Regelson was the son of a prominent professor of physics at Moscow State University. His father, like his grandfather and grandmother, was a committed communist who had lived the Stalinist dream of building a new society. Regelson hardly knew his mother, since he lived in the home of his paternal grandparents who raised him. At Moscow State University, where he matriculated, Regelson specialized in physics and mathematics, intending to follow the same career path as his father. He was seriously committed to his studies, fascinated by the inquiry into the physical universe and the process of discovery. "But narrow scientific endeavors did not satisfy him," wrote Levitin-Krasnov, who knew Regelson well. "He was constantly searching for higher truth."

> Even in his student years, he was often carried away by the study of philosophy. First, he was enthused by Nietzsche, but was soon a little disappointed by the German philosopher, and turned to the study of Freud, whose works were suppressed and illegal at that time in the USSR. Once, he made a public report on Freud's work at a meeting of young students, which attracted wide attention. The young, inquisitive student did not stop with the study of Freud. He turned to the works of the Russian philosopher Berdiaev, then he took up religion seriously.[28]

During his years working as physicist, Regelson considered himself a scientist and a religious person, although he had to keep the latter private. Following his baptism in the Orthodox Church, however, he was removed from his position and forced to live in the most meager circumstances. He wrote a large number of articles for samizdat publications.[29] He joined the Moscow Seminar as one of its oldest and most experienced participants. In the late 1970s he published in Paris *The Tragedy of the Russian Orthodox Church, 1917–1945*, a unique, invaluable collection of documents.[30]

The Moscow Seminar leaders displayed common characteristics. All of them were raised in atheist households. For each of them, the materialist intellectual underpinnings of that world proved unconvincing and led to a resentment of the narrow framework they provided to understand their place in the world. Each of the individuals went in search of something larger, less confining, more open to the world and to mystery, wonder, and the imagination. Ogorodnikov described the painful quest of many of his cohorts and their disappointment in what they found in the official church:

> Each of us has undergone a complex, sometimes agonizing path of spiritual questing, [and] from Marxist convictions, via nihilism and the complete rejection of any ideology, via attraction to the "hippy" lifestyle, we have come to the church. We came to it with our questions and our hopes. However, we were soon convinced that our problems were not being raised in church sermons, which are the only means for the religious education of believers, nor in the pages of the church journal, the *Journal of the Moscow Patriarchate*, which, moreover, is inaccessible to the ordinary Christian.[31]

Lastly, each of the participants had a higher education. They did not fit the common stereotypes of religious believers advanced in the Soviet media as uneducated, superstitious, and unmindful remnants of the past.

Breaking the Chains of Ideology

The quest of these young people is what attracted Fr. Gleb Yakunin. He saw it as the beginning of a new wave of human consciousness in the Soviet people. They had discovered in the Orthodox faith and in other religious traditions a deeper reservoir of thought and being than they heretofore had experienced. Yakunin shared the optimistic view that Ogorodnikov expressed in his assessment of the youth movement: "Russian culture today, while pushing its way out from under the rubble of terror, lies, and delusions, has given birth to an intellectual ferment which neither we ourselves nor the world in general expected."[32]

This statement by Yakunin testified to his conviction that a new day had dawned in the Soviet Union and that, if left unimpeded, its course was irreversible. The awakening had not emerged spontaneously but had been building for some time, at least since the early 1960s when young people began to despair of the lies they witnessed all around them. The thirst for personal freedom, for freedom of the spirit, had developed its own momentum, and the Moscow Seminar, with its searching spirit and the desire of its participants to learn more about Orthodox Christianity, exemplified that momentum.

But Yakunin also saw obstacles on the path that threatened to undermine the religious resurgence among the young. Neither the Moscow
Patriarchate nor the church itself was prepared for the resurgence, and
the former, with its close connections to political authorities, endangered it. Yakunin referred to the first encyclical of the recently elected
Pope John Paul II, "The Redeemer of Man," which defined the redemp-
tive service of humanity as the fundamental goal of Christ's Church. In
Yakunin's view, in its quest to serve the state, the Orthodox Church had
lost sight of its purpose. Such a humane idea about the redemption of
humanity did not fit into what Yakunin described as the " 'cult-pious'
pharisaical mentality" that the church's present leadership exhibited.[33]
Psychologically and spiritually, the Moscow Patriarchate lacked the
capacity to respond effectively to the religious awakening developing
among the young intelligentsia.

Yakunin had little patience with the Orthodox Church's inability
to provide encouragement to the young, a failure he related to several
causes. Most of all, the church's incapability stemmed from its indifference. Because " 'faith without action is dead' a truly believing heart
cannot remain indifferent to the events taking place in the history of
the world around us," he, Lev Regelson, and an associate, Viktor Kapitanchuk, wrote to the newly elected Patriarch Pimen, who succeeded
Patriarch Aleksii I upon his death in 1970.[34] This Christian doctrine,
which called the church to respond to events taking place in history
and to its responsibility "to unmask lies and injustices," would become
a central theme in Yakunin's life.[35] This call to action, guided by what
he called "the light of faith," would lead to his courageous stand against
what he perceived as multiple forms of injustice.

Other than its youthful energy, what inspired hope for the Russian
religious renaissance in which Yakunin so fervently believed? What
precisely underlay the dissatisfaction of the youth, its inability to tolerate the life that the participants in the Moscow Seminar knew and
the conditions in which they had grown up? What distinguished the
seminar from the cultural and educational setting they had previously
known? The meetings in Moscow attracted a sizeable number of converts. Mark Popovskii, a young journalist, described one of the seminars he attended: "In one of the Moscow apartments, in a condition
of strict secrecy, just concluded the usual religious-philosophical seminar of young Orthodox people. For two days, more than forty people,
the majority of them from the provinces, have discussed problems of
philosophy, theory, and the contemporary practice of Orthodoxy."[36]

According to Popovskii, seminars similar to the one in Moscow had also emerged in Leningrad, Smolensk, Kazan, Odessa, Ufa, Grodno, and Lvov. They "show that, in many cities of the country, there are young men and women, for the most part students, teachers, and very diverse kinds of intelligentsia—workers who have moved away from the official ideology, from the left-wing radicalism and the pathos of the counter-culture, to Orthodoxy."[37] The seminar sessions he attended discussed the relationship between newly converted Christians and the church, as well as the writings of the contemporary leftist philosophers Herbert Marcuse, Erich Fromm, Theodore Adorno, John-Paul Sartre, and Michael Jean Pierre Debré. The topic that most excited the participants, however, emerged from a presentation devoted to "The Culture of the Catacombs, or the Search for Free Forms of Life in Soviet Totalitarian Society."[38] The discussants wanted to know how they could success-fully create a dynamic, mutually supportive Christian community in the milieu of a totalitarian society. They wanted to raise their children in such an environment.[39]

During Ogorodnikov's journey, like many other seminar partici-pants, he came to understand the pervasiveness of Soviet ideology. Like them, he had grown sick of what he referred to as the "spellbound spiri-tual captivity of ideology," its penetration into every corner of one's life.[40] Tormented by self-doubt and unable to find an acceptable place in Soviet society, the members of his generation set out in search of a new vision that opened the freedom to explore. The journey he and his friends made required casting off the "state myth" that had imprisoned them since childhood. By this myth, Ogorodnikov meant the "deifica-tion of the state" and its collective forms.[41] The state's sovereign con-trol over every aspect of life demanded total loyalty and left no room for other views of life, but mainly it had expanded into the soul, com-manding everything and suffocating any other human attachments and relationships.

Ogorodnikov described the sense of helplessness that, for a time, had engulfed him. His portrayal of personal despair recalled the period of darkness that Vladimir Poresh had gone through, though it's uncer-tain whether Ogorodnikov's personal account mirrored the journey of other members of the Moscow Seminar. Nevertheless, they all shared the desire to think for themselves about higher values. In Ogorodnikov's case, the novels of Fyodor Dostoevsky played a significant role in over-coming his despair. Dostoevsky's portrayals of Father Zosima and the much-admired Alesha Karamazov in *The Brothers Karamazov* opened up new perspectives that the youth, who heretofore had known only militant atheism, found rejuvenating. Both characters illuminated another world in which harmony and love, rather than perpetual conflict and hatred, predominated. We learned, Ogorodnikov said, that underneath the outward layer of Soviet existence, "spiritual life quietly and secretly flows, streams into the deep Soviet underground, weaving the light."[42] This discovery, he said, is what led them to the "eternal truth" of the church and, from there, to Russia's great spiritual writers and philosophers such as Nikolai Gogol, Petr Kireevskii, Aleksei Khomiakov, Vladimir Solovyev, Nikolai Berdiaev, and Sergei Bulgakov.[43]

But arriving at the threshold of the church, according to Ogorodnikov, Soviet youth encountered disappointment. In search of a brotherly community that welcomed them into a warm-spirited, open-minded, inquisitive body of believers, they encountered passivity, fear, and cold-heartedness. In large part, Ogorodnikov attributed this stultifying atmosphere within the parish community to the fear of persecution by state authorities. "Our thirst for spiritual communion, religious education, and missionary service runs up against all the might of the state's oppressive machinery," Ogorodnikov wrote to Dr. Philip Potter, Secretary General of the World Council of Churches.[44] In order to fulfill their spiritual needs, Soviet youth looked for another way.

The attempt to satisfy these needs led to the creation of the Moscow Seminar in Moscow and other cities of the USSR. According to its founder, the most distinctive feature of the Moscow Seminar was its aspiration to stand between the church and the world. It aimed to speak out and, ultimately, to transform society. In this role, seminar participants perceived themselves as acting within a traditional Orthodox framework and pursuing the same objectives as their predecessors: seeking to develop a welcoming spiritual community, responding to social concerns, and engaging in missionary work. Although Ogorodnikov claimed the seminar had no political objectives, the state authorities saw its intentions differently and sought various means of curtailing its outreach. They placed Ogorodnikov under continuous surveillance. He worked as a table clearer in a canteen until the manager dismissed him, undoubtedly under pressure from the KGB, and he had difficulty obtaining further employment.[45]

Other members of the Moscow Seminar suffered harassment, confinement in psychiatric hospitals, and beatings on the street. Yet the members persisted. Yakunin, too, for reasons to be discussed later, lived under constant pressure and KGB threats. In the late 1970s, the police began a concerted effort to suppress the seminar's activities by confiscating its materials. The power of new ideas, in a Hegelian sense, soon encountered a strong opposing force—namely, an effort to stifle the spread of these ideas.

Raising Questions

On May 21, 1978, Tatiana Shchipkova heard the doorbell ring in her Smolensk apartment. That morning, she had hosted Viktor Popkov, a member of the Moscow Seminar; Aleksandr Ogorodnikov; and the manager of her apartment building. When Shchipkova inquired, "Who is it?" she was greeted with the response, "The police!" followed by the demand that she open the door immediately. Shchipkova refused, and they became aggressive, telling her to let them in or they would break down the door. She then stepped out onto the landing, slamming the door behind her. The lead police official showed her a search warrant. She felt like she had to let them in. "There were five of them who stood facing me," she said: a large, solidly built woman of about forty-five, red-haired with bangs, assertive and with an air of self-satisfaction; the senior investigator Kleshcheva, accompanied by the assistant public prosecutor; and three men in civilian clothes. Again, they demanded that Shchipkova open the door. When she told them the door had locked and she had no key, the assistant public prosecutor called for a hatchet and ordered the police to break down the door.[46]

The public officials then barged into Shchipkova's apartment, joined by three other women whom they had summoned as witnesses. The ensuing interactions contained a mixture of demands, threats, and accusations. A search of the apartment began, immediately yielding the discovery of a typewriter and a cache of articles for the Moscow Seminar's journal *Obshchina*, which had already gone to the printers. The investigators went into every crevice of the apartment, pulling out papers, documents, and any loose piece of paper they could find. Spreading them out on the floor, they carefully examined each one. Ogorodnikov recalled the statement of the assistant public prosecutor, who from time to time mumbled, "Nowadays, when we are sending up spaceships, to believe in such nonsense . . . They thought themselves up a myth, a fairy tale—a fine thing for people to waste their time on!"[47] The search lasted six hours. In the end, the police bundled the books, samizdat materials, carbon paper, and manuscripts and carted them away, including Shchipkova's typewriter.

As they departed Shchipkova's apartment, the emissaries of the KGB handed her an inventory of the books and manuscripts they confiscated. They asked her to voluntarily surrender all books and other materials that defamed the Soviet Union, to which she responded that she did not consider any item in her possession to be defamatory of the Soviet state.

The inventory, as well as Ogorodnikov's list of readings for the seminar, offered a firsthand view of the main questions the participants explored. The materials consisted of 108 books, articles, and letters, including copies of letters sent to various government officials, essays by members of the Moscow Seminar that had been circulated among its members, books by late nineteenth- and early twentieth-century Russian philosopher-theologians, writings on the unique qualities of Russian saints, and works by Western writers. In terms of the questions they raised and their immediate relevance to Russia in the twentieth century, three of the writers warrant special attention: Vladimir Solovyev, Alexei Khomiakov, and Henri Bergson. These three offered alternative views of religion and, most important, they fit into the participants' evolving understanding of freedom of conscience, creativity, and openness of the mind.

Vladimir Sergeevich Solovyev, the son of one of Russia's preeminent nineteenth-century historians, Sergei Mikhailovich Solovyev, had majored in philosophy at Moscow University, with an emphasis on the natural sciences and theology. He was educated during a time when positivism reigned supreme among Russian educated youth, but early on he began to carve out a path much different from the positivists. As a scholar and writer, he had a large influence on a whole generation of Russia's most creative thinkers. He was Russia's first religious philosopher and among its greatest.

Solovyev's belief that God created the universe as a single, interconnected unity lay at the core of his philosophy. When individuals removed any part of this unity, abstracted, and made it into the whole of their perceptions, they engaged in delusion. This view underlay his criticism of empiricism, which had dominated European thought for much of his lifetime. "The whole visual world," Solovyev maintained, "is no haphazard collection of 'made' things; it is the continuous development and growth of a living organism."[48]

The Creator endowed his creation with love, love that did not exist without mutual relations. God had given human beings the gift of freedom, which enabled them to freely enter relationships with others and with Himself. The Divine never intended for human beings to contemplate Him passively, but to act in living relationship with Him toward the completion of His creation. Humans were essentially creative beings, endowed with a divine spirit, capable of making the world a better place, infusing society with this divine spirit, bringing all of humankind more closely together. Solovyev saw this as a fundamental principle of Christianity. He did not view the church as apart from the earth. It had the responsibility to reach out to society. To remain isolated from the world, as the church often sought to do, violated divine will and purpose. When hate and revenge dominated human affairs, they acted in opposition to the will of the holy God.[49]

Members of the Moscow Seminar, raised on a steady diet of dialectical materialism, found Solovyev's ideas immensely attractive. He offered the participants a much different, coherent view of the world than had been previously taught. Solovyev's emphasis on creativity and the individual's role in fulfilling a Divine plan gave the members a positive view of their own responsibilities. He did not see a conflict between science and faith, although he understood that each of them represented distinctive ways of knowing. They were parts of God's creation, divine sources of a universal unity.[50]

The belief that Russia has a special mission to fulfill in the world had roots deep in Russian history. Dostoevsky had emphasized this unique mission, and Solovyev, similarly, conceived of Russia's distinctive calling, a subject to which seminar participants gave considerable attention.[51] Following Dostoevsky, Solovyev believed Russia had a special role to develop a synthesis between the East, with its spiritual qualities, and the West, with its dominating belief in rationalism. Because Russia endured a greater amount of suffering throughout its history than did other nations, this suffering served as a precursor to Russia's redemption and eventual salvation of humanity.[52] Drawing from Solovyev, Vladimir Poresh, one of the seminar leaders, wrote, "Our nation has borne incredible suffering that has formed the moral core, the religious foundation, on which a new rediscovered religious consciousness is being built."[53] This religious consciousness, he asserted, has remained incomplete and infirm, but Poresh had little doubt in Russia's spiritual power to transform the world.

The seminar's discussion of Solovyev raised the question of the individual and modern culture, an issue that Russian Orthodoxy found difficult to resolve. What did freedom of the individual mean in reality, and how, Poresh asked, might it contribute to the creation of a moral order and "a clear moral consciousness"? Speaking of the mindset of the Soviet society of his time, he was adamant in his condemnation and in his faith in Russia's hidden resources: "We do not want talentless vulgarity, the stillness that destroys. We do not want the cynicism and despair that suppress the Word, the meaning of life. We do not want this lying [falsehood] peace: we want a just war. Where are you, Holy Russia, Russia of the saints and holy men? We do not believe you are dead."[54]

In its efforts to foster a communal society, the USSR placed little emphasis on the individual. But in the attempt to rediscover Christianity, members of the seminar gave special attention to the question of the person and her or his relationship to the parish community.[55] What did it mean to have an authentic church community, one that opened itself to freedom and was unrestricted by the state? The participants in the Moscow Seminar desired such a community. Frustrated by the inability to locate it in the contemporary church, members of the seminar looked for guidance in the writings of one of Russia's most prophetic theological minds, Aleksei Stepanovich Khomiakov (1804–60). Khomiakov, a founding member of the influential Slavophiles, belonged to the landed nobility that had deep roots in the Orthodox Church. Poet, historian, artist, linguist, and theologian, his writings spoke with a freshness and power that members of the conservative church hierarchy often criticized. Perceiving these writings as revolutionary, church censorship prohibited most of them from publication. As the Orthodox historian Nicolas Zernov noted, however, Khomiakov's thoughts drew from the deepest recesses of the Orthodox tradition.[56]

Khomiakov, like several of his major predecessors, based his theological writings on the need for human transformation. In sharp, evocative poetry and prose, all of which displayed strong biblical themes, he kept the Gospel's representation of Christ at the center of his writings. Although set in distant, bygone days, this portrayal was timeless, and it particularly related to the spiritual confrontation with violence and power. Both forces, according to Khomiakov, originated in self-centeredness and the desire for domination and set people apart from one another. The Creator endowed human beings with reason and, through this "willing reason," expected them to participate in enhancing the harmony and joy of the world. To such an end, human beings should join into a "living organic spiritual fellowship."[57] When segregated, driven apart by violence and power, this organic unit was shattered, misdirected, and profaned. Khomiakov viewed the isolated, self-directed individual as sick and fundamentally impotent.[58]

The church and industrial society today stood at the top of the list of subjects that Ogorodnikov planned for discussion in the Moscow Seminar. He soon added "the individual and the community of the church" to the list. Both topics concerned the present condition in which Soviet youth had grown up and suggested the chief interests of the seminar's participants, particularly the question of freedom and community. Khomiakov's name was the first one recorded on the topic. The treatment of Christ in the Gospels was central to both questions, and Khomiakov's portrayal of Christ addressed them. As Men later noted in his public lecture on Khomiakov's portrayal of Christ: "He is the victor in the New Testament, but a victor who does not humiliate, who does not destroy, and who preserves human freedom. Freedom is a great gift that distinguishes us from animals—this is the freedom that God has carefully endowed us. Therefore, the appearance of Christ took place without force over the personality and conscience of the human being. Christ always allowed the person the opportunity to turn one's back on Him."[59] The freedom of choice stood in stark contrast to force and violence. When it operated properly, the church community fulfilled a similar purpose.

Khomiakov's essay *Tserkov' Odna* (The church is one) is one of his central pieces. Unpublished in his lifetime, it later became widely distributed and generally recognized as one of his seminal writings.[60] In it, Khomiakov defined the church as a fellowship of love, which allows one, in living communion with others, to separate oneself from one's lonely and ego-driven existence and become part of a living organism. The more a person lives in cooperation with other people, the richer and more fulfilled her life will be. The church lives not under force or constraint. It is not an authority, as some were wont to say: "God is not an authority, and Christ is not an authority, because an authority is something exterior to us." Rather, "The church is truth. She lives in a person more real than the heart beating in his breast or the blood running in his veins."[61] In this community, a person finds his true calling in freedom and in unity with others. The term *sobornost'*, meaning to "bring together," expressed this unity in freedom and love.[62]

It is easy to see the appeal of Khomiakov's ideas to members of the Moscow Seminar. His discussion of love, freedom, and the church community spoke directly to the founding purposes of the seminar and the main interests of its participants. The discussions on the role of the church in the contemporary world, the individual and society, and the relationship between the church and freedom raised other questions.

How might the church speak more effectively to the spiritual needs of the Russian people? What was the relationship between freedom and creativity? What present qualities and ways of thinking impeded the development of a spiritual community?

The last question served as the subject of the great French scientist and philosopher Henri Bergson's *Two Sources of Morality and Religion*. Bergson won the Nobel Prize for Literature in 1927, and several of his works, as well as other significant foreign books, were translated into Russian shortly after their publication. Many of them could still be found in Soviet antiquarian bookstores, and they remained fresh sources of discussion among certain segments of the population. In the Moscow Seminar, Bergson's work closely fit one of the main concerns of the participants, the moral characteristics of two different kinds of social order.

In *Two Sources of Morality and Religion*, Bergson contrasted the evolution and characteristics of what he called closed and open societies.[63] He likened the closed society to a biological organism that attempted to define the functions of each part of the whole and tried to fit them together for the sake of the common good. The closed society focused on a common unity; it adopted a clan mentality aimed at preserving the status quo and safeguarding the community against attack. It set narrow boundaries around morality and religion, excluded its members from interaction with outsiders, and exhibited little care about those outside their clan. In the closed society, according to Bergson, human beings operated as ants in an ant heap.[64] Stability, self-preservation, and reproduction expressed some of the closed society's highest values. The individual was subordinated to the whole and custom determined morality. The religious beliefs of the closed society focused on ritual and keeping everything in proper order. These beliefs had evolved from earlier pagan societies, to which the closed society retained a close connection.

In contrast, the open society had less concern with rigidly defined obligations and put much more emphasis on creativity and progress. It valued tradition but did not see tradition as frozen in time, unshakable, or sacrosanct. The open society accepted that life as well as society had to constantly adapt to changing circumstances; it operated much differently than an ant hill. Narrow functions did not define this society. It encouraged individuals to remain open to change, new possibilities, and discovery. Citizens operated not as cogwheels in a well-organized and disciplined mechanism but as participants in a dynamic community. Religion in the open society emphasized love and grace rather than rigid doctrines and rituals. "The open society is one which is deemed in principle to embrace all humanity," he maintained.[65]

This brief discussion of Bergson fit well with the seminar participants' quest for a new social order. His *Two Sources* spoke directly to the Soviet Union's political condition and particularly the high value its governing elite placed on stability, self-preservation, and clan mentality. The participants in the Moscow Seminar wanted change; they sought new direction for their lives, unencumbered by the narrow, self-confining categories of perception that state ideology tried to impose. They were exhausted by the constant barrage of messages that sought to compel a rigid and prescribed code of thinking that had little relevance to their actual lives. They yearned to define their own personal identity, and this required freedom of thought and belief, the antithesis of existence as members of an ant hill.

Bergson offered seminar members a critique of the closed society, but he did not offer them a prescription of how to construct an open community. This issue remained for them to consider. But by resurrecting certain giants within Russia's own philosophical and theological traditions, as well as incorporating relevant Western writers, members of the seminar rekindled the imagination that would enable productive consideration. By focusing on possibilities, they ignited hope. However nebulous the concepts that they stressed—such as compassion, love, and creativity—may have been, they constructed an alternative moral vision to the society in which they lived. In so doing, they played a small but significant part in the reawakening of Russian society.

In a closed society, the questions that individuals raised were answered within a preestablished framework. In that kind of society, according to Czesław Miłosz, one must not ask embarrassing questions, but rather accept what one is told and submerge one's identity in the political order.[66] It is little wonder, therefore, that the security police considered the materials of the Moscow Seminar subversive and attempted to confiscate and destroy them.

Seminar participants were fully aware that the security police were present all around them and that their leaders and the most energetic members would be arrested. Yet they persisted, and the seeds they sowed—the conversations their questions stimulated and the critiques these conversations generated about power and violence—would continue to germinate. All of these took a different but related form in the struggle for human rights and religious liberty. In that quest, Fr. Gleb Yakunin, Lev Regelson, and other members would play major parts.[67]

Notes

Some material is drawn from my book *Freedom and the Captive Mind: Fr. Gleb Yakunin and Orthodox Christianity in Soviet Russia*, a Northern Illinois University Press book published by Cornell University Press. Copyright (c) 2024 by Cornell University Press.

1. Vladimir Il'ich Lenin, "O znachenii vointsvuiushchego materializma," in *Polnoe sobranie sochineniia*, vol. 45 (Moskva: Izd-vo Politicheskoi Literatury, 1964), 28.

2. "Soviet Official Lectures on Religion," *Religion in Communist Lands* 6, no. 1 (Spring 1978), 32.

3. "Soviet Official Lectures on Religion," 33.

4. Fr. Gleb Yakunin, "Doklad Sviashchennika Gleba Iakunina Khristianskomu komitetu zashchity prav veruiushchikh v SSSR o sovremennom polozhenii Russkoi Pravoslavnoi Tserkvi i o perspektivakh religioznogo vozrozhdeniia Rossii," in *Dokumenty khristianskogo komiteta zashchity prav veruiushchikh v SSSR*, vol. 11 (San Francisco: Washington Street Research Center, 1979), 1128.

5. Tatiana Goricheva, quoted in Jane Ellis, *The Russian Orthodox Church: A Contemporary History* (London: Routledge, 1986), 392.

6. Fr. Michael Aksenov-Meerson, "The Russian Orthodox Church, 1965–1980," *Religion in Communist Lands* 9, nos. 3–4 (1981), 105.

7. Aksenov-Meerson, "The Russian Orthodox Church," 106.

8. Fr. Michael Aksenov-Meerson, interview by author, Bethesda, MD, May 27, 2019. Fr. Meerson immigrated from the Soviet Union and presently is head priest of the Christ the Savior Orthodox Church in the dioceses of New York and New Jersey.

9. Aksenov-Meerson, "The Russian Orthodox Church."

10. Protoierei Aleksandr Borisov, "Dukhovnyi realizm ottsa Aleksandra Menia" in *Tserkovnaia zhizn' XX veka: Protoierei Aleksandr Men i ego dukhovnye nastavniki: Sbornik materialov pervoi nauchnoi konferenstsii "Menevskie chteniia" (Sentiabria 2006 g.)*, ed. M. V. Grigorenko (Sergiev Posad: Izdanie prikhoda Sergievskoi tserkvi v Semkhoze, 2007), 163–65, 170–71. Iurii Mikhailovich Tabak, interview by author, Moscow, October 19, 2008. Tabak, a writer and member of the Moscow intelligentsia, often went to see Men at Novaia Derevna. Andrei Cherniak, interview by author, May 24, 2007, Moscow. Cherniak, a physicist and former atheist, spoke glowingly about his discussions with Men.

11. Anatolii Levitin-Krasnov, "Religion and Soviet Youth," *Religion in Communist Lands* 7, no. 4 (Winter 1979): 232–33.

12. Levitin-Krasnov, "Religion and Soviet Youth," 237.

13. See the details on the people who flocked to his community in Anatolii Levitin-Krasnov, "Otets Dimitrii Dudko," *Posev*, no. 1 (1975): 26–36.

14. Sviashchennik Dmitrii Dudko, *O nashem upovanii: Besedy* (Paris: YMCA-Press, 1976), 235–36. A collection of Fr. Dmitrii's sermons over a twenty-five-year period, 1960 to 1985, is included in Sviashchennik Dmitrii Sergeevich Dudko, *V ternine i pri doroge* (Moskva: Tip. Molodaia gvardiia, 1993).

15. Yakunin, "Doklad," 1160.

16. J. H. Hexter, *Reappraisals in History: New Views on History and Society in Early Modern Europe*, 2nd ed. (Chicago: University of Chicago Press, 1979), 38.

17. Anatolii Levitin-Krasnov, "Sol' zemli (Molodaia Rossiia)," *Russkaia Mysl',* November 15, 1979, 14; Koenraad De Wolf, *Dissident for Life: Alexander Ogorodnikov and the Struggle for Religious Freedom in Russia* (Grand Rapids, MI: William B. Eerdmans, 2010), 55; Jane Ellis, "USSR: The Christian Seminar," *Religion in Communist Lands* 8, no. 2 (Summer 1980): 94–95. In relating the primary influences on the creation of the Christian Seminar, I have followed Ellis's approach.

18. De Wolf, *Dissident for Life*, 64–65.

19. Alexander Ogorodnikov and Boris Razveev, "Letter to Dr. Philip Potter, General-Secretary of the WCC," August 5, 1976, *Religion in Communist La*nds 7, no. 1 (1979): 50.

20. Tatiana Shchipkova's son Aleksandr Shipkov was a student at the institute where she taught, and the two others were Vladimir Poresh, a former student of hers who had entered Leningrad State University, and Viktor Popkov, a staff member of the Smolensk Exhibition Hall, who will be discussed later.

21. Tat'iana Nikolaevna Shchipkova, "Imeet li pravo sovetskii prepodavatel' na svobody sovesti," July–September 1978, in *Dokumenty khristianskogo komiteta zaschchity prav veruiushchikh v SSSR*, vol. 4 (San Francisco: Washington Street Research Center, 1978), 497. An excerpt from this document is published in *Religion in Communist Lands* 8, no. 2 (Summer 1980): 106–9.

22. Shchipkova, "Imeet li pravo sovetskii prepodavatel'," 497–98.

23. Shchipkova, "Imeet li pravo sovetskii prepodavatel'," 498.

24. Tat'iana Shchipkova, "Spiritual Pilgrimage of Vladimir Poresh," appendix to Ellis, "USSR: The Christian Seminar," 101–2.

25. Shchipkova, "Spiritual Pilgrimage of Vladimir Poresh," 101.

26. Shchipkova, "Spiritual Pilgrimage of Vladimir Poresh," 102.

27. In October 1975, members of the "creative intelligentsia" in Leningrad formed a religious-philosophical seminar that they called the "37" seminar, named after the apartment in which it first met. This Leningrad seminar differed in size and focus from its fellow organization in Moscow. See Tatiana Goricheva, *Talking about God Is Dangerous: The Diary of a Russian Dissident* (New York: Crossroad, 1987).

28. Anatolii Levitin-Krasnov, "Father Gleb Yakunin and Lev Regel'son," in *Letters from Moscow: Religion and Human Rights in the USSR*, ed. Jane Ellis (Keston: Keston College and H. S. Dakin, 1978), 8.

29. Levitin-Krasnov, "Father Gleb Yakunin," 8–9. Levitin-Krasnov's biographical portrait offers a firsthand description of Regelson's struggles to be simultaneously both a scientist and a person of faith.

30. Lev Regel'son, *Tragediia russkoi tserkvi, 1917–1945*, afterword by Archpriest John Meyendorff (Paris: YMCA-Press), 1977.

31. Aleksandr Ogorodnikov, "Pis'mo General'nomu Sekretariu Vsemirnogo Soveta Tserkvei D-ru Filippu Potteru," July 27, 1976, *Vestnik russkogo khristianskogo dvizheniia*, nos. 3–4 (119) (1976), 305. In English: Alexander Ogorodnikov, "Letter to Dr. Philip Potter," *Religion in Communist Lands* 4, no. 4 (1976), 46.

32. Ogorodnikov and Razveev, "Letter to Dr. Philip Potter," 49.

33. Yakunin, "Doklad," 1128.

34. Father Gleb Yakunin, Viktor Kapitanchuk, and Lev L. Regel'son, "Appeal for the Glorification of Russian Martyrs in the USSR," May 25, 1975, in Ellis, *Letters from Moscow*, 35.

35. Yakunin, Kapitanchuk, and Regel'son, "Appeal," 35.

36. Mark Popovskii, "Khristianstvo molodeet," *Vol'noe slovo*, no. 29 (1978), 53.

37. Popovskii, "Khristianstvo molodeet," 54.

38. Popovskii, "Khristianstvo molodeet," 54.

39. The participants proposed beginning with a summer school organized during the holidays that would attract like-minded individuals of similar spiritual dispositions. Founded at an isolated location as a camp, those who came here for the summer could engage in discussion about a whole range of topics related to their lives and their society. They wanted their children to "escape from the all-consuming antireligious propaganda" they faced every day. In the postwar period, such small, independent groups, offering instruction on religious topics in informal, after-school sessions, did exist in Moscow. See, for example, Aleksandr Men, *O sebe . . . vospominaniia, besedy, inter'viu* (Moskva: Zhizn' s Bogom, 2007), 32.

40. Ogorodnikov and Razveev, "Letter to Dr. Philip Potter," 49.

41. Ogorodnikov and Razveev, "Letter to Dr. Philip Potter," 49; Aleksandr Ogorodnikov, "Khristianskii kruzhok v Moskve," *Vestnik russkogo kristianskogo dvizheniia*, no. 119 (1976), 296.

42. Ogorodnikov, "Khristianskii kruzhok," 297.

43. Ogorodnikov, "Khristianskii kruzhok," 297. In addition to these writers and philosophers, Ogorodnikov cited Pavel Florenskii, Nikita Struve, and Semyon Frank.

44. Ogorodnikov, "Pis'mo General'nomu Sekretariu," 305.

45. Ogorodnikov, "Pis'mo General'nomu Sekretariu," 305; Ogorodnikov, "Khristianskii kruzhok," 300.

46. Alexander Ogorodnikov, "Informational Report No. 5," May 27, 1978, in *Dokumenty khristianskogo komiteta zashchity prav veruiushchikh v SSSR*, vol. 4, 487. An English-language copy is in *Dokumenty khristianskogo komiteta zashchity prav veruiushchikh v SSSR*, vol. 3 (San Francisco: Washington Street Research Center, 1977, 1978), 303–11.

47. Ogorodnikov, "Informational Report No. 5," 488.

48. Vladimir Sergeevich Solovyev, quoted in Nicolas Zernov, *Three Russian Prophets: Khomiakov, Dostoevsky, and Soloviev*, 3rd ed. (Gulf Breeze, FL: Academic International Press, 1974), 133.

49. Vladimir Sergeevich Solovyev, *God, Man, and the Church: The Spiritual Foundations of Life*, reprint ed., trans. Donald Attwater (London: Trowbridge and Esher, 1974), 114–15, 144–45, 150–51, 156, 160.

50. Aleksandr Men, "Vladimir Solov'ev," in *Russkaia religioznaia filosofii: Lektsii* (Moskva: Khram sviatykh bessrebrenikov Kosmu i Damiana v Shubine, 2003), 31.

51. See Ogorodnikov and Razveev, "Letter to Dr. Philip Potter," 50; Aleksandr Ogorodnikov, "Istoki i nadezhdy: Predvarenie," in *Obschchina: Zhurnal Khristianskogo Seminara po problemam religioznogo vozrozhdeniia*, ed. Aleksandr

Ogorodnikov, no. 2 (1978): 2–5, and, in the same volume, Varsonofii Kapitan-chuk, "Ontologicheskaia problema v russkoi sotsialogii," 89–103.

52. [Unsigned], "Postroenie pravoslavnogo mirovozzreniia i poluchenie bogoslovskogo obrazovaniia," 11–12, and "Dolg missionerskogo sluzheniia," 13–15, box 28, folder 12, SU Ort 11/10, Keston Archive (KA), Keston Center for Religion, State, and Society, Baylor University; Aleksandr Ogorodnikov, "Istoki i nadezhdy," *Obshchina: Zhurnal Khristianskogo Seminara po problemam religionogo vozrozhdeniia*, ed. Aleksandr Ogorodnikov, no. 2 (1978), 4–5, 11–12, 13–15.

53. Vladimir Poresh, "Dai krovi—priimi Dukh," April 1977, in Ogordnikov, *Obshchina*, 21–23. *Arkhiv samizdata*, no. 3452, 123, in box 28, folder 12, SU Ort 11/10, KA.

54. Poresh, "Dai krovi," 22.

55. Ogorodnikov and Razveev, "Letter to Dr. Philip Potter," 50.

56. Zernov, *Three Russian Prophets*, 60.

57. Aleksei Stepanovich Khomiakov, "Neskol'ko slov pravoslavnogo khris-tianina o zapadnykh veroispovedaniiakh," in *Izbrannye sochineniia*, ed. N. S. Arsen'ev (New York: Izd-vo imeni Chekhova, 1955), 256.

58. Khomiakov, "Neskol'ko slov pravoslavnogo khristianina," 242–43.

59. Protoeirei Aleksandr Men, *Bibliia i literatura: Lektsii* (Moscow Khram svi-atykh bessrebrenikov Kosmu i Damiana v Shubine, 2002), 141, quoted also in Wallace L. Daniel, *Russia's Uncommon Prophet: Father Aleksandr Men and His Times* (DeKalb: Northern Illinois University Press, 2016), 275.

60. *Tserkov' Odna* was published in Berlin in 1867, and in Russia only in 1879, nineteen years after Khomiakov's death.

61. Khomiakov, "Neskol'ko slov pravoslavnogo khristianina," 252. In *Tserkov' Odna*, Khomiakov made clear the distinction between the individual as an isolated being and the person as a member of the corporate body of the church. "The wisdom that lives within the human being," he wrote, "is not given to him individually, but as a member of the church, and it is given to him in part, without nullifying entirely his individual error, but to the church wisdom is given in the fullness of truth and without any mixture of error." Khomiakov, *Tserkov' Odna*, 11.

62. Aleksei Stepanovich Khomiakov, *Tserkov' Odna* (Moskva: Gos. Publi-chnaia istoricheskaia biblioteka, 1991), 22.

63. Henri Bergson, *The Two Sources of Morality and Religion*, trans. R. Ashley Audra and Cloudesley Brereton, with the assistance of W. Horsfall Carter (Garden City, NY: Doubleday, 1935).

64. Bergson, *Two Sources of Morality and Religion*, 266.

65. Bergson, *Two Sources of Morality and Religion*, 267.

66. Czesław Miłosz, *The Captive Mind*, reprint ed., trans. Jane Zielonko (New York: Vintage International, 1990), 27–28.

67. Viktor Popkov and Tatiana Lebedeva, interview by author, Moscow, May 17, 2018.

CHAPTER 5

Youth Religiosity

An Ideological Challenge to the Soviet Authorities in the 1970s–1980s

Barbara Martin

In early 1988, Aleksandr Kravetskii's college friends approached him with an unusual request. Their youth creative union, registered with one of the Moscow Communist Youth League (Komsomol) cells, had been entrusted with the organization of an "evening of youth leisure dedicated to the 1,000th anniversary of the baptism of Rus'."[1] Since religion was starting to return to Soviet public space, their idea was to invite a priest to debate with atheists about faith and science, but they had no idea how to find a churchman. Kravetskii, who belonged to a new generation of young converts to Orthodoxy, suggested inviting Fr. Aleksandr Men, a charismatic figure who was certain to find the right words to address atheistic youths.[2] But this was a bold gamble: just two years earlier, Men had been targeted in a propaganda article denouncing him and other religious dissenters for their connections with the West.[3] Nevertheless, Kravetskii and his friends managed to somehow conceal this information from the Komsomol committee, and on May 11, 1988, Men participated for the first time in a public debate in a hall full of youths. According to Kravetskii's account: "The Marxist participants were not ready to hold a discussion on such a level, and the materialist worldview suffered a crushing defeat. When one of the opponents tried to go over from substantive arguments to political ones, the audience simply started [loudly] clapping and did not let him speak. Father Aleksandr Men's victory was absolutely obvious."[4] The commercial success of the evening—1,200 tickets were sold—was such that soon enough, the Komsomol committee entrusted Kravetskii with the organization of courses on Old Church Slavonic.[5]

How can we explain such a spectacular about-face from communist organizations that had for decades been at the forefront of antireligious propaganda? A turning point was certainly the celebration of the one-thousandth anniversary of the Christianization of Ukrainian and Russian lands, but it was made possible by two decades of increasing religious feelings among Soviet youths. Like Kravetskii, many young people who greeted Men that evening had grown up in nonreligious families yet had developed an interest in religion. Some of them had taken the risk to be baptized as adults and a few had joined an underground catechism group, like those Men had been organizing clandestinely in his parish, starting from the late 1970s. For others, religion was still a latent interest that might result in a full conversion later.

How did these young people from what Alexei Yurchak has called "the last Soviet generation,"[6] who were born and raised in Soviet families, develop an interest in religion despite seven decades of antireligious propaganda? In *Everything Was Forever, Until It Was No More*, Yurchak provides some clues by insisting on the ideological disaffection of this generation. Young Komsomol members had for the most part ceased to take the regime's ideological discourse at face value and considered only its performative dimension, reproducing words and rituals that inscribed them into the Soviet collective. In her research on Soviet atheism, Victoria Smolkin also shows how Soviet propaganda tried in vain to inject a measure of sacrality into atheist policies by creating civic rituals to replace religious ones. She documents the failure of this project that started from a realization that decades of atheist policies had not yielded any tangible results and had failed to offer new generations of Soviet citizens the spiritual nourishment they craved.[7]

Yet the failure, I would argue, was also one of image: antireligious propaganda had sought to depict religion as a phenomenon of another era, doomed to extinction. Surely it would die out with the last *babushki* (grandmothers) born in the prerevolutionary era. By the late 1970s, however, the authorities could not fail to notice that not only did generations of *babushki* keep reproducing themselves but more and more young people were joining the ranks of believers. For the younger generation, religion had become fashionable and represented the only officially allowed counterideology. How did Soviet propaganda attempt to counter this phenomenon and how did it adapt its discourse to new circumstances?

Based on press cuttings from the Keston Archive, materials from the Russian state archives, and oral history interviews with Russian Orthodox believers from Moscow and Leningrad, this chapter examines three tropes of antireligious discourse in the late Soviet press, particularly youth newspapers, that were used to discredit youth participation in the religious revival. The first, sectarianism, was the most traditional. It was applied particularly to Protestant believers but could also be used in relation to believers from other confessions. Whether they had been separated from the collective from an early age by their upbringing in a religious family or had left their family and society to join a monastery or apply to a seminary as adults, young Soviet believers were suspected of sectarian tendencies. Second, the religious revival was declared a mere youth fashion, shallow and disconnected from the actual meaning of religious tradition and testifying to a lack of ideological discipline among Komsomol members. Finally, religion was considered an ideological diversion: religious youth groups that came into contact with the West were thus transferring their allegiance to the ideological enemy—a betrayal that could fully justify their arrest.

Religious Revival in the Land of Soviets

Religious studies scholars have identified a phenomenon of recurring religious awakenings throughout history, the most recent of which started in the 1960s.[8] Scholarship on the late Soviet Union points to a parallel and probably related process, which started among predominantly urban and educated Soviet youth in the late 1960s and benefited not only established churches but also nonconfessional religiosity and new religious movements.[9] Despite the Iron Curtain, contacts with the West, in particular through the Baltic states, and with India led to a popularization of Eastern religions and yoga among Soviet young people. These influences often provided a first opening to spirituality, which could later lead to a conversion to a Christian confession, particularly Russian Orthodoxy. Esoteric currents also had local roots: the teachings of Nikolai and Elena Roerich, as well as the legacy of Helena Blavatsky and George Gurdjieff were influential in certain circles.[10] The phenomenon certainly also had political roots, as a number of traditional religions were associated with national and ethnic identities that provided an alternative identity and value system.[11] More generally, it had to do with the ideological disaffection of a whole generation of Soviet youth born in the 1940s–1950s. Elena Beliakova, a historian who converted to Russian Orthodoxy in the 1970s, remembers:

> Ideology had exhausted itself. For the generation of our parents, it still meant something, they thought that there was no other way. But it did not work anymore with our generation. There was almost no one left who really took it [seriously]. There were those who consciously made a career . . . But there was no one left who would have been really committed. People were searching, there was an active search for truth. And this search for truth led them precisely to faith. It is, generally speaking, something common for youth, to search for truth.[12]

As Soviet youths began to question official propaganda, they also began to question the atheist tenets of communist ideology. This tendency did not escape the attention of observers in the West, among them Russian émigrés. In an article published in the émigré journal *Posev* in 1979, a member of a religious-philosophical seminar in Leningrad noted:

> While 10–15 years ago it would have been most unusual to see a young woman or man in a church, especially in large cities, it has now become commonplace, most of all precisely in large cultural centers . . . Conversations on God, religion, and mysticism, which were almost absent from our educated society in the early 1960s, except for a few narrow circles, are now most typical in various literary and artistic salons, circles, at various dissident meetings, and in any kind of company of "spiritual people," often around the same wretched bottle.[13]

As the large corpus of oral history interviews collected in the framework of my research project on Russian Orthodox converts from Moscow and Leningrad has shown, this religious revival had a number of characteristics: it concerned primarily educated youths from large cities who had grown up for the most part in nonreligious families and had come to faith as adults.[14] Some of them had been baptized in their childhood and had had minimal contact with religion, generally through a devout grandmother. Their parents' generation, however, had turned away from the church, whether out of atheist conviction or fear. Most of these young people had ties with dissenting circles or read samizdat and tamizdat literature,[15] although they had often joined the

Komsomol because membership was nearly obligatory to study at a university. This contradiction between outward conformism and inner dissent was often a source of qualms, and those who were most committed to living "in truth" aligned with their spiritual and moral values often chose to join spiritual seminaries and monasteries or accepted menial jobs in order to devote much of their time to the church and escape ideological conformism.

Soviet Reaction

Soviet authorities closely monitored and attempted to control this phenomenon of revived religious interest and activity. Head priests wrote reports to the commissars of the Council for Religion Affairs, an intermediary body exercising control over religious cults, which in turn collaborated with party organs to seek to stem this tendency. A 1967 report on the activity of religious organizations in Leningrad and the Leningrad region thus noted with concern:

> Despite ongoing atheistic [propaganda] work and some improvement in its quality we do not witness any diminution of religious activity. The quantity of religious rites performed has not diminished, the income of religious organizations has been significantly growing every year . . . One of the factors raising concern is that some youths have begun to show added interest toward religion and the church. Different reasons have been drawing youth to the church: there is interest in rituals and religious decorum, interest in the Bible as a literary and historical source, [and] the aspiration to become familiar with Christian philosophy. One also finds all kinds of "truth seekers" who are looking for answers to the questions that preoccupy them. There are also people who disagree with our philosophy and our reality, losers disappointed with life, morally broken people who seek consolation, inclined to superstition.[16]

Despite being well-informed about the phenomenon, Soviet officials often tried to minimize it. As late as 1983, a researcher for the Institute of Scientific Atheism interviewed by *Komsomolskaia Pravda* explained that religion was not popular among young people except in "sectarian groups," but there was a rising interest in the history of religion, which was connected with the rising education level of Soviet youth. He explained youth religiosity most of all by the strict religious education of "sectarians." As for those who came to faith without a religious education, it was "the result of [an] absence of stable convictions, a worldview infantilism."[17]

A decade after the hefty antireligious campaign organized by Nikita Khrushchev in the early 1960s, Soviet authorities opted for a course of limited repression circumscribed to a few "anti-Soviet" elements. This allowed the Orthodox Church's hierarchs to travel abroad and attend conferences organized by the World Council of Churches, and also host delegations of foreign religious dignitaries, a series of propaganda measures designed to perpetuate the myth of freedom of conscience in the USSR.

On the home front, however, Soviet authorities were preoccupied with the revival of established Christian churches, which could potentially escape political control, leading to a coalition of national and religious forces, as happened in Poland with the strategic alliance of the Solidarity movement and Pope John Paul II. The revival could also be easily instrumentalized by Western actors seeking to destabilize the Soviet regime. Indeed, a number of Western organizations dedicated their activity to the defense of Soviet believers' rights, among them Keston College, founded by Reverend Michael Bourdeaux. Such organizations became regular targets of Soviet propaganda but continued to disseminate information about antireligious repression in the Soviet Union.

Despite Soviet claims that the revival was engineered from abroad or was a pure invention of Western propaganda, official reports reveal genuine preoccupation with the situation. Throughout the 1970s and 1980s, the Soviet authorities waged an uphill ideological battle against religion, which they could not afford to lose, for fear of endangering the whole Communist project.

But Soviet atheist propaganda lacked effective arguments against youth religiosity. A journalist who visited the House of Scientific Atheism in Tashkent in 1984 was struck by an exhibition showing the history of religion, with impressive reproductions of a prehistoric cave and torture instruments of the Inquisition but no "materials on prominent atheists of the past or documents denouncing the propaganda of bourgeois clerical centers," and the only visitors were a few auditors from the party school.[18] Even when atheist propaganda journals entered into a dialogue with young believers, they relied only on hackneyed clichés. In 1970, *Science and Religion* published the letter of Viktor N., a twenty-one-year-old believer who suffered discrimination after leaving the spiritual seminary and complained that he could not find a job.[19] The journalist who commented on this letter answered: "You are wrong, Viktor, to affirm that the path to truth and good is in god and through god. For many centuries, religion reigned over the minds of millions of people but society during this time reached neither good nor truth." Nor was it correct to affirm "that it is impossible to live, think, and work normally without faith in god." Were there not "thousands upon thousands of sons of humanity who did not believe in god and showed the best examples of moral service to people"? Certainly, Viktor's personal offenses had led him to look for "the reasons of his own contradictions in the outside world," and his words showed how religious convictions "distort one's worldview, narrow one's horizon, lead to prejudiced, unobjective conclusions, and judgments."[20]

By the mid-1970s, the failure of these classical antireligious arguments was so patently obvious that propagandists had to adapt their discourse to try to regain control over the minds of Soviet youths. A textbook for Soviet propagandists of "scientific atheism" titled *Atheism and Youth*, published in 1978, noted with satisfaction that 97 percent of Soviet youths were atheists, in stark contrast to their Western peers.[21] The author, however, observed with preoccupation that in some religious communities, especially Protestant ones, young believers were particularly active. Moreover, religious objects and rituals had become fashionable among youth. The booklet identified various degrees of commitment among both believers and atheists, pointing to the large share of ideologically indifferent nonbelievers who could potentially go over to the adversary's camp, and who therefore had to be targeted by atheist propaganda. Since the young generation had grown up at a time when religion had already been largely defeated, they had "no experience of ideological struggle with religion [and] are not fully informed about its nature, functions, history, and the clergy's capacity to influence one's spiritual world. Hence youth's underestimation of this ideological enemy of the scientific worldview."[22]

The acute need of Soviet authorities for more convincing arguments led to the development of at least three lines of argumentation against religion in the late 1970s. These arguments appealed to the readers' feelings: the depiction of young believers as victims of sectarian groups or institutions played on the parents' fear of losing their children; articles showing superficially religious youngsters used the weapon of ridicule and shame to discourage such practices; and finally, the third trope rested on a political narrative of ideological betrayal and threatened young believers with severe punishment.

Sectarianism

Traditional antireligious discourse denounced the "sectarian" character of religion and set it in opposition to the Soviet collective spirit.
Some groups, such as Evangelical Baptists or Pentecostals, were generally suspected of fostering such sectarianism. Parents usually raised
their children in strict observance of religious rituals and traditions
that were at odds with the atheist education provided in school. But
Soviet authorities were no less concerned with the conversion of young
adults who, despite growing up in nonreligious families and going to
Soviet schools, turned away from their communist upbringing to join
religious groups. The terms "brainwashing" or "indoctrination" were
often used to designate the actions of these religious groups on young
people. As for their "victims," they were suspected of acting against their
own best interests, lacking the necessary will or intelligence to escape
manipulation. The victims of such brainwashing were usually women,
who were not only predominant in all religious groups but were most
easily suspected of weakness in traditional misogynistic discourse. The
result of such indoctrination was to sever previous ties, both with the
family and society, to prompt young people to leave promising careers
or studies and enter monasteries or the spiritual seminary.

An article published in 1983 in *Molodezh Estonii* (Youth of Estonia)
illustrates this narrative in relation to a young Orthodox woman, Liudmila.[23] The article begins with a quote from Matthew's Gospel (10:34),
which, in the authors' view, showed the hostile and antisocial nature of
Christian teachings: "Do not assume that I have come to bring peace
to the earth; I have not come to bring peace, but a sword. For I have
come to turn a man against his father, a daughter against her mother,
a daughter-in-law against her mother-in-law."

Liudmila's story is told in a heartbreaking tone by her father, a
driver who lived a few hours away from her in the city of Kuibyshev,
now Samara. Liudmila, who worked as a seamstress, announced one
day that she was going to Leningrad for advanced training. However,
after trying to get information about his daughter's situation from
his ex-wife, the man finds out that Liudmila is actually in a women's
monastery in Estonia. What follows is a harrowing account of his trav-
els to meet his daughter, who is already no longer of this world. He
notices "the faded look, the emaciated face, and the seal of doom that
had already appeared on it (later he saw this expression on the faces of
believers more than once)." The journalist wholeheartedly stands by the

side of this bereaved father who has lost a daughter, and comments: "Religion is the name of this force, which still cripples people's souls and indeed broke their family apart."[24]

The article goes on to describe how religion had wreaked havoc on their lives. Liudmila's mother, Klavdiia, raised her children in the Christian faith, despite her husband's protests. And eventually she had asked for a divorce at the insistence of a priest. But Liudmila seemed integrated in the Soviet collective until she met a young girl from a religious family, Liuba, who took her on a trip to visit holy sites. Ultimately, Liudmila decided to dedicate her life to religion, and nothing her father could say to try to convince her to leave the convent had any effect on her. He implied that she was manipulated by the nuns, whereas she argued she was no longer underage and could live wherever she wanted.

This article shows how Soviet propaganda instrumentalized a rather typical case of intrafamily conflict. The reader is left to believe that religion was the sole reason for the parents' divorce and Liudmila is depicted less as a responsible adult making her own decisions than as the victim of her mother first and then of a manipulative religious environment.

Another example of this line of argument is an article published in *Komsomolskaia Pravda* in 1986, titled *Ukhod* (Departure).[25] It featured a young woman from Baku who disappeared with her one-and-a-half-year-old son after converting to Hinduism and taking the name of Lakshmi. The newspaper explained her religiosity by her failure to accomplish what she had hoped for in life, despite numerous talents. This had led her to turn away from active participation in the collective and full engagement in earthly life: "She seemed to have taken offense at life, which did not keep its promises in relation to her, and as a result of misfortunes she went over to those who teach that the material world is an illusion. Both misfortunes and joys are empty, petty, deceptive. What was true and real for her was the god from ancient Eastern eposes."[26]

Lakshmi's family had not seen the danger coming: they did not keep her from fasting, even as she sunk into a "world of hallucinations" as a result. Along with fellow believers she joined a monastery. "Concern about one's soul, salvation promised by 'the teaching,' were akin to individual salvation after a shipwreck when each one grasps at his own inflatable ring of mantras and falls into a deadly whirlpool."[27] Ultimately, Lakshmi left her parents' home with a message sounding like a suicide note: "Please do not accuse anyone of my departure. Do not look for me." Lakshmi's parents were certain that she had been abducted.

The journalist believed that the people at fault were most of all "those who introduced [her] to contraband mystical nonsense (*bredni*)," particularly "pseudo-Eastern mystical spiritual teachings that had appeared in the USA."[28] Sectarian groups offered ready-made answers to parapsychological phenomena that science could not yet adequately explain.

Both Lakshmi and Liudmila are presented as weak characters manipulated by ill-intentioned religious groups, either sects instrumentalized from abroad or traditional confessions. Their religiosity is presented as excessive, leading to a separation from the collective, and this despite a promising potential: Liudmila was a committed worker, Lakshmi studied at a Moscow university. Parents appear helpless in the face of religious indoctrination and literally lose their children to the religious group.

Not all parents failed to act before it was too late, however, and Soviet propaganda implicitly called on parents to follow the example of one mother who called the editorial team of *Komsomolskaia Pravda* to share her deep concern about her son who had joined a yoga group. The editors took her call earnestly, knowing from previous cases that interest in yoga, fasting, and other practices could go along with such "criminal activities" as the distribution of anti-Soviet materials. The article, titled "The 'Miracle' and the Boy: Confession of a Mother Who Almost Lost Her Son," told in a heartbreaking tone the story of a mother who had saved her son from religious indoctrination with the help of psychiatry.[29] The young man, who had graduated from high school with honors, had experienced a bad divorce, which had certainly made him "good material for fishers of souls." He changed after he started attending the home circle of an enigmatic lady nicknamed "sorceress" (*charodeika*), with whom he "flew" into unknown worlds. The mother was in despair to see her son turn away from his favorite meat cutlets, and at night she could hear the rustle of paper as he read *samizdat*. She was shocked when he told her that she was a mere "body shell" (*obolochka*), but the last straw was when he announced that he had psychic powers and could heal anyone. Soon, as a result of his excessive fasting, he transformed into a mere "shell" himself. But three months of psychiatric care had returned this young man to life.

This type of argument was targeted at parents who had noticed changes in their children's behavior and could still try to influence them. Many respondents interviewed for my project confirmed that their parents had experienced shock when they learned that their children had converted to Orthodoxy, and some actively tried to deter their children from attending church. Such arguments could also potentially scare young people away from such seemingly harmless practices as yoga. However, in the 1970s and 1980s, the sectarian lens no longer appeared sufficient, particularly in relation to young people who were not fully "churched" and participated in religious rituals without the full commitment one may expect of members of a religious community.

Fashion

Mocking the superficiality of religious youth through the lens of "fashion" certainly had some truth to it. In certain intellectual circles of Moscow, Leningrad, or Kyiv, getting baptized or practicing yoga were just different facets of a longing for alternative worlds beyond Soviet ideology, an attempt to live *vnye* ("outside"), to use Alexei Yurchak's term, but did not always entail commitment to a religious tradition.[30] As one respondent who later became an Orthodox nun recalled, she had a few friends who were Christians but were not fully churched, and other colleagues with whom she practiced yoga and agni yoga, the esoteric doctrine founded by Elena and Nikolai Roerich. In this context she traveled to a monastery in Estonia where she was baptized. "It was just another spiritual experiment. What you tried in Buddhism, in Islam, you had to try with Christianity . . . Back then I didn't know that baptism is a sacrament. After baptism I felt in a completely different spiritual world."[31]

While religious searching was indeed a defining feature of youth religiosity in many circles, religious rituals could also be performed for nonreligious motives: the pressure of relatives, conformism, or mere curiosity. Such motives regularly came up in official reports of priests to the Commissar for Religious Affairs, perhaps also as a way to justify the persistence of such rituals in the modern era. Soviet youth periodicals regularly denounced the "fashion" for religious objects and rituals among young people: wearing a cross, collecting icons, having a religious wedding, baptizing children . . . The performance of such rituals might have appeared quite innocent, but it was an entry point into an "alien ideology" that, as one journalist put it, "is looking for a loophole, a crack in human soul, to sneak into it." He continued, "Just as blind admiration (*preklonenie*) for the Western way of life can start from the search for branded jeans, a small cross worn around the neck 'just like this' can sometimes turn out to be more than an innocent piece of jewelry."[32]

The article "A Golden Cross on a Thin Chain," published in *Molodezh Moldavii* (Youth of Moldavia) in 1981, discussed young people who were Komsomol members and wore crosses or participated in religious rituals.[33] Young Sveta, who works in a pharmacy, wears her grandmother's golden cross, a beautiful and fashionable piece of jewelry. She eventually agrees to remove her cross at her workplace but refuses to be told what to wear after work. The journalist L. Demidovich paraphrases her argument in these words: "You consider that it's incompatible with Komsomol morals? But what is incompatible? One can be an active Komsomol and think about the beauty and modernity of one's attire." The journalist goes on to describe the church wedding of a young couple. The bride holds a diet cake instead of the traditional *kulich* cake, while the groom lights his cigarette using his church candle as a lighter. Demidovich sneers: "Why did they come? Also to play a role, which they know of from books or the accounts of their elders. Then it will be an amusing story to tell in the company of their peers."[34] Another Komsomol member decorates his room with images of icons and posters of the fashionable singer Alla Pugacheva. Demidovich recognizes that interest in religious works of art is justified by their aesthetic qualities, but he expresses the concern that state programs to restore churches and religious monuments may have "reconciled" atheists with the church as a religious institution.

These articles emphasize the disconnect between the religious meanings of these objects or rituals and the alleged lack of faith of young people who followed fashion. They downplay the religiosity of young people, emphasizing the superficiality of their behavior, the message being that stricter Komsomol discipline could solve this problem. Reducing religiosity to a fashion also demeaned religion as fake and nonexistent.

Many articles also deplore the excessive tolerance shown by young people who did not realize that the values of the Komsomol were in strict opposition to religion and saw a continuum between Christianity and Communism. Journalists frequently reminded readers that the Komsomol charter included the duty to "lead a determined struggle with all manifestations of bourgeois ideology, with parasitism, religious prejudice, various antisocial manifestations and other remnants of the past, always place society's interest above personal ones."[35]

This alleged superficiality of convictions, both communist and religious, was the central theme of an article by I. Rudenko published in *Komsomolskaia Pravda* in 1983.[36] Titled *Nikakie* (None), it featured the three letters of young women who believed that they could safely combine their communist youth affiliation with religious beliefs and practices and even called on the organization to show more tolerance in this regard. Alla, aged sixteen, declares that she goes to church, confesses, and communes, and does not see "anything bad" about her faith, since she does not make a show of it. But she fears expulsion from the Komsomol if her religiosity becomes known. Marina, aged twenty-one, has recently been baptized and writes that it "has not affected in any way [her] views and convictions" and she "has not become a believer." Still, she believes that Komsomol members should be allowed to participate in religious rites. Finally, Lena, aged sixteen, writes that she is "tired of these conversations about religion" and atheistic propaganda at her school. "Why can't I go to church on a holiday? In our class many girls, although they may not say that god exists, agree that there is some kind of supernatural force. And I want to say: 'Leave religion in peace!'"[37]

Rudenko, who commented on these letters, doubted the sincerity of the girls' religious faith. He found no trace in their letters of existential doubts, of personal tragedies, or even disappointment in communist ideals that could explain their need to turn to religion in search of answers. Religious faith and communist ideals, instead of conflicting in their hearts, seemed to coexist peacefully side by side. The three girls called for greater tolerance toward religion, but according to the journalist, they were serious neither about faith nor about ideology: these were just "whims," no real convictions. It was precisely this indifference, this *dvoeverie* ("dual faith") of youth who "make the sign of the cross with one hand and vote with the other one at the Komsomol meeting"[38] that was most threatening to Soviet society.

Religion as Ideological Diversion

Finally, the third interpretation of youth religiosity was through the Cold War lens of ideological confrontation, which targeted two types of actors: Soviet religious dissidents and the Western organizations that publicized their calls and rendered assistance. As a lead article published in *Pravda* in 1977 emphasized, "We should not forget that contemporary bourgeois propaganda is becoming more and more sophisticated in its ideological diversions, trying to undermine [and] weaken Soviet people's convictions, most of all youth's, impose on us alien views and morals, [and] galvanize nationalist and religious prejudice."[39]

The lens of ideological confrontation was not new; even at the peak of détente Soviet propaganda forcefully attacked Western and émigré organizations supporting Soviet believers. In 1972 the state publisher of political literature, Politizdat, published *Diversion without Dynamite*, followed by an updated second edition in 1976.[40] The book's main thesis was that the United States engaged in a policy of "bridge building" with the peoples of the USSR as a new Cold War strategy in the framework of détente, the goal being the "erosion" of communist ideology. Religion was used as a weapon in this "psychological war" meant to introduce "bourgeois ideology" into the minds of Soviet people: "Religion is the only officially existing ideology in the Soviet Union opposed to Marxist-Leninist ideology."[41]

The instruments of such propaganda were most of all organizations such as Keston College, which published religious samizdat, smuggled religious literature into the USSR, and publicized the plight of religious dissidents. In 1983 the newspaper *Sovetskaia Rossiia* warned:

> It is well-known that centers for "religious studies" and subversive organizations under a religious guise have been created in the West, not without the help of secret services, for purposes of ideological diversion against Socialist countries. . . Each "religious" center has its specialization. Some elaborate theoretical methods of ideological diversion, others directly apply them. But their goals are identical: to discredit the communist worldview, to defame Socialist Democracy, to create in the religious milieu a bellicose opposition. These are the main tasks of clerical anticommunism.[42]

Diversion without Dynamite targeted a large number of these organizations: the Vatican, the publishing house Zhizn s Bogom (Life with God), Jehovah's Witnesses, Keston College, Licht im Osten (Light in the East), the Russian Student Christian Movement, the radio stations Radio Vatican, Radio Monte Carlo, Voice of America, and Radio Liberty, the émigré organization Narodno-Trudovoi Soiuz (People's Labor Union), the Russian Orthodox Church Abroad, and others. Individual religious actors were also targeted: those Western and émigré authors, historians, and researchers who wrote about the situation of believers in the USSR since the revolution, such as Rev. Michael Bourdeaux, Rev. Dmitrii Konstantinov, Nikita Struve, and Archbishop Ioann of San Francisco, among others.

The forms taken by this ideological diversion could seem innocent at first glance: an article from 1985 by A. Suvorov described a road trip to the USSR by two Swedish lads whose car was filled with illegal religious literature. However, the trip was terminated at the Soviet border and the "tourists" were sent back home on a train. Indeed, Suvorov cautioned, they were "emissaries of one of the foreign clerical 'missions'" who followed a tactic adopted by many such religious centers abroad: "With enviable tenacity they try to 'enlighten' Soviet people, flooding underground channels with their spiritual production . . . One of the goals of foreign missionaries is to propagandize and impose in our country religious cults in any possible way."[43] Soviet citizens who traveled abroad were also recruited to import contraband religious literature or objects. Suvorov cited the cases of two women who had tried to smuggle crosses and Bibles into the country.

Under the guise of rendering assistance to Soviet believers, these organizations pursued anti-Soviet goals. While at first they preferred "not to disclose their plans" and placed the "emphasis on purely 'religious' themes . . . one has only to dig a little deeper and a very clear picture emerges. The 'brothers' try in any possible way to oppose religious cults to the social regime existing in our country." These foreign organizations insisted in particular on the repressive character of Soviet legislation on religious cults, which was described as "infringing on freedom of conscience and Christian morals." These organizations encouraged believers, particularly Protestant groups, to commit "crimes" that could be instrumentalized via anti-Soviet propaganda as "widespread protests" and "antireligious repression." The names of the same religious dissidents came up repeatedly and were, according to Suvorov, instrumentalized by two "potent syndicates of lies," the Swiss-based center Glaube in der zweiten Welt (Faith in the Second World) and Keston College.[44]

However, these Western actors could not have acted without the support of religious dissidents who issued widely publicized protests to the West and relished the media attention and material gains to be accrued. In *Diversion without Dynamite*, A. Belov and A. Shilkin denounced the actions of Soviet religious dissidents and Soviet believers who had connections with anticommunist centers abroad, some of them in emigration: Frs. Gleb Yakunin and Nikolai Eshliman, Lev Regelson, Fr. Dmitrii Dudko, Anatolii Levitin-Krasnov and his young helpers Evgenii Kushev and Vera Lashkova, but also the Reformed Baptists, also called *initsiativniki* ("initiative takers").

Another propaganda book, published by Evgenii Vistunov in 1984, was titled *Priglashenie v zapadniu* (Invitation to a Trap). According to the description, the book "tells about the anti-Soviet activity of the West's ideological saboteurs (*diversanty*) who, under the guise of religion, try to speculate on the religious feelings of believers. Based on concrete examples, the author shows on whom the ideological saboteurs placed their stakes, whose services they used, [and] how and why they failed."[45]

The figures and organizations denounced varied slightly: the emphasis was on the "Slavic mission" in Leningrad and on members of Narodno-Trudovoi Soiuz in the Soviet Union. Levitin-Krasnov was also accused of collaborating with this organization and of relaying materials about the religious dissidents Yakunin, Regelson, and Aleksandr Ogorodnikov to the West. A whole chapter was dedicated to the feminist journal *Zhenshchina i Rossiia* (Woman and Russia), edited by Iuliia Voznesenskaia, Tatiana Goricheva, Natalia Malakhovskaia, and Tatiana Mamontova.

Soviet propaganda also instrumentalized the public trials and recantations of religious dissidents to denounce their connections with the West, employing a self-explanatory scheme: their arrest allegedly proved their guilt rather than justifying their claims about antireligious repression. The case of Dudko, whose recantation was broadcast on Soviet television, is well known, but there were a number of such cases that reinforced the Soviet line of argument that the connections between Soviet believers and their brothers of faith in the West were in essence criminal.

In a two-part article by N. Dombkovskii titled *Krest na sovesti* (Cross on the Conscience), Boris Razveev, a former participant in an unofficial Christian Seminar organized by Aleksandr Ogorodnikov (see chapter 4), expressed his "heartfelt" repentance for his past "crimes," hoping to deter others from this path. He could now see clearly "the criminal nature of the actions of those who shout about the persecution of believers allegedly taking place in our country." These affirmations were "gross lies" and "no one had ever prevented him from taking part in religious rituals, nor did he know about any such cases." Nevertheless, Dombkovskii noted, Razveev had once put forth a wholly different discourse. The article went on to describe Razveev's "criminal path": the young hippie, lazy and craving attention, listened to Western radio stations, "an ideological poison that had a slow but sure effect." His friendship with Ogorodnikov only strengthened his anti-Soviet views: the young man professed an alternative, "free" kind of religion and handed Razveev a few books published by the émigré anti-Soviet *Posev*. From a person "with a critical view on life," Razveev thus turned into someone who "spreads slander on his own country." Soon enough, the two friends were sending protests to the West about the imaginary antireligious discrimination they were facing. Ogorodnikov convinced Razveev that it did not matter whether what they said was true or false, since the publicity they would receive in the West would shield them from Soviet repression in any case. And the reward was not long in coming. After their protest was broadcast on Western radios, they began to receive parcels with jeans and Western clothes. "Over time Razveev got used to it: he transmitted a slanderous lampoon (*paskvil'*) abroad and received his reward."[46]

Once he became famous in the West, Razveev was invited to a secret meeting with Fr. John (Ioann) Meyendorff, a leading theologian of the Orthodox Church of America. Also present were, among others, the Orthodox dissidents Yakunin and Men. Yakunin presented the agenda of this conspiratorial meeting: he proposed the creation in the USSR of "another church that would conduct the struggle for 'believers' rights'" and a network of "secret parishes" with priests ordained by Meyendorff and affiliated to the Orthodox Church of America. Razveev concluded: "All these plans of creation of an underground 'catacomb' church, as they like to say, have only one goal: to conduct an action that will allow them to reap capital—moral—among their sponsors abroad, and real—in hard cash (*v zvonkoi monete*)."[47] The second part of the article went on to denounce the activities of Men and his spiritual son Sergei Bychkov, both of whom were described as immoral characters.

The journalist accepted Razveev's confession of "guilt before the people." The religious dissident had now fully realized his faults: "Blind faith in these 'defenders' has brought me and my family misfortune. I emphasize once more: they could not care less about the fate of people, the only thing that matters to them is to earn handouts (*podachki*) from the West."[48] In discrediting prominent religious dissenters, articles of this type aimed to deter Soviet believers from having any contact with the West or with religious dissidents who sought to create alternative religious structures, whether unofficial seminars or catechization groups. Moreover, by denouncing religious dissidents who had not yet been arrested, such as Men, these articles directly threatened them and warned everyone to stay away from them.

In the late Soviet period, youth religiosity evolved from a marginal phenomenon limited to traditionally religious groups to a broader movement among predominantly urban, educated youths from nonreligious backgrounds. The loss of the allure of communist ideology went along with a renewed interest in all things spiritual, from Eastern religions and esotericism to Christianity and Judaism. Traditional atheist discourses, which opposed science and religion, modernity and tradition, proved insufficient to stem this movement, and Soviet propagandists had to find new ways to target new audiences who were increasingly escaping their ideological control.

This chapter has examined the main lines of argument used in late Soviet antireligious propaganda aimed at deterring youth from joining religious groups and participating in rituals. Three dominant tropes, appealing to various feelings from fear to shame, emerged in the articles examined. The first line of argument emphasized the sectarian character of religion, the risk of indoctrination and separation from the Soviet collective. Targeting parents, these arguments played on the fear of losing one's child to a religious cult and warned about the need to show vigilance even in regard to seemingly harmless changes in one's child's behavior. The second line of argument depicted youth religiosity as a fashion, a symptom of frivolity and lack of firm ideological convictions. It dismissed the idea that religious views or participation in religious rituals were compatible with membership in the Komsomol. By making fun of young believers, these articles presented the religious renaissance as a myth without any foundation in reality. Finally, the third line of argument used in propaganda articles was ideological confrontation. Religion was an attribute of bourgeois society, and such Western anticommunist organizations as Keston College, under the guise of helping Soviet believers, actually tried to introduce anti-Soviet views. Moreover, these foreign groups instrumentalized the protests of Soviet religious dissidents, who craved attention and had a material interest in denouncing antireligious repression. Such articles, denouncing the activities of real figureheads of Soviet religious dissent after their arrest or emigration, but also sometimes preventively, as a measure of intimidation, served a double purpose: to scare those who already engaged in activities classified as anti-Soviet and to discourage anyone from embarking on this path or from establishing any contact with them or with the West.

Notes

This article was written for the project "Finding Faith in an Atheist Land: Russian Orthodox Intelligentsia and the Late Soviet National-Religious Revival" funded by a Swiss National Science Foundation Ambizione Grant.

1. The "baptism of Rus'" refers to the Christianization of Kyivan Rus', a state encompassing territories in contemporary Ukraine, Russia, and Belarus, following the conversion of its ruler Prince Vladimir in 988.

2. Aleksandr Kravetskii, "'Ia vyidu na stsenu i skazhu: A seichas diskoteka'—kak otets Aleksandr Men vpervye vystupil na vechere raikoma," *Pravmir.ru*, January 22, 2018, https://www.pravmir.ru/ya-vyiydu-na-stsenu-i-skazhu-a-seychas-diskoteka/.

3. Nikolai Dombkovskii, "Krest na sovesti," *Trud*, April 10–11, 1986.

4. Kravetskii, "Ia vyidu na stsenu."

5. Aleksandr Kravetskii, interview by Barbara Martin, Moscow, September 29, 2020.

6. Alexei Yurchak, *Everything Was Forever, Until It Was No More: The Last Soviet Generation* (Princeton, NJ: Princeton University Press, 2006).

7. Victoria Smolkin, *A Sacred Space Is Never Empty: A History of Soviet Atheism* (Princeton, NJ: Princeton University Press, 2018).

8. See, for example, Robert William Fogel, *The Fourth Great Awakening and the Future of Egalitarianism* (Chicago: University of Chicago Press, 2000); William Gerald McLoughlin, *Revivals, Awakenings, and Reform: An Essay on Religion and Social Change in America, 1607–1977* (Chicago: University of Chicago Press, 1978); Mark R. Shaw, *Global Awakening: How 20th-Century Revivals Triggered a Christian Revolution* (Downers Grove, IL: IVP Academic, 2010).

9. Boris Filippov, "O volne dukhovnogo napriazheniia kontsa 1960-kh XX veka-nachala XXI veka," *Vestnik PSTGU I: Bogoslovie, Filosofiia* 5, no. 61 (2015): 112–30.

10. Nikolai (or Nicholas) Roerich (1874–1947) was a Russian painter, archaeologist, and philosopher. Along with his wife Elena (Helena, 1879–1955) he developed an interest in theosophy and Eastern religion, and their religious-philosophical teachings, known as *agni yoga* ("living ethic"), became influential among New Age adepts in Russia. Helena Blavatsky (1831–91) was a Russian religious philosopher and founder of the Theosophical Society, an influential esoteric movement. George Gurdjieff (1877–1949) was a mystic of Greek-Armenian origin whose teachings, known as the "Fourth Way," were influential in the West and in Latin America. On the development of New Age thought in the USSR, see Michael Hagemeister and Birgit Menzel, *The New Age of Russia: Occult and Esoteric Dimensions* (Munich-Berlin: Verlag Otto Sagner, 2012).

11. See, for example, Miklos Tomka, "The Changing Role of Religion in Eastern and Central Europe: Religion's Revival and Its Contradictions," *Social Compass* 42, no. 1 (1995): 17–26.

12. Elena Beliakova, interview by Barbara Martin, Moscow, January 13, 2020.

13. Vladimir Veretennikov, "O religioznykh iskaniiakh v Rossii," *Posev*, no. 6 (June 1979), 37.

14. I have conducted approximately one hundred interviews with Russian Orthodox believers from the intelligentsia who were active in Moscow and Leningrad/Saint Petersburg from the 1970s to the 1990s.

15. *Samizdat* designates uncensored literature reproduced by readers on typewriters and circulated among friends. *Tamizdat* is the publication of

uncensored works by Soviet authors in the West that are then smuggled into the Soviet Union.

16. "On the Activity of Religious Organizations in Leningrad and the Leningrad Region," undated, fond 2017, finding aid 1, file 11, 4–5, Saint Petersburg Central State Archive (TsGA SPB).

17. "Ubezhdenie–smolodu," *Komsomolskaia Pravda*, September 16, 1983.

18. A. Tiurikov, "Delo osoboi vazhnosti," *Pravda vostoka*, May 26, 1984, 3.

19. "Podumaem vmeste," *Nauka i religiia*, no. 12 (1970), 14–15.

20. "Podumaem vmeste."

21. Viktor I. Nosovich, *Ateizm i molodezh* (Leningrad: Obshchestvo "Znanie" RSFSR, 1978), 12.

22. Nosovich, *Ateizm i molodezh*, 11.

23. S. Mironov, "Po tu storonu sveta," *Molodezh Estonii*, June 28, 1983.

24. Mironov, "Po tu storonu sveta."

25. A. Ganelin, "Ukhod," *Komsomolskaia Pravda*, March 19, 1986.

26. Ganelin, "Ukhod."

27. Ganelin, "Ukhod."

28. Ganelin, "Ukhod."

29. B. Pilipenko, "'Chudo' i mal'chik," *Komsomolskaia Pravda*, August 16, 1985.

30. Yurchak, *Everything Was Forever*.

31. Natalia (Sister Anuvia) Vinogradova, interview by Barbara Martin, Moscow, February 1, 2020.

32. Tiurikov, "Delo osoboi vazhnosti."

33. L. Demidovich, "Zolotoi krestik na tonen'koi tsepochke," *Molodezh Moldavii*, October 27, 1981.

34. Demidovich, "Zolotoi krestik."

35. *Ustav Vsesoiuznogo Leninskogo Kommunisticheskogo Soiuza Molodezhi* (Kishinev: Izdatel'stvo TsK KP Moldavii, 1973), 7.

36. I. Rudenko, "Nikakie," *Komsomolskaia Pravda*, April 6, 1983.

37. Rudenko, "Nikakie."

38. Rudenko, "Nikakie."

39. "Vospitanie ideinoi ubezhdennosti," *Pravda*, December 1, 1977. Quoted in Nosovich, *Ateizm i molodezh*, 15.

40. A. Belov and A. Shilkin, *Diversiia bez dinamita*, 2nd ed. (Moskva: Politizdat, 1976).

41. Belov and Shilkin, *Diversiia bez dinamita*, 13.

42. I. Gapochka, "Pod maskoi lozhnoi sviatosti," *Sovetskaia Rossiia*, July 29, 1983.

43. A. Suvorov, "Lozh v sviatoi upakovke," *Sovetskaia Belorussiia*, August 18, 1985.

44. Suvorov, "Lozh v sviatoi upakovke."

45. Evgenii Vistunov, *Priglashenie v zapadniu* (Leningrad: Lenizdat, 1984), 2.

46. Dombkovskii, "Krest na sovesti."

47. Dombkovskii, "Krest na sovesti."

48. Dombkovskii, "Krest na sovesti."

CHAPTER 6

Protest from the Margins

A Human Rights Campaign Led by Evangelical Women in the Soviet Union, 1964–1987

April L. French

In February 1964, three women gathered clandestinely for what they called an All-Union Conference of Relatives of Evangelical Christian-Baptist Prisoners. Four years earlier, a debate had broken out among Evangelical Christian-Baptist (ECB) congregations over whether the church should acquiesce to the intensifying demands of the antireligious Soviet government. The state demanded that local religious organizations maintain their official registration by submitting to the Law on Religious Associations—a 1929 law designed to confine worship to officially sanctioned buildings and to prohibit children's attendance at religious services, among other things. During the intradenominational debate, some ECB believers formed the Action Group (Initsiativnaia Gruppa), which by 1965 would become the Council of Churches of Evangelical Christians-Baptists (CCECB), splitting from the officially recognized All-Union Council of Evangelical Christians-Baptists (AUCECB).[1] Such public defiance provoked Soviet officials to subject many of these breakaway evangelicals to arrest, show trials, and imprisonment for violating the Law on Religious Associations.

Before their initial meeting, the three founding members of a new organization—called the Council of Prisoners' Relatives (CPR) by Keston College personnel—had collected information on at least 155 ECB members who had been imprisoned since 1961. The founders saw this record keeping about ECB prisoners and the reporting of this information to their co-religionists as two central tasks of their fledgling organization. A third task was to petition the Soviet government to review all cases of those imprisoned "for the Word of God" and of children removed from their parents "for a religious upbringing," with the goal of complete rehabilitation of the prisoners and full restoration of their co-religionists' parental rights and the unconditional return of their children.[2] Although the CPR was initially a provisional committee, the women would continue their activism with a steady rotation of leading members until September 1987. Their organization thus ran for over twenty-three years, making it the longest-standing human rights organization established and operating within the confines of the Soviet Union. In comparison, the well-known human rights samizdat publication, *The Chronicle of Current Events*, was active for sixteen years from 1968 to 1983—eight years fewer than the entire activity of the CPR, whose samizdat *Bulletin* ran for a total of seventeen years (1971–87).[3]

This essay examines the work of the Council of Prisoners' Relatives and considers its underexplored influence. Despite its significance— including the frequent citation by Western organizations of their letters and petitions during the Cold War as evidence of human rights violations in the Soviet Union, thanks in large part to Keston College— most historians of Soviet Protestantism have mentioned the group only briefly in their wider analyses. Setting the stage with historical and organizational context, the essay goes on to explore the story of Aleksandra Kozorezova, opening a window into the way women's daily realities often sharpened their rights consciousness and dually subversive activism in the Council of Prisoners' Relatives.

Historical Context

The evangelical movement emerged in the Russian Empire in the late 1860s and early 1870s in three separate locales: Ukraine, the Transcaucasus region of Georgia and southern Russia, and St. Petersburg. Although these early groups had clear links to Western European believers—to German Baptists and Mennonites in the southern regions, and to Lord Radstock, an evangelical Anglican, in St. Petersburg—they quickly acquired their own Slavic forms. From these three initial geographic centers, evangelicalism spread to the rest of the Russian Empire. By the first decade of the twentieth century, the strongest two denominations—the Baptists and the Evangelical Christians—had formed. These denominations maintained their distinctiveness while continuing their cross-denominational relationships well into the Soviet period. During World War II, after fifteen years of crushing repression against believers, the Soviet state allowed a joint denomination of Evangelical Christians-Baptists to be established. Following its establishment, the ECB denomination experienced a period of sustained rebuilding and evolution, despite internal factions and external oppression, as their congregations navigated a tenuous relationship with an atheistic state.[4]

Believing it "impossible to build a communist future without . . . freeing [people's] consciousness from 'religious prejudices and superstitions,'" Mikhail Suslov, the head of the Communist Party's Agitation and Propaganda Department from 1947 to 1982, unleashed an antireligious campaign in late 1958 with the approval of Nikita Khrushchev.[5] During this campaign, authorities employed multiple tactics, from antireligious propaganda to sharpening the legal code concerning religious believers, from the removal of registration and the closing of churches to instigating very public confessional modifications that led to internal conflict. In 1960 authorities added two laws to the criminal code, designed to thwart the activities of religious believers: Article 142, on the separation of church from state and church from school, and Article 227, on religious leaders inciting citizens to neglect civic duties or to abstain from social life. From 1961 to 1964 alone, over eight hundred Jehovah's Witnesses, Pentecostals, Seventh Day Adventists, and unregistered ECB believers were arrested under suspicion of violating Articles 142 and 227, many of them sentenced to three to five years in labor camps.[6] During the antireligious campaign, authorities began closing prayer houses for all religious confessions and stripping congregations of their registration across the Soviet Union, especially from early 1961 when the Council of Ministers passed a secret resolution "on the improvement of monitoring the fulfilment of the Law on Cults."[7]

Among the most pernicious aspects of the antireligious campaign was the way religious-affairs officials manipulated the leadership of national religious organizations with a "divide and conquer" strategy, playing on long-simmering tensions.[8] In December 1959 the AUCECB approved a Letter of Instruction to all pastors across the Soviet Union, the contents of which "fully reflected Soviet religious policy."[9] In early 1960 they distributed the letter, informing pastors of policies and procedures that must be followed to facilitate or maintain each congregation's official registration. The Letter of Instruction demanded, inter alia, the cessation of "zealous proselytism," a reduction in "the baptism of young people between the age of eighteen and thirty," and a ban on children's presence at church services.[10] This letter, and the development of new statutes for the AUCECB from 1960 to 1963, ignited a union-wide split.[11]

AUCECB leaders chose to send these letters to assure institutional survival. Once ECB pastors and congregations found out about the letter and the new constitution, however, some justifiably regarded these documents to be a result of state pressure on registered communities. The documents precipitated a split between those who believed it traitorous to register with an atheist state that would dare mandate how to worship and those who chose to remain in the AUCECB to worship in registered communities. The AUCECB leadership refused to revoke their controversial instruction letter and new statutes until 1963. By then, it was too late. The rupture was sealed in 1965 when the breakaway faction formed into a separate denominational organization, the CCECB. Since this separatist organization rejected the state's demand to register, its members experienced much more official repression than AUCECB members, including nearly two hundred who were imprisoned by the end of 1964.[12] The CCECB subsequently saw its members as martyrs and identified their group as the true Christian church, willing to suffer imprisonment and even death for the sake of their faith.[13]

Despite multiple failed attempts at unity, boundary lines were drawn and leaders and activistic laity took sides. Most ECB believers across the nation were forced to choose camps by 1966, the split occasionally crossing family lines. The 1960s and 1970s were particularly taxing for those from unregistered ECB congregations. In 1967 alone, eight hundred of the thirteen hundred religious believers subjected to fines or warnings were ECB believers.[14] CCECB leaders justified their tenacious civil disobedience by the call to remain faithful to the end and to suffer for the faith, as the martyrs of early Christianity had done. With such calls, they implied or stated outright that AUCECB believers were not faithful, having capitulated to religious-affairs officials, and could not therefore be considered true Christians. As early as 1961, congregations that sided with the Action Group began writing complaint letters to Soviet officials.[15] The newly established CPR began adding their own letters on behalf of their imprisoned and oppressed family members in 1964.[16]

The CPR—established and run by women—became the most active evangelical political action group in the Soviet era. By 1966 its members had selected a highly respected woman, Lidiia Vins (1907–85), to lead the organization. She was the widow of Petr Vins (1898–1937), a missionary to the Far East in the early Soviet period who was sentenced to death by shooting in Siberia in 1937, and the mother of Georgii Vins (1928–98), a key leader of the CCECB who was serving his first stint in prison at the time. From 1967, the CPR began sending out semiregular "emergency messages" to Soviet leaders to inform them "about concrete instances of new illegal actions and repressions" by officials against ECB believers.[17] Lidiia Vins was imprisoned in 1970 for nearly three years for her provocative work with the CPR.[18]

In 1971 other women—who kept the work of the CPR going while Lidiia Vins was in prison—started collating letters from CCECB-affiliated congregations to reprint in the samizdat *Bulletin*. Despite unrelenting attempts by the state to undermine the group's epistolary activism, the underground publication of the *Bulletin* went on uninterrupted for seventeen years due to clandestine networks and an extensive system of hidden mimeograph printing presses around the Soviet Union. Women functioned as the primary compilers and printers of the *Bulletin*. The underground publisher Khristianin (Christian) started printing the *Bulletin*, among other publications including portions of the Bible, as early as 1972 (figure 6.1).[19]

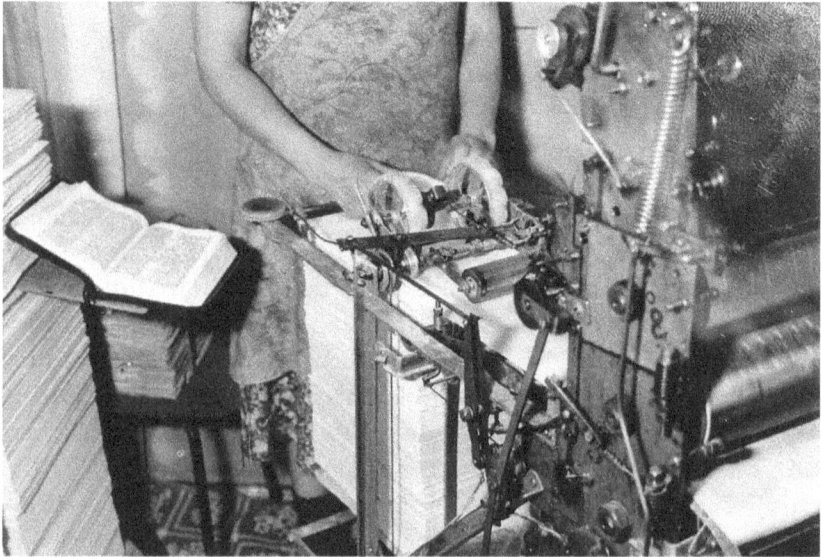

FIGURE 6.1.   Anonymous woman working at a Khristianin printing press somewhere in the Soviet Union. Photo from The Keston Center for Religion, Politics, and Society, Baylor University, Waco, Texas.

From 1971 to 1987, the CPR produced 143 issues of the *Bulletin*.[20] With an average of over eight issues per year, the *Bulletin* consisted primarily of a reproduction of various petitions, complaints, and declarations made by CPR and CCECB churches to Soviet leaders and international organizations. Through the *Bulletin* and a flood of separate letters, they spread the news of the plight of religious believers in the Soviet Union to an international audience. Considering the anti-Western stance of Communist authorities, this dissemination of information to the West greatly annoyed state and party officials. In 1980 Soviet religious-affairs officials noted the "systematic" nature of the CPR "network of information gathering" established for their "libelous speculations and illegitimate demands set forth in illegally published bulletins."[21]

The women of the CPR used their extensive network to gather signatures for open letters, including one dated May 1977 and addressed to Brezhnev and others "from Christian mothers living on the territory of the USSR," which gathered an astonishing 4,131 signatures on 166 pages. In the letter, they demanded that any limits on parents giving their children a religious upbringing should be abolished, among other things.[22] The network of trust fostered by the CPR among their co-religionists in the preceding thirteen years increased their ability to gather so many signatures within a short time. I. A. Gordeeva argues that the CPR "activated within the underground brotherhood [the CCECB] the mechanisms to form horizontal structures of trust, networks of mutual assistance and support, [and] the reproduction of traditions of social solidarity."[23]

CCECB women in Omsk were active members and assistants of the CPR from the mid-1960s until the late 1980s, influenced by their connection with Lidiia Vins, who had lived in Omsk in the 1930s and 1940s. Aleksandra Timofeevna (Andrienko) Kozorezova, the mother of ten children and a tireless advocate for religious freedom in the Soviet Union, spearheaded this activism.[24] She and her family had been members of the breakaway ECB faction since at least 1963, refusing to join the local congregation that regained registration in 1964, while demanding they be granted the freedom of conscience enshrined in the Constitution of the USSR.[25] Kozorezova's husband Aleksei—who led CCECB congregations in Omsk, Siberia, and Voroshilovgrad (now Luhansk), Ukraine—was imprisoned three times, spending a total of twelve and a half years in prison between 1966 and 1985. In 1966, by virtue of her husband's first arrest, show trial, and imprisonment,

Kozorezova became a member of the CPR. Despite the daily hardships she and her family faced, she accepted the role as head of the CPR in 1979 when Lidiia Vins emigrated to the United States. Kozorezova led the organization until 1987.

Aleksandra Kozorezova

Multiple episodes from Kozorezova's life not only reveal the way believers adapted to antireligious Soviet state tactics, but they also open a window into the development of CPR activism. In November 1958 Kozorezova was kicked out of the Communist Youth (Komsomol) organization at the Omsk Medical Institute, where she was in her final year of study to become a physician. The provincial religious-affairs commissioner reported this as a necessary measure, since Kozorezova had "entered the Baptist sect."[26] Having been raised in a Baptist family and baptized in 1956, she likely had not been active in the Komsomol for some time. In the earliest months of the antireligious campaign, however, Komsomol representatives would have found it politically expedient to report that they had culled from their membership a religious believer deemed to be in blatant violation of communist ideals. After her expulsion from its Komsomol organization, Kozorezova was also expelled from medical school, having completed all but one semester.[27]

By late 1963 the Kozorezov family and several others decided not to join their co-religionists who were appealing for registration, knowing that to remain unregistered would lead to further oppression at the hands of local authorities.[28] In May 1966 Aleksei Kozorezov traveled to Moscow to protest the violation of believers' rights at the headquarters of the Central Committee of the Communist Party.[29] Aleksei recounts that when he and two others from Omsk made the decision to go, he told them, "Only one who believes he will not return home should go." On May 27, nine days after Aleksei returned safely to Omsk, local authorities arrested him. Several months later, at a show trial against him and two Mennonite women, he was sentenced to three years in prison (figure 6.2). He recalls that for someone who expected death, three years was an easy form of suffering, even in the notorious Vladimir prison.[30]

In August 1967, acting as a CPR member after her husband's arrest, Kozorezova joined four other women in signing a lengthy petition to the United Nations Commission on Human Rights. The petition enumerated the ways the Soviet state had been violating the rights of their

FIGURE 6.2.   Show trial of Aleksei Kozorezov, Omsk, autumn 1966. Arkhiv Omskogo gosudarst-vennogo istoriko-kraevedcheskogo muzeia (OGIKM), OMK 7528.38.

co-religionists, including the imposition of exorbitant fines; the break-ing up of religious meetings and weddings; the searching of homes and confiscation of property; the arrest, show trials, and unjust imprison-ment of leaders; the interrogation of their children at school; and the removal of children from their parents.[31] Although copies of some let-ters written by Soviet dissidents to their government had earlier made their way to the West, this appeal to the United Nations was apparently the first by religious dissidents addressed to an entity in the West and requesting intervention in the defense of the human rights of Soviet citizens. Nadezhda Beliakova and Miriam Dobson argue that through this "pioneering appeal," CPR members "went further than many dis-sidents; in addition to condemning the regime's failure to implement its own legislation, they also noted and condemned inconsistencies between Soviet laws and decrees." The letter also demonstrated that "the CPR had fully adopted the concept of human rights" well before the Helsinki Accords.[32] The final paragraph of the letter reads: "We would not have considered appealing to international organizations had we even the slightest bit of hope that our petitions before the Gov-ernment of the USSR would bear positive results. But the ruthless war against unregistered congregations is spreading . . . The facts of per-secution we have here delineated are only a tiny speck of all that has taken place."[33] This was the first of a flood of appeals from the CPR to the West.

Kozorezova's signature on the letter provoked authorities in Omsk to launch a criminal investigation against her for "libel against Soviet legitimacy." She recalled, "They had decided to take [my] children [from

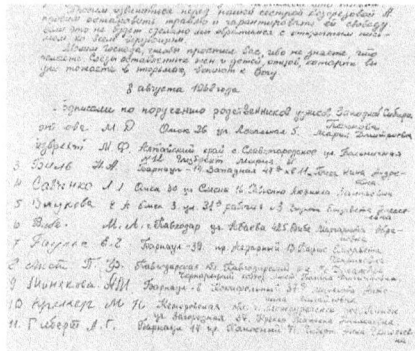

FIGURE 6.3. Xerox copy of the final paragraphs and signature page of the 1968 handwritten declaration letter by Kozorezova's co-religionists. Photo from The Keston Center for Religion, Politics, and Society, Baylor University, Waco, Texas. KCRPS, SU-Ini-6-8-S, 1968.

me] and to place them into a communist boarding school. So I secretly left Omsk with my eight young children and we lived illegally in the homes of believers until my husband was released [from prison] in 1969."[34] In August 1968, eleven of Kozorezova's friends sent a letter to Brezhnev and others about the libel in an Omsk newspaper that accused her of "carrying on subversive work" (figure 6.3).[35] Kozorezova's friends demanded that the state apologize to her, that "this persecution cease and that her freedom be guaranteed," closing with a provocative statement reflecting Jesus's words from the cross: "We beg the Lord to forgive you, since you do not know what you are doing."[36]

After Aleksei Kozorezov's release from prison in 1969, Kozorezova and their children returned to Omsk. One reason their church had chosen to remain unregistered was the Soviet mandate that children not be allowed to attend religious services. They felt God commanded them to give their children a religious upbringing. A May 1970 report to the provincial Communist Committee described teachers' efforts to instill an atheistic upbringing at the school attended by the Kozorezov children:

> Concrete atheistic work is being conducted at School No. 66, where the children of A[leksei] Kozorezov study.... The class leaders [teachers] for the classrooms where the Kozorezov children study observe these children's behavior and social-activity level. They have noticed that the younger children, Misha Kozorezov (a pupil in grade 1) and Galia Kozorezova (grade 3) conduct

themselves more freely in their collectives. They are highly social with their comrades, and in their behavior one does not sense a difference from the other children in their classrooms. The conduct of Petia (grade 3) and Liuba (grade 5) is much more withdrawn. They do not participate in the life of the collective, try to avoid social assignments, and do not go on excursions to films or the theater. In conversations with their teacher(s), they explain this as a desire "only to study." Class leaders . . . have had several conversations with these children's parents about this and have argued that such behavior separates the children from the collective and makes their schoolwork more difficult. In response, the parents categorically stated that the school's job is to teach a child grammar, but the parents' job is to give their children a proper upbringing. When . . . Liuba Kozorezova's class leader led a conversation [with the parents] about their daughter joining the Pioneers, Aleksandra Kozorezova replied, "I do not forbid my children from joining the Pioneers, but then they must forget God. They can choose for themselves who is most important to them."[37]

Kozorezova's reported response to her daughter's teacher reflects both a strong stand to give her children a Christian upbringing and an uncompromising desire that they choose to follow God, without denying that it was ultimately each child's choice whether to join the Communist children's organization.

Soviet scholars who conducted a study of religiosity in the 1960s concluded that many believers were young people, which not only went against the Marxist-Leninist notion of religion withering away but also pointed to religion being transmitted via the family. The leader of this study "considered this a failure of the Soviet school system and argued that teachers had to familiarize themselves with the family lives of their students by regularly visiting their homes."[38] In the late 1960s and early 1970s, the tactic of teachers conducting welfare checks at the homes of "sectarians" spread across the Soviet Union. Although such visits were conducted under the guise of ensuring that children were being properly cared for, school officials often used home visits to attempt to draw students away from religious belief. The report about representatives from the school in Omsk frequenting the Kozorezov home in 1970 betrays such mixed motives: "Teachers and class leaders have visited the Kozorezov family several times to learn their living conditions and to observe the children. Unfortunately, however, conversations with them and attempts to pull them away from religion have thus far brought about no tangible results."[39] In light of the challenges Kozorezova and her children had faced the previous few years, it was foolish to have expected tangible results.

Because CCECB believers refused to register their congregations, officials considered their religious meetings illegal gatherings. Women and married couples regularly hosted worship services and prayer meetings at their homes, often resulting in steep fines.[40] The illegal status of the Omsk CCECB congregation posed significant challenges for its members, since local officials frequently disrupted their worship services.[41] In one instance, two women from the Omsk city council were assigned "to present [themselves on February 13, 1971] at the gathering of the sectarian group . . . at the home of the Kozorezov family and officially to certify the illegality of such an assembly."[42] Based on these women's reports, they had no idea what they and their male companion were about to get themselves into. As they entered Aleksandra Kozorezova's kitchen, they heard people singing a hymn behind a closed and guarded door. That winter evening, however, they would never see who was behind the door.[43] After a decade of repressive tactics, Kozorezova was prepared. She came out of the room with five or six of her children, who stood in front of her while she guarded the door. Kozorezova reportedly spoke for most of the forty-five minutes that the unwelcome strangers stayed at her home. All the while, her co-religionists remained completely silent, having stopped singing as soon as they realized officials had arrived. After gathering the officials' names and employment numbers, Kozorezova defiantly told them that they could stay there until 10 p.m. and no later, that they would not get beyond the kitchen, that this was her house to which she had invited friends, that this gathering was in no way illegal, and that these city officials were therefore acting disrespectfully by coming to her home uninvited. She continued:

> You can fine me, throw me into prison, remove my children from me, but I will never deny God, because God gives me life. . . . You officials would find a better use of your time by putting other places in order, where there is drunkenness, prostitution, and corruption. In our faith, there is absolutely no such disorderliness, so leave us believers alone and in peace. You have absolutely no right to interfere with our faith and to follow us everywhere. I officially declare that I refuse to attend any administrative commission, and you will not do anything to me.[44]

FIGURE 6.4. Show trial of Iurii Mikhailovich Terekhov, Nikolai Romanovich Savchenko, Fedor Akhimovich Poiunov, and Aleksei Timofeevich Kozorezov (left to right), Omsk, July 23, 1971. OGIKM, OMK 7528.41.

Both officials' reports concluded that Soviet authorities should not tolerate such impudence, since it could lead to mass disturbance. Arguing that these sectarians bring only harm, the officials recommended that the danger must be countered with further antireligious work.[45]

Kozorezova's husband Aleksei sat among those behind the door on that February evening. He and three other leaders from this congregation were arrested at their workplaces three months later—on May 14, 1971—charged with *tuneiadstvo* (social parasitism—i.e., not working but freeloading off society and the government). At their show trial, Kozorezov was sentenced to five years in a labor camp (figure 6.4).[46]

In the CCECB world, prisoners and their families were seen as heroes of the faith, but life was difficult. When their husbands were incarcerated, women were in essence civilly widowed—left to raise their large families alone with little or no financial means.[47] CCECB congregations and the women of the CPR called the children of ECB prisoners "orphans" while their fathers were away, although their mothers usually remained in the home.[48] The use of this term indicates that the father was the parent whose presence offered the greatest economic security and protection. Given these families' subsistence living and decreased sense of safety, co-religionists offered support and encouragement. And many of these civilly widowed women, including Aleksandra Kozorezova, took up the pen and continued their epistolary activism through the CPR.

By 1975, partly due to Kozorezova's open activism with the CPR, Omsk officials again threatened her with arrest, so she packed up her ten children and elderly mother and fled to Voroshilovgrad, Ukraine.[49] Soon after she arrived there, KGB officials threatened criminal charges if she did not stop her work with the CPR. Recalling that time many years later, she wrote: "[At that time,] the image of Esther came to me. Esther told the king, 'How can I endure to see the calamity that will befall my people, and how can I endure to see the destruction of my kindred?' With my whole heart, I internally repeated those words. I then told the KGB official, 'I cannot be indifferent when it comes to those who are imprisoned for the work of the church.'"[50]

Kozorezova became the director of the CPR in 1979. The early 1980s were particularly trying for her family.[51] Her husband was arrested in late December 1980, at which time local authorities were already building a case against her.[52] In a January 1981 letter to Communist officials, Kozorezova wrote: "I cannot cease the work of petitioning as long as there is even one Christian prisoner in the Soviet Union, as long as believers are victimized. My husband and I never had, nor could we ever have, evil intentions against the authorities. . . . We, as believers who love the Lord and Christ's Church, are opponents of godlessness [and] atheistic dogma."[53]

In August 1981 Kozorezova was sentenced to a three-year suspended sentence of probation.[54] Less than a year after her sentence came to an end, authorities began compiling another case against her. The prosecutor in Voroshilovgrad coordinated a multi-site search of at least eleven believers' homes across the Soviet Union in connection with her case on July 12, 1985. That day, officials searching a home in Donetsk told believers that Kozorezova would be arrested on July 15, and the news spread quickly to her. Thus began a period when she was forced underground for more than a year and a half, as authorities launched a widespread criminal investigation and pestered her co-religionists about her whereabouts.[55] In a letter to Soviet officials, dated December 15, 1985, Kozorezova acknowledged she had to leave her children "to continue [her] entrusted ministry in illegal conditions."[56] Only in 1987—with the easing of restrictions that accompanied glasnost and perestroika under Gorbachev—was Kozorezova able to return home. She remained the CPR's leader until the last ECB prisoners were released after a targeted amnesty by the Supreme Soviet in February 1987 and a more far-reaching amnesty in July 1987.[57]

Discourse Analysis

Kozorezova took part in the compilation of the *Bulletin* from as early as 1974 for as many as 131 of the *Bulletin's* 143 issues. Based on their letters and publications, the women of the CPR and their co-religionists defined a true evangelical as one who opposes the "world"—that is, the antireligious state—and is called to defend the right to true freedom of religion, being prepared to suffer bodily harm and potential social deprivation for the sake of Christ. They perceived themselves to embody true evangelicalism as an expression of heroic suffering at the hands of a "godless" state that was persecuting them. These dual themes of suffering and persecution are clear in CPR and CCECB epistolary activism. Indeed, the discourse in the *Bulletin* lines up well with Olena Panych's examination of several memoirs of CCECB leaders. She argued that their "biographical canon" included:

1. An active interpenetration of the mystical into everyday common practices.
2. The image of a "faith hero" as a persecuted . . . fighter for the right to confess [one's] own religious beliefs, in spite of repeated repression by the atheistic authorities—almost always including the element of suffering "for the sake of the faith and God's work" or "for the sake of God's Word."
3. A self-understanding of the faith hero as "a physical and spiritual successor to the historical destiny of [one's] parents who also lived as faith heroes and martyrs," thereby perpetuating a "special kind of 'martyr habitus' [that] was transmitted over generations with the help of consciously maintained historical memories from the Soviet period, . . . bec[oming] part of a habitual, axiomatic tradition of recalling past sufferings."
4. An artistic and rhetorical form [that] contributes to an "aura of factuality" projected onto a depicted reality.[58]

Kozorezova's writing in the CPR *Bulletin* in 1974 and 1975 reflects similar themes. In a letter to the Chairman of the Presidium of the Supreme Soviet, Nikolai Podgorny, she wrote in exceptional detail about events that took place on June 5, 1974, when a female investigator came with a crew of strong male *druzhinniki*—a voluntary people's patrol called on to protect public order—to search the Kozorezov household in Omsk in connection with a case against Georgii Vins. Toward the end of the search, a confrontation ensued. The *druzhinniki* violently twisted the arms of Kozorezova's children and elderly father before dragging her away to a government vehicle by her hands and feet for interrogation, to the dismay of her wailing children. In Kozorezova's complaint letter, she writes to Podgorny:

> It does not cease to amaze me that the heads of your just, democratic state allow such actions. Where are the justice, equal rights, and defense of the rights of women and children that you proclaim so loudly to the whole world? Or do those rights only extend to the ruling class of atheism? In their fierce malice, it is apparent that atheists have decided to destroy our family physically. But, Comrade Podgorny, I have now informed you of this personally. And if anything happens to my husband, to me, or to our children, you will be responsible.[59]

A later edition of the *Bulletin* printed an August 1974 reply to Kozorezova from Podgorny's office, stating that local officials had not violated the law during the search of her home.[60]

By fall 1974 believers complained that local officials were building a case against Kozorezova.[61] As that threat grew stronger, she fled with her family to Voroshilovgrad sometime in 1975, as described above.[62] In October 1975 Kozorezova informed Podgorny and other authorities that she had just sent a letter to Amnesty International about her family's situation:

> I consider it my duty to notify you that I have sent a declaration to Amnesty International. . . . My husband . . . is serving a second term of punishment for his convictions, for his sincere faith in God. . . . After the Christian wives of prisoners from the city of Omsk sent a declaration to you,[63] agents of the Prosecutor of the Lenin District of Omsk conducted a search of our home in June 1974. My children had to witness them dragging me away from home by my hands and feet to interrogate me at the prosecutor's office. Yet, in response to my complaint to you about that illegal action, you [i.e., Podgorny's office] stated that the prosecutor's agents had acted correctly and according to the law. . . [Since you

have responded negatively to my many previous petitions,] I have therefore decided to turn to Amnesty International at this time.[64]

In her declaration to Amnesty International, Kozorezova cited the Helsinki Accords, signed a few months earlier by Brezhnev,[65] and enumerated the arbitrary ways her husband, family, and co-religionists had been treated by Soviet officials:

> My husband . . . is now being deprived of his freedom for a second time . . . On May 14, 1971 he was once again arrested, and on July 23 of that same year he was sentenced by the Omsk Provincial Court to five years . . . in a strict-regime camp. He has once more been separated from his family. Ten young children have been left without their father. The family is without its breadwinner. The intolerable burden of raising children alone has once again been placed upon my female shoulders. Our seven sons are growing up without their father, and of course our daughters also need their father. . . . The head of the prison camp has announced to me that my husband has the Gospels in his possession and that they will find them and will punish my husband again for reading literature considered illegal for the camp . . . I would not be surprised if in the last months before my husband's [scheduled] release, [prison officials] were to attempt to destroy his health or to kill him. Having briefly described the state of my husband and family, I ask you today to petition before our government for the release of [my husband and other falsely accused believers who are now in prison] . . . Their wives and children have also been deprived of their breadwinning fathers by the harshness of their sentences. Once I send this letter to you, the Soviet authorities might accuse me of libel and charge me with a crime, but I fear God above all and therefore scorn [any accusations of] libel.[66]

This letter demonstrates her courage to stand up to Soviet authorities as she petitioned for her family's and co-religionists' rights. She describes her family's plight in desperate terms. The varied language and tone in the two documents from October 1975—equal portions strength and desperation—is representative of thousands of similar letters sent by ECB believers and widely distributed by the CPR.

One cannot help but notice the gendered complexity in the letters Kozorezova wrote. On the one hand, she led an organization run by women that appealed insistently for the religious freedom of their co-religionists. On the other hand, her letters exhibit a traditionalist evangelical view of gendered norms. Although Kozorezova was highly educated, she was able to work only menial jobs as the mother of ten children, one with special needs. As a result, she found it difficult to run her household without the support of her breadwinning husband. Many ECB women faced similar challenges in negotiating the complexities of their faith, their families, and a society run by an antireligious government.[67]

Ann Komaromi claims that "the style of [unregistered Baptist] reporting remained far more emotional and personal" than that of other dissident groups in the Soviet Union.[68] Beliakova and Dobson concur, arguing that the "assertive attitude" adopted by the Baptists "distinguished [their statements] most from other samizdat appeals, whether secular or religious."[69] Certainly CCECB writers were assertive while standing up for their rights and demanding that Soviet central officials take charge of renegade local officials before God's wrath came down on Soviet leaders and the entire Soviet Union. With the threat of God's wrath pouring out on those who infringed on the freedom of religion declared by the 1948 UN Declaration or the Helsinki Accords, biblical motifs and the contemporary language of human rights frequently coalesced. From 1964 to 1987, the CPR facilitated the distribution of thousands of letters to Soviet officials and entities in the West. Gordeeva argues that through their assertive activism, the CPR "created a cult of martyrs for the faith on the examples of heroic self-sacrifice that bound the movement together and inculcated their youth."[70]

Dual Subversion and Questions of Effectiveness

The story of the CPR is one of dual subversion. Kozorezova and her friends overtly challenged Communist hegemony. In the CPR perspective, the atheistic state sought to obliterate believers, and hence they saw this as a fight for the survival of fellow Baptists as well as evangelical traditions, values, and convictions. This was apparent when Kozorezova invoked Esther as an example in 1976, reflecting a mindset that informed the impassioned letters she and other CPR members wrote. Likewise, Lidiia Vins argued that their letters "needed to have teeth, . . . so that those who read [them] felt they had been bitten."[71] Mikhail Shaptala, who led the CCECB denomination from 1966 to 1969, took issue with Lidiia Vins and the radical way the CPR "started to dictate conditions to the government" in that period. In his memoir, he relates what he said to Vins: "Who are we that we should write all these reports? You are forgetting in which country we are located."[72]

Shaptala's memoir demonstrates that the women of the CPR also subverted the norms of CCECB culture, which invoked biblical justifications for female submission. Although the civilly widowed women saw it as an extension of their call to be good "helpmeets" to their absent husbands, whom they extolled as heroic models of true evangelicalism, they turned that call into a purposeful activism for religious freedom. Membership in the CPR gave these wives a vehicle to exercise bold leadership in a way that was otherwise proscribed. Some ECB men were not particularly pleased at the women's provocative audacity and called the CPR a bunch of "strong-willed women."[73] According to Walter Sawatsky, women's leadership of the CPR, which became "the second spokesman for the CCECB and reflect[ed] a more intense negativist tone than the CCECB itself," was problematic, since men "placed a very heavy emphasis on the subordination of women and fe[lt] uncomfortable that women [we]re *de facto* leaders of their movement."[74] Indeed, within a month of Aleksandra Kozorezova being named the leader of the CPR, nineteen pastors from Central Asia signed a petition to the leadership of the CCECB requesting that the CPR be brought under the strict control of the CCECB, that a pastor be named as the chief editor of the *Bulletin*, and that "acerbic language" be removed from CPR petitions addressed to the Soviet government.[75] Based on the strong language that continued to be used in their petitions and Kozorezova's ongoing leadership of the CPR for eight more years, this petition seems not to have been given significant weight at the time.

Varying interpretations of CPR effectiveness began in the 1960s and continue in the post-Soviet era. Was the CPR a model of suffering heroism that effected the liberation of ECB prisoners, or at least drew national and international attention to their plight, as many CCECB believers and some conservative Western Christians insisted? Or in writing such sharply worded letters, was the CPR unnecessarily provocative, inciting persecution by Soviet officials and stirring up Baptist leaders against their movement, as argued by registered Baptists and members of the World Council of Churches?

These opposing assessments of CPR activism are two sides of the same coin: the CPR was both heroic and provocative. On the one hand, its bold letters and advocacy did occasionally bring change. An ECB leader in Novosibirsk, for example, recounted how the CPR's fast-acting network saved him and his Baptist brothers from being put on trial in Kazakhstan for attempting to smuggle censored religious literature into Siberia, because Kazakh authorities did not want to be reported to high-level Soviet officials or international observers, as the CPR had threatened.[76] On the other hand, the CPR also provoked a negative assessment by AUCECB leaders, whom the CPR regularly labeled as traitors to the true Gospel for their complicity with the state.[77] CPR letters and the *Bulletin*, as well as letters to them from co-religionists, regularly called out state and party leaders for violating human rights. Such writings only further inflamed state officials against the "extralegal and antisocial" sectarians who were spreading "fabrications," as Vladivostok's commissioner of the Council for Religious Affairs described them in 1983.[78]

As the atmosphere in the Soviet Union shifted toward greater freedoms, the CCECB decided in September 1987 to cease the work of the CPR and to form a new division, the Otdel Zastupnichestva (Department of Intercession). The CCECB leadership announced this decision to believers in the first publication of the Department of Intercession in April 1988. In the announcement, they expressed "gratitude to the Lord and to all who labored" in the CPR, whose "temporary mandate and limited mission" had now been "fulfilled." The Department of Intercession would be a new permanent commission led by "brother ministers on a collegial basis," with some CPR staff continuing to serve.[79] This decision thereby allowed men—by 1988 no longer primary targets for arrest, show trials, or imprisonment—to make a clean break by taking the leadership away from strong-willed women.[80]

Aleksandra Kozorezova's work of drawing attention to the plight of her co-religionists continued unabated until the last ECB prisoner was released in late 1988. Soon after the collapse of the USSR in 1991, evangelicals started to emigrate in a steady flow, primarily to the United States and Germany. The Kozorezov family joined them, emigrating from Ukraine to the United States in 1991. Aleksandra Kozorezova died in an auto accident near Seattle in 2006 at age seventy.

The life and advocacy of Kozorezova and her fellow CPR members exhibit the importance of evangelical women's networks of mutual support. Their acute sense of rights consciousness was forged by years of discrimination at the hands of the Soviet government. As these women imparted their faith and tradition to the next generation, they also subverted both patriarchal standards and state norms and laws through their work with the CPR. Despite the establishment of the Department of Intercession, at least partially designed to supersede the women's leadership, CPR women have continued to be celebrated by successive generations of ECB believers for their historical legacy.[81]

Notes

I dedicate this essay to Rev. Canon Dr. Michael Bourdeaux, a generous colleague to me for the last twelve years of his life. Many thanks to the Keston Institute for a research scholarship, the Institute for International Education for a Fulbright Study/Research Grant to Siberia, and Brandeis University for the Irving and Rose Crown Fellowship. I also want to thank colleagues with the Hadassah-Brandeis Institute, the Evangelical Studies Unit of the American Academy of Religion, and the history department at the University of Wyoming for their enthusiastic reception of earlier versions of this work. Additional gratitude to Miriam Dobson for feedback on this essay.

1. Those who subscribed to the views of the Action Group were called *initsiativniki*. The group, however, soon changed its name to the Organizational Committee (Orgkomitet), before finally becoming the Council of Churches (Sovet Tserkvei) in 1965. One can find all of these organization and adherent names in archival documents across the former Soviet Union, dated well into the 1970s.

2. Arkhiv Gosudarstvennogo muzeia istorii religii (GMIR), kol. 1, op. 8, d. 689. Several of the women connected with this organization were arrested or placed in a psychiatric hospital in the spring of 1964 and were only released after a nationwide petition campaign by CCECB believers. I. A. Gordeeva, "Religioznoe podpol'e kak sreda formirovaniia grazhdanskogo obshchestva," *Vestnik RGGU* 62/11, no. 1 (2011), 78.

3. The Russian term *samizdat* means "self-published" and refers to documents that Soviet dissidents used to work around the extensive censorship of anything that did not fall in line with Marxist-Leninist ideology. Nadezhda Beliakova has argued that the *Bulletin* was "the longest-running rights-defending samizdat organ in the USSR." Nadezhda Beliakova, "Kollektivnye praktiki tipichnoi obshchiny evangel'skikh khristian-baptistov v pozdnem SSSR," *Gosudarstvo, religiia tserkov' v Rossii i zarubezhom* 30, nos. 3–4 (2012), 307. The CPR's main publication, *Biulleten' Soveta rodstvennikov uznikov Evangel'skikh khristian-baptistov v SSSR*, is cited hereafter as "CPR *Bulletin*."

4. Several works explore aspects of this history, including *Istoriia evangel'skikh khristian-baptistov SSSR* (Moscow: Vsesoiuznii sovet evangel'skikh khristian-baptistov, 1989); S. N. Savinskii, *Istoriia evangel'skikh khristian-baptistov Ukrainy, Rossii, Belorussii (1867–1917)* (St. Petersburg: Bibliia dlia vsekh, 1999); S. N. Savinskii, *Istoriia evangel'skikh khristian-baptistov Ukrainy, Rossii, Belorussii (1917–1967)* (St. Petersburg: Bibliia dlia vsekh, 2001); Heather J. Coleman, *Russian Baptists and Spiritual Revolution, 1905–1929* (Bloomington: Indiana University Press, 2005); Tat'iana Nikol'skaia, *Russkii protestantizm i gosudarstvennaia vlast' v 1905–1991 godakh* (St. Petersburg: Evropeiskii universitet Sankt-Peterburga, 2009); Albert W. Wardin, Jr., *On the Edge: Baptists and Other Free Church Evangelicals in Tsarist Russia, 1855–1917* (Eugene, OR: Wipf & Stock, 2013); Walter

Sawatsky, *Soviet Evangelicals since World War II* (Scottsdale, PA: Herald Press, 1981).

5. Tatiana A. Chumachenko, *Church and State in Soviet Russia: Russian Orthodoxy from World War II to the Khrushchev Years*, ed. and trans. Edward E. Roslof (Armonk, NY: M. E. Sharpe, 2003), 149.

6. Emily B. Baran, *Dissent on the Margins: How Soviet Jehovah's Witnesses Defied Communism and Lived to Preach about It* (New York: Oxford University Press, 2014), 81–82; Nikol'skaia, *Russkii protestantizm*, 188–90; Petr Dashkovskii and Natal'ia Zibert, *Gosudarstvenno-konfessional'naia politika na iuge zapadnoi Sibiri v kontse 1917–seredine 1960–kh gg.*, vol. 3 of *Etnokul'turnye i religiovedcheskie issledovaniia v Evrazii*, ed. A. V. Gorbatov (Barnaul: Altaiskii gosudarstvennyi universitet, 2020), 80.

7. Dashkovskii and Zibert, *Gosudarstvenno-konfessional'naia politika*, 80, 98. Authorities closed some two thousand prayer houses of all religions from 1960 to 1962 alone (91). At the Twenty-Second Congress of the CPSU in October 1961, Khrushchev declared the necessity of a "more effective system of scientific atheist propaganda . . . , one that . . . will prevent the dissemination of religious views, especially among children and adolescents." N. S. Khrushchev, *Report of the Central Committee of the CPSU to the 22nd Congress of the Communist Party of the Soviet Union*, Documents of Current History 18 and 19 (New York: Crosscurrents Press, 1961), 177.

8. A move against Orthodox priests came in 1961. On its leadup, see Chumachenko, *Church and State in Soviet Russia*, 165–88. On the bishops' council in 1961 that stripped priests of power in their parishes, see Jane Ellis, *The Russian Orthodox Church: A Contemporary History* (Bloomington: Indiana University Press, 1986), 45–46, 53–69.

9. Tat'iana Nikol'skaia, "Istoriia dvizheniia baptistov-initsiativnikov," in vol. 3 of *Al'manakh po istorii russkogo baptizma*, ed. M. S. Krakhmal'nikova (Saint Petersburg: Bibliia dlia vsekh, 2004), 71.

10. Michael Bourdeaux, *Religious Ferment in Russia: Protestant Opposition to Soviet Religious Policy* (New York: Macmillan, 1968), 20. The earliest known version of this letter was reprinted by Arkhiv Samizdata: Vsesoiuznyi sovet EKhB, "Instruktivnyi list starshim presviteram," in *Dokumenty Baptistov (EKhB)—chast' 1*, vol. 14 of *Sobranie dokumentov samizdata* (Munich: Arkhiv Samizdata, Radio Free Europe, 1973), AS no. 773, scanned at the Keston Center for Religion, Politics, and Society (KCRPS), Baylor University, Waco, Texas. Cited henceforth by AS no.

11. For a review of developments in AUCECB statutes, see "Appendix I: Constitution of the ECB Church in the USSR," in Bourdeaux, *Religious Ferment*, 190–210.

12. For a synopsis of this history, see A. V. Sinichkin, "Istoriia evangel'skikh khristian-baptistov v SSSR s dekabria 1959 po 1966 god: Istoriia i analiz krizisa v bratstve EKhB," Bachelor's diploma, Moskovskaia Bogoslovskaia Seminariia Evangel'skikh khristian-baptistov, 2001.

13. See Olena Panych, "A Time and Space of Suffering: Reflections of the Soviet Past in the Memoirs and Narratives of the Evangelical Christians-Baptists,"

in *State Secularism and Lived Religion in Soviet Russia and Ukraine*, ed. Catherine Wanner (New York: Oxford University Press, 2012), 218–43.

14. I. M. Sovetov, "Sovet po delam religii pri SM SSSR: Struktura, funktsii i osnovnye napravleniia deiatel'nosti (Epokha V. A. Kuroedova, 1966–1984 gg.)," Rossiiskoe Ob"edinenie Issledovatelei Religii, https://rusoir.ru/president/president-works/president-works-268/ (accessed January 31, 2022). It is unclear how many from the CCECB were fined, but they likely constituted a significant majority of those eight hundred administrative punishments. In this same period, ninety Pentecostals, twenty Adventists, and eighty Orthodox believers encountered the same punishment.

15. "Dokumenty Initsiativnoi gruppy i Orgkomiteta po sozyvu vsesoiuznogo s"ezda evangel'skikh khristian-baptistov (August 1961 to May 1966)," AS nos. 770–72.

16. Vremennyi sovet rodstvennikov uznikov, "Soobshchenie o 95 baptistskikh uznikakh," July 5, 1964, AS no. 780.

17. GMIR kol. 1, op. 8, d. 698, ll. 1ob–2ob, dated August 20, 1967. Other emergency messages are available at KCRPS SU-Ini-11-4-CPR-S (August 1968); AS no. 617 (March 1970); KCRPS SU-Ini-6-1972-S CPR (1972).

18. Lidiia Vins became a member of CPR in 1966 when her son Georgii was imprisoned, the same year she signed her first letters via CPR (e.g., GMIR kol. 1, op. 8, d. 719) and was selected as its leader. "Sovet rodstvennikov uznikov Evangel'skikh khristian-baptistov," Fond podderzhki gonimykh khristian Rossii i stran SNG, https://www.fondsp.ru/news/read/sovet-rodstvennikov-uznikov-evangelskih-hristian-baptistov (accessed March 14, 2017).

19. On the secretive nature of the printing-press network, see Nikol'skaia, "Istoriia dvizheniia baptistov-initsiativnikov," 87–88.

20. This included two unnumbered supplementary issues. Collections of these samizdat bulletins can be found in repositories around the world, primarily KCRPS, Arkhiv Samizdata (Radio Free Europe, Munich), and the Archive of the Russian Union of Evangelical Christians-Baptists (A-RSEKhB, Moscow), in addition to single issues located in archives throughout the former USSR. The full collection of the CPR *Bulletin* was recently published online, allowing scholars to engage with their discursive evolution more substantially. *Biulleten' Soveta rodstvennikov uznikov Evagel'skikh khristian-baptistov (1971–1987)*, Russkii Baptist, http://rus-baptist.narod.ru/08.htm (accessed January 25, 2021).

21. Beliakova, "Kollektivnye praktiki," 308–9, citing Gosudarstvennyi arkhiv Rossiiskoi Federatsii (GARF), f. R-6991, op. 6, d. 1759, ll. 95–96.

22. Beliakova, "Kollektivnye praktiki," 309, citing GARF f. R-6991, op. 6, d. 1121, ll. 37–38, 44–54. See the text of the letter (without signatures) reprinted in Nadezhda Beliakova and Miriam Dobson, ed., *Zhenshchiny v evangel'skikh obshchinakh poslevoennogo SSSR, 1940–1980-e gg.* (Moscow: Indrik, 2015), 328–35. An incomplete version of a translation of the letter is in the Keston collection: KCRPS SU-Ini-6-33-S-1977.

23. Gordeeva, "Religioznoe podpol'e," 79.

24. Liudmila Leont'evna Savchenko, oral history interview (OHI) by April L. French, June 2 and 9, 2015, Omsk; Beliakova and Dobson, *Zhenshchiny v*

evangel'skikh obshchinakh, 324n202. Lidiia Vins and her family moved to Kyiv from Omsk in 1946, when Aleksandra Andrienko (later Kozorezova), whose family was a part of the ECB congregation in Omsk, was ten years old.

25. On August 31, 1949, officials stripped the Omsk ECB Church of its registration, as a result of which believers lived outside the law in that city for nearly fifteen years. Gosudarstvennyi istoricheskii arkhiv Omskoi oblasti (GIAOO), f. R-2603, op. 1, d. 43, l. 1; GIAOO f. P-17, op. 1, d. 7250, l. 32.

26. GIAOO f. P-17, op. 1, d. 7541, l. 12. The report calls her by her maiden name, Andrienko, ignoring that she had changed her surname to Kozorezova when she married Aleksei Timofeevich Kozorezov a year earlier.

27. GARF f. R-6991, op. 6, d. 3127, ll. 8–9; CPR *Bulletin*, no. 29 (1976), 11–12.

28. N. R. Savchenko, "Istoriia Omskoi Tserkvi (iz vospominanii N. R. Savchenko)," unpublished document provided to the author by Liudmila Savchenko.

29. This protest, on May 16–17, 1966, ended up being "the largest civil protest action of the 'stagnation' era," according to Nikol'skaia. Organized by leaders of the CCECB to protest the violation of believers' rights, between four hundred and six hundred individuals made it to Moscow. Several believers were prevented from leaving their city of residence or interrupted on their way to Moscow by local or regional officials. For more information, see Tatyana Nikolskaya, "Human Rights Advocacy of Baptist Initiators," *Changing Societies & Personalities* 1, no. 4 (2017): 340–43.

30. Aleksei T. Kozorezov, "Lesnaia Tserkov'," Nasledie vernykh, April 27, 2016, https://www.youtube.com/watch?v=6G6S4bYmFyc&list=PLXzQfCGp mticr0tvz-SwHChCrr92Kg4ow&index=7 (accessed October 22, 2024). On the charges against Kozorezov, see GIAOO f. R-2603, op. 1, d. 50, ll. 52–54, 58; L. L. Savchenko, *U Boga pishetsia pamiatnaia kniga: Biografiia N. R. Savchenko* (Moscow: Khristianin, 2012), 24, 26.

31. Sovet rodstvennikov uznikov Evangel'skikh khristian-baptistov, "Veruiushchie prosiat zashchity ot bezzakoniia," August 15, 1967, AS no. 515. Reprinted in Beliakova and Dobson, *Zhenshchiny v evangel'skikh obshchinakh*, 368–92, and translated into English as "Appeal II: From Five Baptist Women to U Thant," in *Christian Appeals from Russia*, ed. Rosemary Harris and Xenia Howard-Johnston (London: Hodder & Stoughton, 1969), 33–62.

32. Nadezhda Beliakova and Miriam Dobson, "Protestant Women in the Late Soviet Era: Gender, Authority, and Dissent," *Canadian Slavonic Papers* 58, no. 2 (2016), 131.

33. Sovet rodstvennikov uznikov Evangel'skikh khristian-baptistov, "Veruiushchie prosiat zashchity ot bezzakoniia," AS no. 515, 22.

34. "Sovet rodstvennikov uznikov Evangel'skikh khristian-baptistov."

35. The author has not yet located the specific newspaper article referenced in this letter.

36. Rodstvenniki uznikov Zapadnoi Sibiri, "Zaiavlenie," August 8, 1968, copy sent to Brezhnev and others, KCRPS SU-Ini-6-8-S. This letter was translated into English as "Appeal V: From Western Siberia," in Harris and Howard-Johnston, *Christian Appeals*, 77–83.

37. GIAOO f. P-17, op. 1a, d. 999, ll. 82–83. The word "God" was not capitalized, but it is capitalized here since this is what Kozorezova would have done.

38. Victoria Smolkin, *A Sacred Space Is Never Empty: A History of Soviet Atheism* (Princeton, NJ: Princeton University Press, 2018), 153. See also Rossiiskii gosudarstvennyi arkhiv sotsial'no-politicheskoi istorii (RGASPI), f. P-606, op. 4, d. 80.

39. GIAOO f. P-17, op. 1a, d. 999, ll. 83–84.

40. GIAOO f. R-437, op. 9, d. 2340, ll. 28–30; Gosudarstvennyi arkhiv Novosibirskoi oblasti (GANO), f. R-1418, op. 1, d. 192, l. 7; Arkhiv Omskogo gosudarstvennogo istoriko-kraevedcheskogo muzeia (OGIKM), OMK-7406/1-15, September 1960; OGIKM OMK-7528/13–35, May 1962; KCRPS SU-Ini-6-4-S and SU-Ini-6-17-S.

41. Savchenko, OHI, June 2 and 9, 2015, Omsk.

42. GIAOO f. R-437, op. 9, d. 2340, l. 25.

43. These women's reports can be found at GIAOO f. R-437, op. 9, d. 2340, ll. 23–30.

44. GIAOO f. R-437, op. 9, d. 2340, l. 26. The reports do not capitalize the word "God" here, but the author has capitalized the word based on how Kozorezova would have intended in her own speech.

45. GIAOO f. R-437, op. 9, d. 2340, ll. 27, 30.

46. On the arrest, trial, and imprisonment of these men, see Savchenko, *U Boga pishetsia*, 47–49, 74–77. The irony of these men being arrested at their workplace and accused of freeloading was not lost on their co-religionists.

47. Thanks to ChaeRan Freeze, who suggested the concept of women being "civilly widowed" in a discussion of their realities.

48. Within the CPR *Bulletin* alone, petitioners used the term "orphan" to describe children whose fathers were imprisoned more than four hundred times over the course of seventeen years.

49. Savchenko, OHI, June 2 and 9, 2015, Omsk; "Sovet rodstvennikov uznikov Evangel'skikh khristian-baptistov."

50. "Sovet rodstvennikov uznikov Evangel'skikh khristian-baptistov." She was referencing Esther 8:6.

51. CPR *Bulletin*, no. 79 (1980), 29; no. 87 (1980), 6, 25; no. 88 (1980), 5–14, 35–37; no. 89 (1980), 7–8; no. 90 (1980), 5; nos. 91–92 (1981), 11–12, 15–16; nos. 93–94 (1981), 8, 10, 13–15; nos. 94–95 (1981), 7; nos. 95–96 (1981), 25; no. 106 (1982), 6, 55; no. 107 (1982), 48–51; no. 110 (1982), 18–19; no. 111 (1982), 81–2; no. 112 (1983), 18; no. 115 (1983), 50–51, 60–61; no. 117 (1983), 52–56; no. 118 (1983), 5, 78–79; no. 119 (1984), 5, 30; no. 120 (1984), 24, 33, 43; no. 122 (1984), 22–23, 57; no. 123 (1984), 5, 63–64; no. 124 (1984), 65; no. 126 (1984), 49–51; no. 128 (1985), 68; no. 130 (1985), 5.

52. "Sovet rodstvennikov uznikov Evangel'skikh khristian-baptistov"; CPR *Bulletin*, nos. 92–93 (1981), 10–11. Aleksei Kozorezov was sentenced to three years, but officials fabricated additional charges for another year soon before he was to be released.

53. CPR *Bulletin*, nos. 92–93 (1981), 11.

54. CPR *Bulletin*, no. 97 (1981), 7. A suspended sentence in the Soviet Union meant the individual was allowed to serve their sentence via probation rather than incarceration. The individual was allowed to live at home, but with certain restrictions of freedom.

55. CPR *Bulletin*, no. 131 (1985), 7, 9, 11–12, 20–23, 29–30, 33, 80–82; no. 132 (1985), 21, 22, 26, 69.

56. CPR *Bulletin*, no. 133 (1985), 16–18.

57. Bill Keller, "Soviet Releasing Some Prisoners under New Law," *New York Times*, February 8, 1987; Celestine Bohlen, "Soviets Set First Amnesty for Political Prisoners," *Washington Post*, June 25, 1987.

58. Panych, "A Time and Space of Suffering," 223–26, 238. Regarding the "aura of factuality," Panych is drawing on Geertz's definition of religion. Clifford Geertz, *The Interpretation of Cultures* (New York: Basic Books, 1973), 90.

59. CPR *Bulletin*, no. 16 (1974), 25.

60. CPR *Bulletin*, no. 18 (1974), 11.

61. CPR *Bulletin*, no. 17 (1974), 6–7.

62. "Sovet rodstvennikov uznikov Evangel'skikh khristian-baptistov"; Savchenko, OHI, June 2 and 9, 2015, Omsk.

63. KCRPS SU-Ini-6-8-S, dated March 1974 (signed by both Kozorezova and Vins).

64. CPR *Bulletin*, no. 27 (1975), 28.

65. Although CCECB believers had long been citing the violation of their human or civil rights in letters and appeals, they began using the Helsinki Final Act as a clarion call in their complaints addressed directly to Brezhnev nearly immediately after the accords were signed. In the CPR *Bulletin*, believers had discussed the violation of their civil or human rights in approximately twenty reproduced letters from 1971 to September 1975, sometimes citing the UN's Declaration of Human Rights or the Soviet Constitution. In contrast, within a few weeks of the signing of the Helsinki Accords in July–August 1975, petitions and complaints began citing the accords prolifically: twenty-one letters printed in the *Bulletin* mentioned the accords from August to December 1975, and at least fifty letters mentioned them in 1976.

66. CPR *Bulletin*, no. 27 (1975), 29–31.

67. This analysis is slightly modified from April L. French, "Council of Prisoners' Relatives," in *Voices of the Voiceless: Religion, Communism, and the Keston Archive*, ed. Julie deGraffenried and Zoe Knox (Waco, TX: Baylor University Press, 2019), 39–41.

68. Ann Komaromi, "Samizdat and Soviet Dissident Publics," *Slavic Review* 71, no. 1 (2012), 83.

69. Beliakova and Dobson, "Protestant Women," 131.

70. Gordeeva, "Religioznoe podpol'e," 82. Gordeeva goes on to argue that this led them "to exaggerate and even distort" reality and that "an underground syndrome led the *initsiativniki* to a genuine mania [about perpetual] surveillance."

71. Beliakova and Dobson, "Protestant Women," 131.

72. Mikhail Shaptala, *Kak eto bylo* (Cherkasy: Smirna, 2011), 66; N. A. Bondarenko, "Formirovanie sistemy religioznogo dissidentstva v ramkakh

'otdelennogo' bratstva EKhB vo vtoroi polovine 1960–kh gg.: Ukrainskie realii," *Khristianskoe chtenie*, no. 1 (2017), 398.

73. Beliakova and Dobson, "Protestant Women," 131.

74. Sawatsky, *Soviet Evangelicals*, 242.

75. Central Asian Association of ECB Churches, "O Sovete rodstvennikov uznikov," July 9, 1979, reprinted in Nikolai Klassen, *Gonimaia tserkov'* (Heimerzheim: Self-published, 2004), 153–54.

76. Vitalii Nikolaevich Karman, OHI, May 15, 2015, Novosibirsk. This incident was reported in a religious-affairs report (GANO f. R-1418, op. 1, d. 242, l. 21), the accuracy of which Karman strongly disputes. Nikol'skaia discusses some additional positive changes brought on by CCECB advocacy, including that of the CPR. Nikolskaya, "Human Rights Advocacy," 349.

77. An example of provocative language against the AUCECB is in Sovet rodstvennikov uznikov, "Sbornik dokumentov vtorogo Vsesoiuznogo s"ezda rodstvennikov uznikov Evangel'skikh khristian-baptistov v SSSR" (samizdat, 1970), part 1, 32; KCRPS SU-Ini-11-4-CPR-S Second Congress. Nikol'skaia provides examples of times that officially registered ECB Christians were also caught up in the net of state retribution against CCECB believers. Nikolskaya, "Human Rights Advocacy," 348–49.

78. GARF f. R-6991, op. 6, d. 2562, ll. 1–9. See also GANO f. R-1418, op. 1, d. 242, ll. 34–42.

79. This announcement was reprinted in "Sovet rodstvennikov uznikov," *Vestnik Istiny*, no. 3 (2001), 33. It is unclear how many CPR women continued their work with the Department of Intercession or for how long. The Department of Intercession continues to disseminate information about believers who are reportedly under oppression in various locations, including various post-Soviet countries, China, India, Germany, and the United States. Many separatist Baptists emigrated to the latter two countries, taking their long-developed "martyr habitus" with them.

80. Nikol'skaia claims this transition was a mere reorganization, but the 1988 announcement claims a clear distinction between the two organizations. Nikolskaya, "Human Rights Advocacy," 348,

81. In one celebratory publication by the International Union of Churches of Evangelical Christians-Baptists—the successor organization to the CCECB—on the forty-fifth anniversary of the ministry of both the Council of Prisoners' Relatives and the Department of Intercession, all but seven of the seventy-four pages are dedicated to the legacy and influence of the Council of Prisoners' Relatives. The special edition of *Vestnik Istiny*, nos. 4–5 (2009) is titled "45 let sluzheniia Soveta rodstvennikov uznikov i Otdela zastupnichestva MSTs EKhB."

CHAPTER 7

Seeing Is (Un)believing

Anticlericalism in Soviet Antireligious Posters

Julie K. deGraffenried

The Soviet antireligious crusade radically reshaped the visual landscape of the USSR. Antireligious posters provide insight into Soviet efforts to suppress and manage faith communities and belief in the USSR and are one among many elements of an unparalleled sensory renovation accompanying the antireligious campaigns. From 1917 until 1985, dozens of graphic artists produced hundreds of posters that disparaged religious practices, persons, institutions, and attitudes and offered the posters' creators, viewers, and curators a means to participate in Communist Party efforts to combat these vestiges of the past.

The Bolsheviks' drive to hurry the decline and fall of organized religion in the Soviet Union was characterized by an aggressive anticlericalism. Antireligious propaganda posters featured a visual onslaught of images against clergy unprecedented in modern history. Here I consider the place of antireligious posters within the larger visual environment created to support antireligious policies in the USSR. Then I compare revolutionary-era (1917–1930s) and postwar-era (1954–85)—or first-wave and second-wave—antireligious posters, considering them as one element of a larger body of agitational graphic art intended to expand citizen involvement in Communist Party priorities.

While the fifty-seven Soviet antireligious posters preserved by Michael Bourdeaux and Keston College inspired my initial inquiry, this chapter is based on a survey of approximately 3,100 posters mass produced by professional artists and distributed in the Soviet Union, of which 232 are antireligious in nature. It considers but excludes those pages in the journal *Bezbozhnik* (Godless) that were intended to be torn out and displayed as posters, as well as any amateur creations.[1] The posters are primarily contained in the Keston Digital Archive, a dozen published poster collections, and the Ne Boltai! online archive.[2]

Seeing Is (Un)believing

The Soviet campaign against religion was unprecedentedly visual in nature. Though it obviously also included policy making, legislation, ideological texts, punitive suppression, and education, what set the party-state's antireligious struggle apart from previous critiques of religion or clergy was its attempt to remake the visual landscape, what people saw as they went about their daily lives.[3] Consider how the look of the Soviet Union dramatically changed because of Soviet antireligious policies and the assault on the "visible superstructure" of religious life.[4] Tens of thousands of places of worship dotted the cities, towns, and villages of the Russian Empire at the time of the Bolshevik Revolution. By one observation, Moscow had a church or chapel on every street in the early twentieth century.[5] By the late 1930s, however, a "nearly church-less landscape" predominated.[6] The closure and destruction of religious sites and the ban on new church construction meant dramatically altered urban skylines, reoriented rural village centers, and a loss of quotidian landmarks. The re-tasking of vestigial religious structures modified—or even erased—their original meaning in the community, creating generations who were unfamiliar with their original purpose in religious life.[7] State-sponsored architecture would have included few, if any, structures related to faith communities after 1917. New Soviet urban centers such as Magadan (est. 1929), Ukhta (1929), Norilsk (1935), Sumgait (1949), and perhaps the most famous, Magnitogorsk (1929), would have differed radically from their prerevolutionary counterparts not only in architectural style but also in omission of houses of worship.[8] The damage and post-victory reconstruction associated with the Great Patriotic War (1941–45) also offered opportunities to shape rural and urban design in the complex negotiations between central and local authorities.[9]

Not only would village vistas and cityscapes change, but the population inhabiting them would change as well. The execution and persecution of clergy radically decreased the number of such figures seen in everyday life. Waves of repression, particularly during the collectivization drive after 1928 and during the Great Terror (1937–38), reduced the number of priests, imams, rabbis, pastors, monastics, and lamas dramatically.[10] Those clerics who remained were prohibited from wearing habits or vestments and barred from cities, which essentially rendered them invisible. A ban on religious assemblies and processions, and the dozens of holidays that often inspired them, sought to remove another visual element of faith communities: public displays of piety or tradition by crowds of the faithful bearing crosses, icons, and sacred images, typically led by clergy and punctuated with prayer and signs of the cross.

This modified visual landscape was not formed simply by omission and erasure. Replacements abounded: new architectural forms, new statues, new gathering places, new banners, new community figures, new holidays, and new parades were provided by Soviet authorities in their quest to replace the old.[11] And those who sought to keep belief alive adapted to the new conditions, moving sacred spaces out of the public eye, repurposing sites of pilgrimage, and creating new monuments invested with spiritual meaning.[12] Thus, the quest for modernity *sans* traditional religion continually revised and refashioned the visual landscape over the seven decades of Soviet authority.

Posters were part of this visual renovation. Graphic art in poster form, more generally, played a significant role in the didactic purposes of the party as a relatively inexpensive means of disseminating information and influencing behaviors and attitudes.[13] The "frescoes of the poor," they communicated revolutionary ideology in pictorial language for a population that, at least in the early Soviet era, was largely illiterate and already familiar with a lively graphic design tradition.[14] Further, posters fit well into longtime views on agitprop among members of the Bolshevik leadership, as a kind of bridge between the oral agitation needed for work with the ignorant masses and the written propaganda aimed at the literate.[15] Drawing on the centuries-old artistic inspirations of the icon and the *lubok*—the popular illustrated woodcut or broadside—prerevolutionary satirical journal graphics and advertising, and contemporary movements in the art world such as Futurism, Constructivism, Suprematism, photography, and so on, Soviet artists created thousands of propaganda posters designed to teach the population about the emergent socialist society in which they lived.[16] Posters became a ubiquitous feature of Soviet life, distributed by the millions and posted in all sorts of public spaces. The poster could provide instantaneous communication through a compressed image with the unique ability to present time, space, and message as both "now" and "always," as both temporal and eternal.[17]

Important work on the cultural repertoire and iconography of the Soviet viewer has been done, yet Mollie Arbuthnot reminds us that the viewer was not conceived of as a passive recipient.[18] The simple transmission of ideas was not the ultimate goal. Instead, the modern Soviet person was to participate in the entire process and practice of propaganda as a viewer, displayer, owner, and creator. Those acts, according to theorists, would "integrat[e] political discourse into the everyday."[19] Posters were designed to be legible, challenging, and appealing, based on audience reception. They were not meant to be solely urban street art but were also interior, contemplative display pieces in both private spaces like homes and public spaces like libraries, clubs, reading rooms, and canteens. Walls "completely papered" with political posters in such sites were considered a marker of Soviet modernity.[20] Arbuthnot notes that posters "could appropriate the function of icons, and sometimes compete with the icon in domestic space."[21] The ultimate sign of a New Soviet Person, then, could be the voluntary act of replacing the icon in the home's traditional holy corner with a Soviet poster—all the more so if that poster happened to employ antireligious themes.

Most Soviet posters, however, focused on subjects other than the perfidy of religion and superstition. Most propaganda posters in the Soviet era engaged other topics: war and conflict, economic initiatives, ideology, health and hygiene, and the Soviet people themselves. This was especially true in the period of late socialism as the total amount of antireligious posters declined when agitational tactics expanded and shifted emphases.[22] Antireligious campaigns, we should remember, coexisted with dozens of other campaigns, all of which ebbed and flowed over time. The public or private display of hundreds of thousands of antireligious posters was part of the larger visual reorientation effected by the state's struggle against organized religion.

Antireligious posters occurred in two waves corresponding to the revolutionary era (1917–30s) and the postwar era (1954–85), reflecting the cycles of "militant attack and retrenchment, crackdown and thaw, stagnation and reform" that characterized not only the campaign against religion but the Soviet system more broadly.[23] The years of revolution, civil war, NEP, and early Stalinism witnessed consistent, though not continuous, persecution of religious practice and personnel and spawned hundreds of antireligious posters. There are virtually no mass-produced professional posters that engage faith or its deficiencies from the mid-1930s to mid-1950s, although journals containing antireligious images, such as *Bezbozhnik*, were published through June 1941. The liberalization of religious policies during World War II, or the Great Patriotic War as it was called in the USSR, was reflected in the notable lack of antireligious posters, not the revival of religious imagery or themes. There are miniscule references to the existence of Orthodox churches in a few *Okno TASS* posters during the war—for example, the use of onion domes as locational details or a portrayal of rural dwellers locked inside a burning church by the enemy—while the depiction of Christian crosses is most often affiliated with the death of Nazi troops, a not entirely positive association for the religious symbol.[24] Religion remained off limits in political posters and nearly absent in print propaganda as well during the immediate postwar period of late Stalinism.[25] A renewed visual campaign via the poster accompanied the reinvigorated attack on religion and the call for atheist activism that was launched in 1954 under Khrushchev and continued until Gorbachev's reconciliation with religion on the eve of the 1988 millennial celebration of Christianity. The two waves of antireligious posters, then, correspond with the two major periods of antireligious activity by state authorities, thus providing a good opportunity for comparison across nearly the whole Soviet epoch.

First-Wave vs. Second-Wave Anticlericalism in Soviet Antireligious Posters

Anticlericalism, while well developed in terms of organized political action and mass appeal in other parts of Europe, remained limited to a "diffuse hostility" aimed at "clerical foibles or individual clerics" in the Russian Empire, what Gregory Freeze terms a "stunted" and "inchoate" anticlericalism. Despite an abundance of anticlerical proverbs and *chastushki*—limericks, often sung—circulating in popular culture, no mass anticlerical movement emerged in the prerevolutionary era.[26] The Bolsheviks initiated an aggressive anticlericalism beginning with limits on the Russian Orthodox Church in early 1918 and the persecution of Russian Orthodox clergy, many of whom were sympathetic to Bolshevik opposition during the Russian Civil War. The visual outpouring of anticlerical images exhibited in thousands of seemingly omnipresent political posters was unprecedented not only in the former Russian Empire but beyond the borders of the empire as well.

The figure of the cleric appears consistently in antireligious posters throughout the Soviet period. Though some continuity in style and tone exists, more striking are the differences in the clerical images by artists of the first and second waves of intensive antireligious struggle. Despite these changes over time, the visual rhetoric of anticlericalism persists from revolution to reconciliation, from 1917 to the mid-1980s.

In early Soviet posters, the figure of the Orthodox priest—or more rarely, the rabbi, the mullah, or Roman Catholic priest—stood in for religion writ large and symbolized an unwanted relic of the old regime. As a representative of organized faith communities, a "bulwark of conservatism," and an "irreconcilable enemy" of the Bolsheviks, the cleric was to be demonized in first-wave posters.[27] Soviet anticlericalism, and the critique of religion more generally, manifested several key themes in the revolutionary era.

The first, and most prevalent, was guilt by association. One of the first posters issued by the Bolshevik Party in 1918, *Tsar, pop i kulak* (Tsar, priest, and wealthy peasant), distinctly connects the clergy with the oppressive regime so recently overthrown (figure 7.1).[28] In it, a jauntily crowned, shifty-eyed tsar is flanked by a menacing fanged priest and a dubious-looking stout man, identified in the text as a kulak, or wealthy peasant. Above the stark black-and-white stereotypes swirls an abstract blue-gray thunderstorm. Literate viewers would be familiar with the term "pop" as a pejorative for clergy since at least the mid-nineteenth century.[29]

This early poster was designed for specific national or ethnic groups and issued in different versions, with text in languages such as Ukrainian, Polish, Lithuanian, Mari, or Tatar.[30] The religious figure was portrayed as a skull-capped, crucifix-wearing cleric, bearded or cleanshaven; or as an Orthodox priest with a long white beard or a short dark beard and spectacles; or as a turbaned mullah, depending on the audience. A version of the poster titled *Kenenš, baznīckungs un kulaks* (King, churchman, and wealthy peasant), produced for Latvians (figure 7.2), features a Roman Catholic priest—with a face similar to the Orthodox priest of the Russian version—and a far more nattily dressed kulak in a top hat flanking Nicholas II. For viewers who could not read the text, as in the Russian version, lightning bolts around their heads

FIGURE 7.1.   *Tsar, pop i kulak*, 1918. Russian. Image from Wikimedia Commons.

FIGURE 7.2.   *Kenenš, baznīckungs un kulaks*, 1918. Latvian. Poster image provided by Poster Plakat.com.

symbolizing retribution helpfully point out the sinister troika, literally connecting them via a series of vertical and diagonal lines.

First-wave posters almost exclusively couple clerics with elements of the old regime and enemies of the new. The connection between the tsar and kulak, beyond the obvious, harkened back to those opponents of the masses in the prerevolutionary era who put arbitrary authority and profit before the people: the official (*chinovnik*), the landowner (*pomeshchik*), and the factory owner (*zavodchik*). Orthodox clergy, in particular, were often viewed as state functionaries, given the relationship between the Russian Orthodox Church and the tsarist regime.[31] In posters designed during the civil war, priests regularly accompanied White Army generals or troops, capitalists, monarchs, and foreign powers. In the NEP era of the 1920s, posters paired the clergy with capitalists and rank opportunists, while in the 1930s they were depicted alongside enemies of the Five Year Plan, such as slackers, spies, and the wealthy.[32] The images, collectively, reflected the antireligious print propaganda of the revolutionary era, alleging the conspiracy between the clergy and enemies bent on the destruction of the new Soviet society.[33]

Another way Soviet posters promoted anticlerical sentiment was to dehumanize, or "other," the cleric. For the first several years after 1917, graphic artists regularly depicted enemies of the Soviet government as unwelcome or threatening creatures such as reptiles, birds, insects, or serpents.[34] One of the most famous examples of this sort of dehumanization is Viktor Deni's 1919 lithograph *Pauk i mukhi* (Spider and flies), in which an image of a spider-like priest accompanies the text of Demian Bedny's poem "Pauk i mukhi" (figure 7.3).[35] The long black legs of the arachno-priest grasp groups of unwitting men and women with claw-like hands, pulling them into the arched entry of an Orthodox Church compound that resembles a gaping maw. His face is truly gruesome, the radial lines of his arched eyebrows and facial hair mimicking his appendages, the eyes squinting in concentration, and the full cheeks suggesting an overfed abdomen. Ranging from ghastly to comical, such nonhuman depictions of the clergy not only demystified the sacred but also segregated the local priest from his flesh-and-blood neighbors.[36] Attacks on such vermin, represented in posters by acts of caging, sweeping, beating, crushing, piercing, unmasking, burning, or death by lightning, helped to rationalize their actual destruction.

As well known as Deni's spiderman may be, a more conventional priest image dominates first-wave posters. Corpulent, bearded, and black-robed, the clergyman in most posters was drawn from visual stereotypes that pre-dated the revolution.[37] Corpulence—which was not limited to priests in propaganda posters—suggested ill-gotten wealth or greed. In an unattributed 1919 poster, one pudgy frocked priest reclines on a pile of bread, groats, and cash while another priest greedily accepts coins flowing from a capitalist's hands (figure 7.4).[38] Their avarice is highlighted by their indifference to the bedraggled, pitiful figures of a man, woman, child, and dog who symbolize the working class. The image of the "feeding" priest recalled the longtime critiques of the church as an institution that put other interests ahead of those of its flock, local annoyance over the fees and financial support that Russian Orthodox clergy drew from parishioners, and antisemitic conspiracy theories linking Judaism to global capitalism.[39] Graphic artists most often used satire and caricature to reveal, mock, and shame the

FIGURE 7.3. V. Deni, *Pauk i mukhi*, 1919. Image from Wikimedia Commons.

Figure 7.4. M. Cheremnykh, *Tak bol'she ne budet*, 1919. Image from The Sergo Grigorian Collection.

voracious appetites of the clergy. It is precisely this overfed gluttonous cleric that is most often pictured working in concert with other nefarious opponents of Soviet power and people.

The protracted visual criticism of clergy as opponents of the revolution, the working people, and the new socialist society mirrored revolutionary-era edicts. "On the Separation of Church from State and School from Church," the 1918 order that disestablished the Russian Orthodox Church as the state religion, provided no personhood for the institutional church, thus effectively orphaning its clergy. Active persecution of clergy during the civil war, followed by interference in church affairs and atheist agitation, culminated in the 1929 Russian Soviet Federative Law on Religious Associations, the "principle normative source of Soviet restriction on churches as organizations."[40] This law served as a model for all other republic-level legislation affecting all communities of faith, Orthodox or otherwise, and instituted ongoing regulation of clergy through permits and monitoring. Church closures meant loss of income and accusations of parasitism for clerics. To be sure, some clerics did engage in violent and anti-Soviet acts during the civil war, antireligious campaigns in the 1920s, and the collectivization drive in the late 1920s and early 1930s.[41] But the majority did not, and the constant visual association of clergy with noted enemies placed them and their families in an irredeemable position outside of the society envisioned by the party.

The visual rhetoric of anticlericalism predominated in first-wave antireligious posters. The distinct lack of anticlericalism in general prior to 1917 meant that state authorities had little to work with in any attempt to vilify clergy, and that perhaps helps to explain the virulence of artists' representations. Anticlerical sentiment had to be generated and sustained, which was a difficult task, particularly in rural areas characterized by fruitful relationships and networks between clergy and local inhabitants. First-wave posters communicate a clear sense of the priest as a threat; their aggressive malevolence is depicted in concert with a set of clearly defined male enemies. Clergy steal, oppress, hoodwink, and starve the working class. They encourage husbands to beat their wives and they violently conspire against good Soviet people, implying an ongoing plot between institutional religion and other challenges to Soviet power.[42] To display or own first-wave antireligious posters, then, was to evince a transformation in worldview, and it marked a person as pro-Soviet, pro-people, pro-woman, and pro-modernity.[43]

FIGURE 7.5.   V. Menshikov, *Boga net!*, 1975. Image from The Keston Center for Religion, Politics, and Society, Baylor University, Waco, Texas.

Second-wave antireligious posters, beginning with the Khrushchev-era campaigns targeting religious faith and practice, though fewer in number, present a far more diminished and complex anticlerical-ism.[44] Priests are noticeably less present in second-wave posters, and they are often absent entirely. Perhaps the most famous of all antireligious posters, Vladimir Menshikov's 1975 *Boga net!* (There is no God!) nods to religion via rooftops—onion domes, a crescent, a Latin cross (figure 7.5). Eight of the ten antireligious posters in a 1985 collection from the Moscow publishing house "Plakat" feature no clergy what-soever, extending the blame for spiritual distractions to female palm readers or elderly believers, foreign agents, poor antireligious activists, or thoughtless youth.[45] Similarly, six of twelve antireligious posters in a 1981 collection present no clergy, yet convey disapproval of spiritual practices or attitudes.[46]

The disembodiment of the clergy is a feature of second-wave posters as well. Unlike earlier images that utilized zoomorphic representations to deprive priests of their humanity, some later posters divested cler-ics of their bodies. In a number of postwar posters, Russian Orthodox priests are represented solely by hands, often hairy or clawed and nearly always wearing an Orthodox prayer rope as identification, or exten-sions of hands.[47] In a 1962 poster by Korchemkin, a greenish, bony hand with talon-like fingernails makes the sign of the cross over the face of a young wide-eyed girl (figure 7.6).[48] Her anxious expression and the positioning of the hand creates an air of ambiguity and tension. Is this hand meant to bless the child or rake across her tender skin in an act of violence? The viewer is left to imagine the monstrous body that

FIGURE 7.6. L. Korchemkin, *Ogradim detei ot popovskikh kogtei!*, 1962. Image from The Sergo Grigorian Collection.

could possess such a menacing claw. In Trunev's 1975 poster *Sekt*, an implied yet invisible fisherman lures gullible fish and their young to a baited hook that holds a ticket to paradise.[49] The bodiless angler, a religious leader or perhaps an overzealous proselytizer in one of the many so-called sects or religious cults such as Jehovah's Witnesses, Seventh Day Adventists, or Pentecostals, is represented solely by his or her instrument—or weapon—of temptation, which is understood as an intrusion into a peaceful society.

The relative decline of representations of clergy in postwar posters is pronounced. Despite a slight rebound in numbers during the Great Patriotic War and late Stalinism, it is worth recalling that the Stalinist Terror of the late 1930s had repressed or killed tens of thousands of religious leaders who had managed to survive earlier bouts of persecution, perhaps to eliminate internal enemies in expectation of imminent war.[50] Perhaps the decrease in images of clergy reflects the losses from such repression. More likely, however, it can be explained by a general sense among Soviet authorities responsible for the antireligious effort that the clergy had been, in large part, successfully neutralized and managed in the postwar era. Registration, monitoring, the infiltration of seminaries by KGB agents, and the stripping of what shreds of local authority remained in the hands of clerics over the course of the 1960s and 1970s meant less resistance and little opposition from religious leaders. Further, the mid-1960s marked a shift among antireligious activists who were keen to present a relevant atheism that met the emotional, spiritual, and moral needs of youth raised in the relatively lax religious atmosphere of late Stalinism. Thus, as they diversified their tactics, antireligious propaganda developed a multiplicity of characters and messages designed to discourage religious activity and support atheism.[51]

When priests are pictured, they fall into familiar markers—heft, hair, and robes, if Orthodox, for example—although rather than seeming scary, they often appear comical or incompetent.[52] Overall, postwar posters exhibited a lighter sensibility than revolutionary-era posters. Their humorous satires and caricatures used distortion and pure colors in a decidedly "unpainterly" way, perhaps as a mark of destalinization and a repudiation of a tired socialist realism.[53] Two workshops, Agit-Plakat and Boevoi Karandash (Fighting pencil), in Moscow and Leningrad, respectively, produced nearly all of the professionally designed antireligious propaganda posters in the postwar era.[54] Drawing encouragement from Khrushchev's endorsement of satire as an appropriate method of self-criticism and inspiration from a variety of artistic predecessors, artists of these two collectives aimed fairly lighthearted digs at religion as one of many social problems in late socialism.[55] Agit-Plakat drew a largely urban audience in Moscow for its small-run silkscreens, while the "diverse, ingenious" work of Boevoi Karandash reached factories, clubs, schools, palaces of culture, and other public spaces across the Soviet Union with lithographs and offsets in print runs of tens of thousands and member-conducted traveling exhibitions and teaching seminars in locales as diverse as Cheliabinsk, the Siberian Far East, and the Far North. The few audience-reception studies from this era suggest that viewers appreciated the look and amusing sensibility of these posters.[56]

Hence the prevalence of the blundering, innocuous cleric in these posters. In Sychev's 1977 poster, an elderly robed priest sits on the ground with a needle and thread, sewing together two oversized books, one labeled "Religion" and the other labeled "Science" (figure 7.7). The entire image mocks the futility of the effort—the priest's wild hair, posture, and technique suggests his incompetence—yet also acknowledges the clergies' attempts to adapt to state critiques.[57] Even the idiomatic title, *Shit'e belymi nitkami* (Sewing with white threads), suggests an inept deception or a con so obvious as to be absurd. A larger variety of clergy populate second-wave posters, with collared Catholic priests, Jehovah's Witnesses in suits, and robed mullahs vying for space with Orthodox priests, yet they are equally nonthreatening. Unlike revolutionary-era posters, postwar images of priests usually appear isolated in their efforts to uphold old ways, but occasionally they suggest new foreign collaborators, such as the CIA, other clergy, or kerchiefed *babushki*.[58] Instead of dangerous conspirators, however, these new associates usually seem to be harmless bumblers.

Second-wave posters present an emasculating anticlericalism— literally, by featuring women as more important than male clergy in maintaining faith practices—that ridicules priests more often than attacking them. This reflects the managed and neutralized position of many clerics in registered church organizations in the postwar era as well as evolving tactics in Soviet efforts to combat religiosity (see chapter 5). Removing the singular priest image from propaganda posters, however, also complicated the nature of the critique against faith communities, religious belief, or spiritual practices in general. It required the consumer to agree to vilify his or her grandmother, peers, and those of other faiths to correctly perform Soviet modernity.[59] Further,

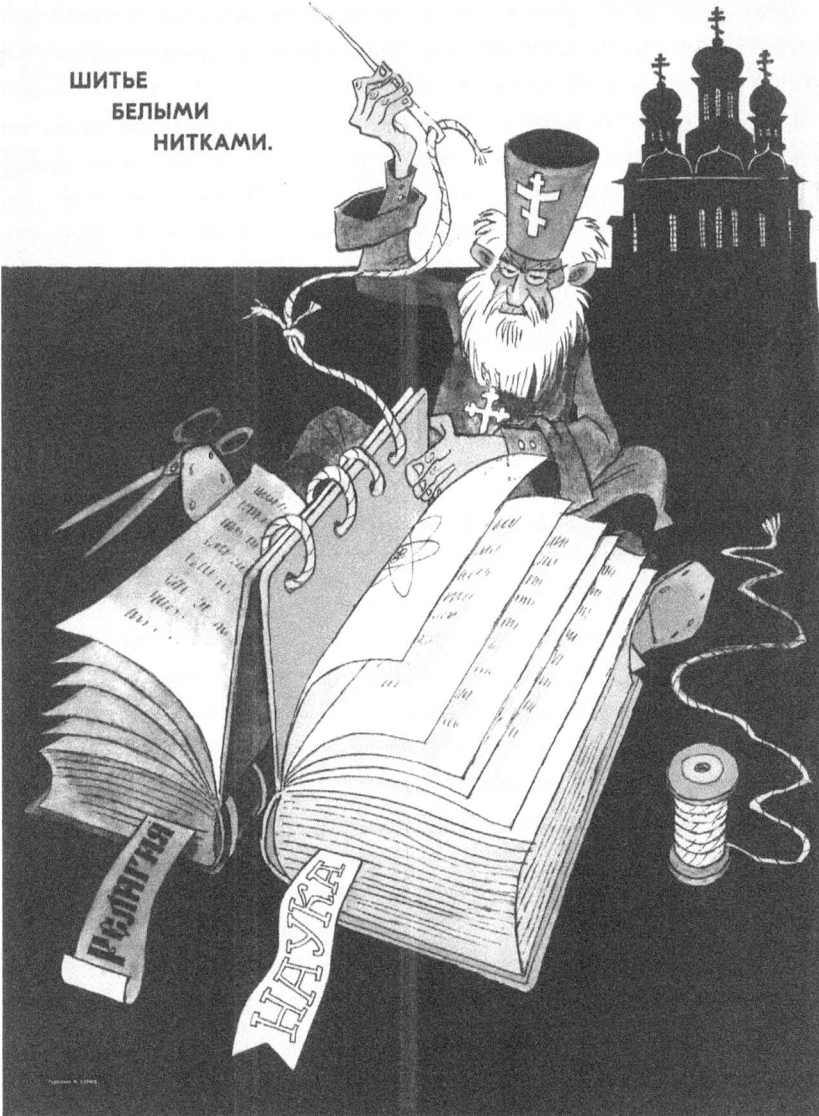

FIGURE 7.7. I. Sychev, *Shit'e belymi nitkami*, 1975. Image from The Keston Center for Religion, Politics, and Society, Baylor University, Waco, Texas.

it meant that youth participating in antireligious efforts had to reject not only spiritual-seeking and faith but also the fashionable trends and social activities that were typical of those indifferent to religion in order to prove their sympathy for party priorities.[60]

The Russian Revolution of 1917 launched a decades-long effort to squelch organized religion for ideological and pragmatic political reasons. From the beginning, this drive was characterized by the sudden emergence of a vigorous anticlericalism in printed artwork and other forms. An unprecedented visual onslaught of clergy images occurred in hundreds of propaganda posters in the two periods in which state authorities prioritized robust antireligious activity. While the visual disparagement of religious leaders remained consistent over time, the manner, intensity, and complexity of Soviet anticlericalism evolved in line with shifting state antireligious policies and practices.

As one component of a dynamic, refashioned religious landscape, antireligious posters bridged the gap between party policies and everyday practices. There is a good reason why these posters can tell us something about both state policies and lived experience, despite their usual dismissal as simple propaganda. The artists who designed them and the editors who assigned and approved them, no matter their personal feelings about religious belief or socialist duty or job security, did so in specific historical contexts that shaped the content and themes of the posters, whether the intent was conformity or subversion. As antireligious authorities sought the legibility and appeal that made a poster "good," the ongoing evolution in antireligious policy and practices complicated their efforts, making it more unlikely that consumers would choose to affirm either their choices or their messages.

Notes

Work on this project was funded the Baylor Class of 1945 Centennial Professors Award, for which I am grateful. My thanks, too, to my Works in Progress cohort in the Department of History at Baylor University and to a lively ASEEES panel and audience for their insightful comments.

1. Mollie Arbuthnot reminds us that Soviet people were encouraged to make their own posters, to cut images out of publications and paste them into new creations and configurations, which explains why magazines such as *Bezbozhnik* began printing full-page or double-spreads that could be easily removed for such purposes. That entire body of work—the amateur, homemade antireligious poster—is excluded from this chapter. Arbuthnot, "The People and the Poster: Theorizing the Soviet Viewer, 1920–1931," *Slavic Review* 78, no. 3 (Fall 2019), 734–35.

2. Published sources include Nina Baburina, *The Soviet Political Poster, 1917–1980,* trans. Boris Rubalsky (London: Penguin, 1985); N. I. Baburina, *Rossiia 20 vek: Istoriia strany v plakate* (Moskva: Panorama, 2000); Roland Elliot Brown, *Godless Utopia: Soviet Anti-Religious Propaganda* (London: Fuel, 2019); Elena Chernevich, Mikhail Anikst, and Nina Baburina, *Russian Graphic Design, 1880–1917* (New York: Abbeville Press, 1990); David King, *Red Star over Russia: A Visual History of the Soviet Union from the Revolution to the Death of Stalin: Posters, Photographs, and Graphics from the David King Collection* (New York: Abrams, 2009); David King, *Russian Revolutionary Posters: From Civil War to Socialist Realism, from Bolshevism to the End of Stalin* (London: Tate Publishing, 2012); E. M. Luchshev, *Sovetskii antireligioznyi plakat v sobranii gosudarstvennogo muzeia istorii religii* (Sankt Peterburg: Izd. Poligraficheskii tsentrom SPbGUTD, 2010); Maria Lafont, *Soviet Posters: The Sergo Grigorian Collection* (Munich: Prestel Verlag, 2007); A. E. Snopkov, P. A. Snopkov, and A. F. Shkliaruk, eds., *Materinstvo i detstvo v russkom plakate* (Moskva: Kontakt-Kul'tura, 2006); Erika Wolf, ed., *Koretsky: The Soviet Photo Poster, 1930–1984* (New York: The New Press, 2012); Peter Kort Zegers and Douglas Druick, eds., *Windows on the War: Soviet TASS Posters at Home and Abroad, 1941–1945* (Chicago and New Haven, CT: The Art Institute of Chicago and Yale University Press, 2011). Any posters drawn from internet searches rather than collections are indicated in notes.

3. French anticlericalism and church persecution, for example, had a visual component but was primarily legislative in nature, both in the French Revolution and in subsequent episodes. Anticlericalism in Mexico under Plutarco Elías Calles was intentionally nonvisual because of the (well-founded) fears that secularization and church disenfranchisement would cause unrest and rebellion. My thanks to my colleagues Daniel J. Watkins and Ricardo Álvarez-Pimentel for discussions on this topic.

4. Nathaniel Davis introduces this idea in the introduction to *A Long Walk to Church: A Contemporary History of Russian Orthodoxy,* rev. ed. (Boulder, CO: Westview Press, 2003), 7–8, 11, 13. The phrase "visible superstructure" is from Daniel Peris, "'God Is Now on Our Side': The Religious Revival on Unoccupied Soviet Territory during World War II," *Kritika: Explorations in Russian and Eurasian History* 1, no. 1 (Winter 2000), 103.

5. Alexandra Guzeva, "How Many Churches Are There in Russia?" *Russia Beyond,* November 30, 2021, https://www.rbth.com/arts/334461-how-many-churches-russia. Guzeva explains that the idiom "forty times forty" (*sorok sorokov*) originates in an expression for Moscow's seemingly countless and ubiquitous churches.

6. Peris, "'God Is Now on Our Side,'" 98. Only two hundred to three hundred churches, one hundred of them functional, remained by the late 1930s in the USSR. All 1,025 monasteries and convents were closed by then as well. Of the Soviet Union's ninety regions, twenty-five had no Orthodox church and most regions had only one. Davis, *A Long Walk to Church,* 11–13; Tatiana A. Chumachenko, *Church and State in Soviet Russia: Russian Orthodoxy from World War II to the Khrushchev Years,* trans. Edward E. Roslof (Armonk, NY: M. E. Sharpe, 2002), 4. Mosques were closed en masse and the last Buddhist temple and monasteries were shuttered. Igor Troyanovksy, ed., *Religion in the Soviet Republics: A Guide to Christianity, Judaism, Islam, Buddhism, and Other Religions*

(San Francisco: HarperCollins, 1991), 169, 178. Jewish synagogues, heders, and seminaries were largely dissolved in the 1920s. Robert Weinberg, "Demonizing Judaism in the Soviet Union during the 1920s," *Slavic Review* 67, no. 1 (2008), 120.

7. See Sonja Luehrmann, *Secularism Soviet Style: Teaching Atheism and Religion in a Volga Republic* (Bloomington: Indiana University Press, 2011), 100, on parents having to make up an answer to "What is that?" questions about a church. See also children's letters in Deborah Hoffman, ed., *The Littlest Enemies: Children in the Shadow of the Gulag* (Bloomington, IN: Slavica, 2008), 125, that discuss the People's Commissariat for Internal Affairs (NKVD) processing center housed in the thirteenth-century Danilov Monastery in Moscow. Today, Danilov is the official headquarters of the Russian Orthodox Church and the official residence of the Patriarch.

8. Cities varied, containing no or very little religious architecture. For example, Stephen Kotkin notes that a church—one presumes an Orthodox church—was built in Magnitogorsk during the Great Patriotic War and a second one in the early 1980s. Kotkin, *Magnetic Mountain: Stalinism as a Civilization* (Berkeley: University of California Press, 1995), 485n159. On the other hand, the Azerbaijan city of Sumgait (Sumgayit) had no mosque until the post-Soviet era. Shahin Abbasov, "Azerbaijan: Sumgayit Becomes Font of Syria-Bound Jihadists," Eurasianet.com, May 5, 2014, https://eurasianet.org/azerbaijan-sumgayit-becomes-font-of-syria-bound-jihadists (accessed November 4, 2023).

9. See, for example, Karl Qualls, *From Ruins to Reconstruction: Urban Identity in Soviet Sevastopol after World War II* (Ithaca, NY: Cornell University Press, 2009), 134–36, for a discussion of how local authorities nixed the prominent Moscow architect Grigorii Barkhin's plans to demolish the historic Vladimir Cathedral to make way for an outdoor naval museum.

10. Davis, *A Long Walk to Church*, 10, 164; Hiroki Kuromiya, *Conscience on Trial: The Fate of Fourteen Pacifists in Stalin's Ukraine, 1952–1953* (Toronto: University of Toronto Press, 2012), 36.

11. New landscapes depicted in Daniil Cherkes, *Stroiteliam sotsialisticheskoi industrii—kul'turnye sotsialisticheskie goroda*, 1932, in King, *Russian Revolutionary Posters*, 90–91; and in Sergei Iaguzhinskii (?), *Traktory i iasli—dvigateli novoi derevni*, 1930, in Snopkov, Snopkov, and Shkliaruk, *Materinstvo i detstvo v russkom plakate*, 34. New processions depicted in V. Khrapovitsky, *Da zdravstvuet vsesoiuznyi den' fizkul'turnika!*, 1947; Viktor Korestsky, Oleg Savostuk, and Boris Uspensky, *Slava velikomu sovetskomu narod—stroiteliu kommunizma!*, 1955; Maria Nesterova-Berezina, *SSSR—da zdravstuet vsepobezhdaiushchee znamia leninizma!*, 1957, all in King, *Russian Revolutionary Posters*, 140–43.

12. See Yuliya Komska, *The Icon Curtain: The Cold War's Quiet Border* (Chicago: University of Chicago Press, 2015), for an example of such adaptation in the forest between Czechoslovakia and West Germany.

13. "Propaganda" and "agitation" had no negative connotations in the nineteenth-century Russian Empire or the early Soviet Union. Arbuthnot, "The People and the Poster," 717. A number of scholars have discussed political posters as a tool of the Soviet authorities, including most of the published poster collections listed in note 2. See also Peter Kenez, *The Birth of the Propaganda*

State: Soviet Methods of Mass Mobilization, 1917–1929 (Cambridge: Cambridge University Press, 1985); Stephen White, *The Bolshevik Poster* (New Haven, CT: Yale University Press, 1988); Victoria Bonnell, *Iconography of Power: Soviet Political Posters under Lenin and Stalin* (Berkeley: University of California Press, 1999); and Klaus Waschik and Nina Baburina, *Werben für die Utopie: Russische Plakatkunst des 20. Jahrhunderts* (Bietigheim-Bissingen: Edition Tertium, 2003).

14. Quote from the French author Anatole France, in Zegers and Druick, *Windows on the War*, 15.

15. Michael David-Fox, "Religion, Science, and Political Religion in the Soviet Context," *Modern Intellectual History* 8, no. 2 (2011), 476–77. The Russian Social Democratic Labor Party principles of proselytizing were laid out in the 1890s in a kind of hierarchy: oral agitation for the masses, written propaganda for the literate, political enlightenment for the dedicated, and theory and science for the intellectuals.

16. More on prerevolutionary influences can be found in José Alaniz, *Komiks: Comic Art in Russia* (Jackson: University Press of Mississippi, 2010), 34; White, *The Bolshevik Poster*, 1–3, 7, 14; Zegers and Druick, *Windows on the War*, 68–70; Wolf, *Koretsky*, 1; Luchshev, *Sovetskii antireligioznyi plakat*, 2.

17. Alaniz, *Komiks*, 15. See also Robert Bird, ed., *Adventures in the Soviet Imaginary: Children's Books and Graphic Art* (Chicago: University of Chicago Press, 2011), 31; Ulf Abel, "Icons and Soviet Art," in *Symbols of Power: The Esthetics of Political Legitimation in the Soviet Union and Eastern Europe*, ed. Claes Arvidsson and Lars Erik Blomqvist (Stockholm: Almqvist & Wiksell International, 1987), 150.

18. The most important example remains Bonnell's *Iconography of Power*. For Bonnell, "visual language" includes a poster's lexicon (key figures or representations) and syntax (the positioning of figures relative to other figures/the environment), and "cultural repertoire" refers to "habits of seeing and interpreting images that viewers brought to visual material" as well as past and present experiences of the viewer that provide context for a personal interpretation.

19. Arbuthnot, "The People and the Poster," 718, 722, 737.

20. Arbuthnot, "The People and the Poster," 730–31.

21. Arbuthnot, "The People and the Poster," 733.

22. Luchshev, *Sovetskii antireligioznyi plakat*, 14, and author's observation. Print runs of posters on religion appear comparable to that of most other topics, ranging from a few thousand to tens of thousands, although numbers are not always available for early Soviet posters. Relatively fewer posters (on any topic) were printed in the hundreds of thousands or millions. Overall, one was perhaps less likely to see an antireligious poster in daily life not because of limited distribution but simply because the struggle against religion was one of many such struggles led by the party.

23. David-Fox, "Religion, Science, and Political Religion," 483, quote on Soviet system.

24. See Aliakrinskii and Zharov, *Zapomnim!*, May 1943, Okno TASS no. 730, in Zegers and Druick, *Windows on the War*, 239, for church depictions. The most famous of the cross-shaped grave markers is undoubtedly Kukryniksy, *Prevrashchenie «Fritsev»*, January 1943, Okno TASS no. 640, in Zegers and Druick,

Windows on the War, 235. See also Mao and Mashistov, *B Tupike*, October 1943, Okno TASS no. 847, in Zegers and Druick, *Windows on the War*, 256; Astapov, Kurdov, Petrov, *Skazano Sdelano*, 1943, in Lafont, *Soviet Posters*, 96; Sokolov-Skalia and Bednyi, *Nemetskaia rozhdestvenskaia elka*, January 1944, Okno TASS no. 892, in Zegers and Druick, *Windows on the War*, 265; and Shirokorad and Spasskii, *Groznyi prizrak*, February 1944, Okno TASS no. 901, in Zegers and Druick, *Windows on the War*, 267.

25. See Juliane Fürst, "Not a Question of Faith—Youth and Religion in the Post-War Years," *Jahrbücher für Geschichte Osteuropas* 52, no. 4 (2004), 558, 564. Fürst notes that *Molodaia Gvardiia* (the Young Guard publishing house) published zero antireligious pamphlets in the 1940s and early 1950s, that only seven publications on atheism were published in 1948, and that antireligious or atheist topics were not in the rotation for public lectures to youth.

26. Gregory L. Freeze, "A Case of Stunted Anticlericalism: Clergy and Society in Imperial Russia," *European Studies Review* 13 (1983), 177–78, 191. On *chastushki*, see William B. Husband, "Mythical Communities and the New Soviet Woman: Bolshevik Antireligious Chastushki, 1917–32," *Russian Review* 63, no. 1 (January 2004), 93. According to Husband, the songs were spirited and irreverent but not political.

27. Bonnell, *Iconography of Power*, 191; Kenez, *The Birth of the Propaganda State*, 183.

28. *Tsar, pop i kulak*, 1918, Izd. VTsIK, at Virtual'nyi muzei sovremennoi istorii Rossii, GIK 1575/78, http://vm.sovrhistory.ru/sovremennoy-istorii-rossii/katalog#/item/75. There is some question about the author of this poster. The Virtual Museum provides no details for the artist, simply indicating "author unknown." Other collections or online repositories list the author as M. Pet/Pat or E. G. Scheimann.

29. Freeze, "A Case of Stunted Anticlericalism," 178. *D'iachok* and *ponomar*—two ranks of sacristans—were also pejorative terms by the mid-1800s.

30. For Ukrainian, see Pat [sic], *Tsar, Pip ta kulak (glitai)*, 1918, Ne Boltai! collection, Object ID 43320. For Latvian, see n. a., *Kenenš, Baznīckungs un Kulaks*, 1918, in B. S. Butnik-Siverskii, *Sovetskiĭ plakat ėpokhi grazhdanskoĭ voĭny, 1918–1921* (Moskva, 1960), 214–15; view at PosterPlakat.com, Item PP 890, https://www.posterplakat.com/the-collection/posters/the-tsar-the-priest-and-the-kulak-pp-890. For Lithuanian, see *Caras, kunigas ir bagocius* (Moskva, 1920), Collection of Russian and Ukrainian Posters, 1917–1921, New York Public Library Digital Collections, https://digitalcollections.nypl.org/items/510d47de-8391-a3d9-e040-e00a18064a99 (accessed May 16, 2024).

31. Freeze, "A Case of Stunted Anticlericalism," 181, 191.

32. N. a., *Vot chto zhdet krest'ian i rabochikh blagodaria dezertiram*, 1918, in Lafont, *Soviet Posters*, 17; Dmitri Moor, *Tsarskie polki i krasnaia armiia*, 1919, in King, *Russian Revolutionary Posters*, 18; Moor, *Kto protiv sovetov*, 1919, USC Digital Library, https://doi.org/10.25549/pcra-c14-15904; Nikolai Kupreyanov, *Tak bol'she ne budet*, 1919, in Lafont, *Soviet Posters*, 22; Viktor Deni, *Tov. Lenin ochischaet zemliu ot nechisti*, 1920, in Baburina, *Rossiia 20 vek*, 46; M. Volkov, *Vel'mozhnye gromily*, 1920, USC Digital Library, https://doi.org/10.25549/pcra-c14-16080; Boris Yefimov, *Novii zemel'nii zakon radians'koi vladi na ukrainii*, 1920,

in Baburina, *The Soviet Political Poster*, 24; Moor, *Prezhde odin s syshkoi, semero s lozhkoi*, 1920, in Luchshev, *Sovetskii antireligioznyi plakat*, 23; n. a., *Delo sovetskoi vlasti budet dovedenogo kontsa, kogda v nem primut uchastie millionyi milliony rabotnits i krest'ianok*, 1925, in Snopkov, Snopkov, and Shkliaruk, *Materinstvo i detstvo v russkom plakate*, 19; Deni, *Vragi piatiletki*, 1929, in Luchshev, *Sovetskii antireligioznyi plakat*, 40; Yuri Pimenov, *Protiv religii*, 1930, in Baburina, *The Soviet Political Poster*, 56; Kukryniksy, *15*, 1932, in Baburina, *Rossiia 20 vek*, 114; L. Lisitsky and S. Lisitskaia, *Kto slaven i znaten v strane sotsializma*, 1938, in Baburina, *Rossiia 20 vek*, 112.

33. William B. Husband, "Soviet Atheism and Russian Orthodox Strategies of Resistance," *The Journal of Modern History* 70, no. 1 (March 1998), 84, discussing the journals *Derevenskii bezbozhnik*, *Radio v derevne*, and *Bezbozhnik u stanka*.

34. See Bonnell, *Iconography of Power*, 193–94, 197, for further discussion of this artistic strategy.

35. A 1920 postcard of Deni's image from the previous year is available in the Ne Boltai! collection, Object ID 7393. Deni used a similar tactic in a portrayal of an avaricious capitalist in his poster *Kapital* (1919), which also accompanied a poem by Bedny (pen name of Yefim Alekseevich Pridvorov), and in his portrayal of a "bread-spider" in *Kulak-miroed* (1919).

36. For other examples, see D. S. Moor and I. Kasatkin, *Ptakhi tsarskie*, 1919, at Ne Boltai! Object ID 19546; D. Moor, *Popy pomogaiut kapitali i meshchaiut rabochemu. Proch' s dorogi!*, 1920, and M. Cheremnykh, *Ne poddavaites' popovskomu obmanu—osvobozhdaites' ot religioznogo durmana!*, 1933, available to view at https://www.rbth.com/history/329413-how-soviet-undermined-god. These three portray clergy as, respectively, birds; a collective mass and grasping robes, claws, and crosses; and puppets.

37. Bonnell, *Iconography of Power*, 193–94, 197, suggests the stereotype image is derived from Vasilii Perov's paintings of the nineteenth century, while Luchshev, *Sovetskii antireligioznyi plakat*, 4, asserts the "ignorant and mammonish drunkard priest and Black-Hundreder" was familiar anticlerical visual fare in the prerevolutionary era.

38. Poster in Lafont, *Soviet Posters*, 22. Similar posters include D. Moor, *Prezhde odin s syshkoi, cemero s lozhkoi. Teper' kto ne rabotaet, tot ne est*, 1920, Ne Boltai! collection, Object ID 11493; n. a., *Prezhde, teper'*, 1921, Ne Boltai! collection, Object ID 18619; V. Deni, *Liubliu s nikh brat'*, drawing, 1926, Ne Boltai! collection, Object ID 47140; N. Kogout, *Posle ispovedii, Bezbozhnik u stanka: 1923–V–1927* (Moskva: VKP(b), 1927), https://mcbcollection.com/early-soviet-anti-religious-propaganda.

39. Freeze, "A Case of Stunted Anticlericalism," 180; Weinberg, "Demonizing Judaism," 121.

40. Albert Boiter, "Law and Religion in the Soviet Union," *The American Journal of Comparative Law* 35, no. 1 (1987), 106, 109.

41. Husband, "Soviet Atheism and Russian Orthodox Strategies of Resistance," 85–86.

42. See, for examples, K. Urbetis, *Cherez reku* (1936) and *Byla u popa vlast'* (1937), reproduced in Dmitri Vladimirovich Mikhnovskii, *Oruzhiem satiry—protiv religii: Mastera russkoi sovetskoi grafiki protiv religii i sueverii* (Leningrad:

Khudozhnik RSFSR, 1963), 56–57; A. Deneika, *Batiushka nashego prikhoda* (1930), reproduced in Lafont, *Soviet Posters*, 74; D. Moor, *Razoblachim antisovetskie zamysly . . .* (1932); M. Cheremnyhk, *Tak uchit tserkov'* (1931); V. Koretsky, *Tserkovniki i sektanty* (1929).

43. See Lisitskaia and Lisitsky, *Kto slaven i znaten v strane sotsializma* (1938) for a poster illustrating this point.

44. No one appears to know the total number of antireligious posters for the postwar era, but all scholars agree that it is quite a small number. See, for example, Luchshev, *Sovetskii antireligioznyi plakat*, 14.

45. "Podborka satiricheskikh plakatov," Izd-stvo "Plakat," 1984.

46. "Svet protiv t'my," Izd-stvo "Plakat," 1981.

47. See, for example, L. N. Korchemkin, *Ogradim detei ot popovskikh kogtei*, 1962, Red Avant Garde, Sergo Grigorian Collection, Cat. no. 404, viewable at http://redavantgarde.com/en/collection/show-collection/378-let-s-protect-children-from-the-priest-s-claws-.html; L. F. Aleksandrova, *Sekundy v kupeli— nedeli v posteli*, 1965; Iu. Travin, *Sekt*, 1975; K. Nevler, *Sobral tserkovnyi khlam pizhon . . .* , 1977.

48. Korchemkin, *Ogradim detei ot popovskikh kogtei*, 1962.

49. Trunev, *Sekt*, 1975, Keston Center for Religion, Politics, and Society, ml-keston-pos_031, https://digitalcollections-baylor.quartexcollections.com/Documents/Detail/soviet-poster/1064121.

50. Hiroki Kuromiya, "Why the Destruction of Orthodox Priests in the Soviet Union in 1937–38?" *Jahrbücher für Geschichte Osteuropas* 55, no. 1 (2007), 87, 92.

51. Victoria Smolkin-Rothrock, "The Ticket to the Soviet Soul: Science, Religion, and the Spiritual Crisis of Late Soviet Atheism," *Russian Review* 73, no. 2 (April 2014): 187–92.

52. See E. Rabinovich, *Ateist spit . . . a sluzhba idet!*, 1975; T. Svetozarov, *Sotvorenie kadrov*, 1975; V. Travin, *Pop-musika*, 1975; I. Sychov, *Shit'e belymi nitkami*, 1977; F. Neliubin, *Dedushka, a ia tsarstvie nebesnoe narisoval!*, 1979; n. a., *Raketnym reisam serdtse rado*, 1981. All available at the Keston Center for Religion, Politics, and Society.

53. Masha Kowell, "Agit-Plakat: The Destalinization of Soviet Posters (1956–1966)," PhD diss., University of Pennsylvania, 2013.

54. Luchshev, *Sovetskii antireligioznyi plakat*, 14–15. Other professional antireligious posters were published by the Institut Sanitarnogo Prosveshchenia (Institute of Health Education) and Sovietskaia Khudozhnik (Soviet Artist). Local production of visual aids such as posters was a highly encouraged part of atheist activism on the provincial, district, city, or village level, both for the activist to use in presentations and for engaging local audiences. Locally produced posters both mitigated state shortfalls in supplying professional posters and supplied relevant, timely materials tailored to specific communities. See Luehrmann, *Secularism Soviet Style*, 11; and Sonja Luehrmann, "The Modernity of Manual Reproduction: Soviet Propaganda and the Creative Life of Ideology," *Cultural Anthropology* 26, no. 3 (2011), 367, 370–71, 375.

55. Sergei Il'ich Stykalin and Inna Kirillovna Kremenskaia, *Sovetskaia satiricheskaia pechat' 1917–1963* (Moskva: Gospolitizdat, 1963), 29–32. Mikhnovskii,

Oruzhiem satiry, 74, calls the castigation of remnants the "most important task of satire."

56. Vadim Stepanovich Matafonov, "Introduction," in *Vystavka satiricheskikh plakatov kollektiva leningradskikh khudozhnikov i poetov "Boevoi karandash": Katalog* (Leningrad: Khudozhnik RSFSR, 1981), 10–13, 22; Kowell, "Agit-Plakat," 34–35, 75, 103.

57. On the recognition of the adaptability of religion by activists, see Smolkin-Rothrock, "The Ticket to the Soviet Soul," 186.

58. See, for example, K. Nevler, *Neprasnyi trud*, 1965; V. Bokovnia, *Govorit 'golos brat'ev vo khriste'!*, 1979; N. Lisorgskii, *Skoro! Veleno otiskat' pokrovitelia kosmonavtov*, 1965; A. Svetkov, *Etogo lektora nam sam Gospod' Bog . . .* , 1965. All available in the Keston Center for Religion, Politics, and Society.

59. On grandmothers, see Julie deGraffenried, "Combatting God and Grandma: Soviet Anti-Religious Policies and the Battle for Childhood," in *The Dangerous God: Christianity and the Soviet Experiment*, ed. Dominic Erdozain (DeKalb: Northern Illinois University Press, 2017), 32–50.

60. See Victoria Smolkin, *A Sacred Space Is Never Empty: A History of Soviet Atheism* (Princeton, NJ: Princeton University Press, 2018), 205–15, on Soviet youth as spiritual consumers during late socialism.

PART III

Freedom of Conscience beyond the Soviet Union

CHAPTER 8

Overcoming One's Own Fear

Exile Publishing, Samizdat, and the Illegal Transport of Literature to Czechoslovakia, 1971–1989

Michael Long

The Keston Archive contains a curious volume. The book measures 9 x 7 centimeters, has a simple adhesive binding, and a plain, rose-colored chipboard cover (figure 8.1). A small paper label bears traces, barely visible, of the title *Mráz přichází z Kremlu* (Frost approaches from the Kremlin). The miniature book was published in 1981 by the exile publishing house Index and was prepared and bound by the Erlangen workshop, both in the Federal Republic of Germany (FRG). The miniature *Mráz* is the former Czech reform Communist Zdeněk Mlynář's memoir of negotiations between the leadership of the Czechoslovak Communist Party (CCP) and government and Soviet Politburo officials in Moscow after the Warsaw Pact invasion of Czechoslovakia in 1968.

Holding the miniature volume of Mlynář's memoir in one's hand elicits many questions. Why was this book produced and for whom? What is Index? What does this book represent? What is the larger story behind this book?

This chapter will answer these questions by focusing on the exile publication of Czechoslovak literature, essays, and documents. Attention is given to two of the larger exile publishers, 68 Publishers in Toronto, Canada, and Index in Cologne, FRG: their founders and operations, their titles and genres, and the mechanism by which they

Figure 8.1. Zdeněk Mlynář's memoir *Mráz přichází z Kremlu* miniaturized and prepared for smuggling. Image from The Keston Center for Religion, Politics, and Society, Baylor University, Waco, Texas.

made their publications available to readers in Czechoslovakia. In addition, the chapter discusses the two-way transport of manuscripts and other materials from the opposition, or "dissident," community within Czechoslovakia out of the country for publication abroad, and materials by exiled authors, political analysts, historians, and others to the citizens of Czechoslovakia. Inspired by the miniature *Mráz*, this paper synthesizes information from previous works on exile publishing with the story of the illegal transport of materials.

The story of the underground transportation of illegal literature to and from Czechoslovakia during 1971–89 begins in 1968. "Sixty-eight" saw the reform period of the Prague Spring that was initiated by reform Communists under the leadership of Alexander Dubček. The reforms in Czechoslovakia became the envy and the fear of the citizens and leadership of other East bloc countries. The Prague Spring ended with the Warsaw Pact invasion of Czechoslovakia during the pre-dawn hours of August 21, 1968. Dubček, the General Secretary of the CCP, and other members of the CCP leadership and government were arrested and whisked away to Moscow for negotiations with representatives of the Soviet government. In Moscow, it was made clear to the Czechoslovak delegation that the reforms had to be reversed and that Czechoslovakia's relations with its Socialist brother nations had to be "normalized." The post-invasion period of Normalization, under the leadership of Gustáv Husák—installed as General Secretary to replace Dubček in April 1969—and other hard-line Communists obedient to Moscow, was marked by repressive measures intended to punish anyone who had supported or taken part in the Prague Spring reforms, including CCP and government officials, professors, writers, journalists, film directors, actors, and others. Legislative Measure 99/1969 mandated that those persons complicit with the Prague Spring reforms be banned from working and their works also banned from publication, sale, or performance.[1] It is estimated that 350,000 people emigrated from Czechoslovakia as a direct result of the Husák regime's purge of the CCP and official discrimination against reformists.

In the early 1970s, the Czech and Slovak exile community consisted for the most part of persons who left Czechoslovakia in two waves after 1945. The first wave of exiles emigrated in response to the Communist takeover of Czechoslovakia in 1948. Exiles from the 1968 period, very many of whom were reform Communists but also those noncommunists persecuted during the early years of the Normalization period, comprised the second wave. Francis Raška maintains that many exiles from the 1948 period distrusted the post-1968 exiles who were reform Communists and who had held positions of privilege in Czechoslovakia.[2] This distrust colored the relationships between various exile groups, as well as relationships between exile publishing houses.

Nevertheless, Czechoslovak exiles living in the West, desiring to maintain an active intellectual life that could potentially challenge the Normalization regime in their homeland, established publishing houses. The primary objective of exile publishers was the publication of works by exiled writers and by dissident authors still resident in Czechoslovakia. It very quickly became clear to exile publishers that their titles should be made available, even by illegal means, to the citizens of Czechoslovakia. Thus was born a system of underground transport of materials to and from Czechoslovakia that continued virtually unabated from 1971 right up to the Velvet Revolution in 1989. A key player in the illegal movement of materials across the Iron Curtain was the sociologist and dissident Jiřina Šiklová, who was the exile publishers' primary contact person in Czechoslovakia for more than ten years. Šiklová's role in the smuggling operation was pivotal, and her desire to maintain her own freedom of conscience while assisting her compatriots to do the same explains in large part her remarkable endurance and survival.

Overview of Exile Publishing

The history of exile publishing of Czech and Slovak literature and other materials is multifaceted. Francis Raška's *Long Road to Victory* (2012) is a comprehensive study of exile publishing, focusing on the founders, their aims, and their disagreements with one another, and will not be provided here. This chapter, however, builds on Raška's work to provide background information on two of the largest exile publishing firms, concentrating on the courageous story of the illegal transport of materials to and from Czechoslovakia and illuminating the remarkable longevity and success of the smuggling operation.

Of the more than forty organizations dedicated to exile publishing, Index and 68 Publishers were two of the largest in terms of the number of titles published and the number of subscribers, with 170 and 227 titles, respectively. Other major exile publishing firms were Křest'anská Akademie (Christian Academy), in Rome, with 270 titles, Konfrontace (Confrontation), in Zürich, with over 100 titles, and Poesie Mimo Domov (Poetry Away from Home), in Munich, with 136 titles. Rozmluvy (Conversations), established in London in 1982 by Alexander Tomský,[3] published 70 titles specifically for illegal transport to Czechoslovakia.[4]

Exile publishers were distinguished from one another primarily by their publication profiles. Index and 68 Publishers both produced literary works—novels, novellas, poetry, and short stories—by exiled writers and dissident writers in Czechoslovakia. Index also published studies in philosophy, politics, and history by exiled former reform Communists. Křest'anská Akademie focused on religious works and on writers banned from publishing in Czechoslovakia. Rozmluvy published primarily "reprints of successful and widely-distributed titles originally published by other exile publishing houses," as well as works by conservative or Catholic exile or dissident writers.[5]

68 Publishers

While 68 Publishers is well known to Slavists around the world as a major publisher of Czech and Slovak exile literature, the story of its establishment and operations and the backgrounds of its founders is less known. Josef Škvorecký (1924–2012) and his wife, Zdena Salivarová Škvorecká (b. 1933), emigrated from Czechoslovakia in 1969 in the wake of the 1968 invasion. Settling in Toronto, the pair founded 68 Publishers in 1971. Zdena, a former singer, actress, and published short-story writer, was the primary business force behind the project and Josef was the editor-in-chief.

Before emigrating, Škvorecký had "consolidated his reputation as a courageous, entertaining and often controversial novelist and screenwriter in Prague during the slow thaw of the late 1950s and 60s."[6] Škvorecký wrote more than forty novels and screenplays, short stories, essays on literature and cinema, as well as translations of Hemingway and Faulkner into Czech. Paul Wilson, the primary translator of Škvorecký into English, notes that a "series of seven semi-autobiographical, jazz-soaked books," all but one narrated by a single author, and a "series of crime novels" that "can be read as a single, vast epic covering the most crucial and painful periods of modern Czech history" comprise the core of Škvorecký's work.[7] Škvorecký also taught literature and film studies at the University of Toronto.

In addition to works by Škvorecký and Zdena Škvorecká, the catalog of 68 Publishers contains notable works in Czech such as Ludvík Vaculík's *Guinea Pigs* (1977) and *The Czech Dream Book* (1983); Václav Havel's *Plays, 1970–1976* (1977) and *Letters to Olga* (1985); and Milan Kundera's *Life is Elsewhere* (1979), *The Book of Laughter and Forgetting* (1981), and *The Unbearable Lightness of Being* (1985). 68 Publishers also produced works by Arnošt Lustig, Jiří Gruša, Ivan Klíma, Pavel Kohout, Jan Patočka, Eda Kriseová, Jaroslav Seifert, Bohumil Hrabal, Tom Stoppard, and many others. In addition to Czech and Slovak authors, 68 published Czech translations of American literature—for example, Philip Roth's *Prague Orgy* (1988) and Arthur Miller's drama *The Archbishop's Ceiling* (1989)—that were relevant to citizens in East bloc countries. Several publications were second editions of works previously published in pre-invasion Czechoslovakia—for example, Arnošt Lustig's novel *Dita Saxová*, first published in Prague in 1967.[8]

Index

The exile publishing house Index—Society of Czechoslovak Literature Abroad, more often referenced simply as "Index"—in operation from 1971 to 1991, was founded in Cologne by the reform Communists Adolf Müller (1929-2002) and Bedřich Utitz (1920-2017). Adolf Müller emigrated from Czechoslovakia in 1968 and settled in the FRG. A founding member of *Listy*, he lectured on political science at German universities until the mid-1990s.[9] In 1999 President Václav Havel decorated Müller with the Medal of Merit. He returned to Czechoslovakia in 2002, only eight weeks before his death.[10] Bedřich Utitz, born in Vienna to a Jewish family of Czech origin, moved with his family to Prague in 1931, then, fleeing the German occupation of Czechoslovakia, emigrated to Palestine in 1939. After World War II, Utitz embarked on a career with the Czech Press Agency in 1946 as a correspondent in the Soviet sector of divided Berlin. From 1954, Utitz worked for Czechoslovak Radio as head of the German broadcasting service, then took a post in Cuba (1963–65), and finally settled in Cologne in 1968. In 2005 Utitz resettled in Prague, where he remained until his death.[11]

On the beginnings of Index, Utitz stated, "Both of us [Müller] were known to have been active in the Prague Spring. They were still exhorting some of us from the exile: 'Do something. Found a political party or some association.'"[12] The original intent of Müller and Utitz was to publish one work per month for a total of twelve publications per year. Financial difficulties through the mid-1970s brought Index to near collapse. By the end of the 1970s, however, Index was meeting its publication target, and through the 1980s was publishing nine to twelve titles per year.[13] Index, like 68 Publishers, released the titles of both exiled writers and dissident writers in Czechoslovakia.

The Index catalog lists notable works by Czech writers, beginning with Jiří Hochman's *Deer Creek* in 1971 and followed by, among others, Arnošt Lustig's *Street of the Lost* (1973), Bohumil Hrabal's *How I Served the King of England* (1974), Ludvík Vaculík's *The Axe* (1977) and *Dear Classmates* (1986), Jaroslav Seifert's *The Plague Column* (1979), and Eva Kantůrková's *My Companions in the Bleak House* (1984). Other Czech writers, including Eda Kriseová, Pavel Kohout, and Lenka Procházková, also found their works in the Index catalog. Index also published non-Czech and non-Slovak writers, making their work available in translation to readers in Czechoslovakia. Among these are Angelo Rippelino's *Magic Prague* (1978), Nadezhda Mandelstam's *Hope Abandoned* (1975), George Orwell's *Animal Farm* (1981) and *1984* (1984), Czesław Miłosz's *Hymn about a Pearl, Selected Poems* (1986), Yevgeny Zamyatin's *We* (1985), and many others.[14] Eva Kantůrková commented on the importance of Index to her personally: "Besides the Canadian Sixty-Eight publishing house of the Škvoreckýs, Index was for me one of the great important exile publishers that managed to map the majority of what was published here in samizdat."[15]

Index is distinguished from 68 Publishers and other exile publishers by its specialization in journalistic, political, and economic studies by exiled Czech and Slovak writers and other European writers.[16] These include, among others, Roy and Zhores Medvedev's *A Question of Madness* (1974), Zdeněk Mlynář's *Night Frost in Prague* (1978),[17] and works by the journalist Jiří Lederer, the philosopher Milan Šimečka, the journalist and poet Karel Hvížd'ala, and others.[18]

Apart from novels, stories, poetry, and nonfiction analytical works in book form, Index also produced three journals: *Listy* (Letters), *150,000 Slov: Texty odjinud* (150,000 Words: Texts from elsewhere), and *Mosty* (Bridges). The bimonthly *Listy* was founded in Rome in 1971 by Jiří Pelikán[19] as the "journal of the Czechoslovak socialist opposition."[20] From 1971 to 1989, Index produced *Listy* in six issues per year, and numbers 1–12 in German (1980–82).[21] Antonín Liehm, who emigrated to Paris in 1969, edited *150,000 Slov*. *Mosty*, prepared and edited by Jiří Gruša,[22] in exile in the FRG since 1981, appeared in two issues. Index also produced and distributed eighteen titles in Zdeněk Mlynář's series "The Crisis of Soviet-Type Systems" as well as four video cassettes dedicated to political topics, most notably "A Look at the Year 1968 after 20 Years," comprised of interviews with Adolf Müller, Jiří Pelikán, Vilém Prečan,[23] Josef Škvorecký, and others (1987–88).[24]

Index typically printed one to two thousand copies of prose works and five hundred copies of poetry collections. Of these, two to three hundred copies were set aside for illegal transport to Czechoslovakia, where they would be distributed free of charge.[25]

Propašováná Literatura (Smuggled Literature)

One of the most courageous acts of resistance to the Communist regime of Czechoslovakia during the years 1971–89 was the organized illegal transport of literature and other materials to and from Czechoslovakia. The smuggling operation provided a means for exile writers to make their publications available to readers in their homeland who would otherwise not have access to those materials. It also provided a means for members of the opposition within Czechoslovakia to have their work sent abroad for publication and then returned via the same mechanism.

The Palach Press Agency, founded by Jan Kavan in 1975 in London, played a key role in organizing and transporting smuggled materials. Kavan, as an active member of the Communist Party, took a leading role in the student movement leading up to the Prague Spring and in 1968 emigrated to the United Kingdom.[26] The agency bore the surname of Jan Palach, a Prague student who committed suicide by self-immolation in 1969 to protest the occupation of Czechoslovakia by Soviet troops in the aftermath of the August 1968 invasion.

The Agency's mission "was to provide information to Western media on Czechoslovak dissent and to provide Western institutions with unofficial Czechoslovak literature."[27] Since the early 1970s, Kavan and a circle of his British and exile friends had been translating materials created by the Czechoslovak opposition and providing it to Western media outlets. In addition, they established the Solidarity Fund, which "emerged in response to the needs of Czechoslovak citizens who suffer imprisonment, employment discrimination, unemployment, and social disadvantage because of their political and social convictions," and whose main activity was the "delivery of documents from the opposition through the Iron Curtain."[28]

Kavan was the only person outside of Czechoslovakia who knew all the details of the smuggling operation. Inside Czechoslovakia, a single person always handled the delivery of materials. From 1971 to 1972, this person was Jiří Müller.[29] Petr Pithart took over from Müller until he signed the Charter 77 Declaration and terminated his involvement with the operation.[30]

Charter 77 played a prominent role in the Czechoslovak opposition. Charter 77 was a Helsinki Watch organization founded by Václav Havel, Petr Uhl, Ludvík Vaculík, and others, including Zdeněk Mlynář and other disenfranchised reform Communists. The founders crafted the Charter 77 Declaration, which stated the group's aim to monitor, report on, and address human rights violations committed by the Czechoslovak government in contradiction to international agreements, the articles of which had become integrated into Czechoslovak law. The Chartists collected more than 240 signatures of supporters, then published the document in January 1977. The Charter group chose three *mluvčí* ("speakers") to represent the Charter publicly and sign its letters and reports. Because of the arrests and interrogations of the original speakers—Václav Havel, Jan Patočka, and Jiří Hájek—the Chartists adopted a system of rotating groups of three speakers.[31] Charter 77 and the Chartists played a vital role in the effort to spread information about human rights abuses and the state of the opposition in Czechoslovakia globally. At the risk of losing their personal liberty and livelihood, many Chartists were intimately involved in the production of samizdat and in the smuggling operation described here.

Most often, camping vans were used for the transport of materials. Over a period of twenty years, Kavan recruited approximately two hundred couriers, most of these from among British peace activists, then later from among students associated with the French Left, "Trotskyites" from the Organisation Communiste Internationaliste, who also helped finance the operation. Registration plates on the vehicle carried a forged insurance card. The cars were changed every two to three years and made the trip to and from Czechoslovakia four to six times a year.[32]

The smuggling vehicle had space to carry materials under its seats, behind drawers, and in the roof. Traveling from Czechoslovakia, the cargo consisted of manuscripts, copies of samizdat periodicals, grant applications, documents concerning human rights violations, financial records, photographs, and videos. Literature by exile authors, professional books and manuals, specifically requested medications, money, copy machines, cameras, computers, and video cameras comprised the cargo transported into Czechoslovakia. Two exile journals, Jiří Pelikán's *Listy* and Pavel Tigrid's *Svědectví* (Testimony), also made up a large portion of the materials transported into Czechoslovakia.[33] Articles by dissident writers smuggled out of Czechoslovakia in manuscript form often returned to the country in the contents of *Listy* or *Svědectví*. Raška maintains that Pelikán and Tigrid depended on Kavan and the Palach Press Agency for the delivery of their respective journals, *Listy* and *Svědectví*, to Czechoslovakia.[34] *Listy* published the Charter 77 Declaration in its entirety, and thereafter virtually all Charter documents appeared in *Listy*, the primary vehicle for information about the Charter to the exile community.[35]

Pavel Tigrid (1917–2003), a journalist, publicist, and the Minister of Culture of the Czech Republic (1994–96), emigrated to the FRG after the Communist takeover of Czechoslovakia in 1948. Tigrid was instrumental in establishing Radio Free Europe and was director of the Czechoslovak desk in Munich until his dismissal in 1952 over differences of opinion. Tigrid founded *Svědectví* with fellow exiles in New York in 1956 and in 1960 moved the journal's operation to Paris.[36] *Svědectví*, which published articles by both reform Communists and signatories to Charter 77, was read widely by exiles as well as by dissident and opposition leaders within Czechoslovakia.

Miniature versions of certain publications, including Mlynář's *Mráz*, were produced specifically for smuggling by Josef Jelínek's workshop in Erlangen, Germany. In cooperation with Index, and later also Prečan, Jelínek produced "tens of thousands" of copies of the miniature editions using simple techniques and inexpensive materials. The miniatures—light, small, and uniform—were easily stackable and could fill tight spaces in the smuggling vehicle. Altogether, Jelínek's workshop produced thirty titles.[37]

"Postwoman" Jiřina Šiklová

Jiřina Šiklová (1935–2021) was a key figure in the smuggling operation for more than ten years. Šiklová states, "I did this a relatively very long time. It is not good to do it long. It is against all the rules of conspiracy."[38] Born into a middle-class family—her father an ophthalmologist, her mother a primary-school teacher—Šiklová studied history and philosophy at Charles University in Prague. Šiklová was a co-founder of the Department of Sociology at Charles University. During the Prague Spring, she joined the Communist Party and took part in and supported student activities calling for reforms within the party. In 1969, Šiklová was fired from her position.[39] After Jan Palach's suicide, Šiklová resigned from the party.[40] After working for some time as a cleaner and at other odd jobs, Šiklová found work as a social worker in the Geriatric Department at Thomayer University teaching hospital in Prague.[41]

Šiklová's involvement with the underground transfer of literature as a "postwoman," or courier, began in the early 1970s but her activities intensified in 1977 after Pithart terminated his direct involvement with the operation. Using the code name "Kateřina," shortened to "Kat," Šiklová acted as the primary contact between Kavan and the Palach Press Agency and the dissident community in Czechoslovakia, at times in cooperation with Ludvík Vaculík,[42] Petr Uhl, and others. "Jiřina organized a complete postal service whereby books, manuscripts, documents, and letters found their way over the border, and back came books, journals, and various requisites for cultural aktivity—for example, even ink," Vaculík recalls.[43] It was important for the operation to have as few persons involved as possible and to keep the names of primary contacts secret. When asked how dissidents knew they could send out materials with her help, Šiklová replied: "Almost no one knew. If many people knew, it would be unsafe for them as well as for me, and it would cease to function. In the opposition there were more groups, not only those who signed Charter 77. I had a sense of who belonged to which group. I would offer the person, the 'link' between the group and me, 'Give it to me, I will arrange it somehow.'" Šiklová elaborated further, "I tried to make the connection between the 'link' and me functional and logically justifiable, why we were meeting and how we know each other."[44] Instructions and information about incoming and outgoing shipments were transmitted in encrypted messages and the names of contact persons and recipients of materials were coded. "Both sides had to have two identical books, the title of which no one else knew," Šiklová relates, "then they passed messages with rows of numbers: the page number, line number, and the letter number. And in this way words were formed. It was completely secure. As long as they didn't break your mouth and you didn't say the title of the book, they didn't have a chance to decipher the message."[45]

Šiklová began her work as postwoman by taking responsibility for the delivery of packages marked "most important," which she carried hidden on her person (*na těle*). "I always received these directly into my hands," she states, "these were encrypted letters, messages, sometimes articles, manuscripts on punched paper, no books."[46]

Larger shipments weighing 200 to 300 kilos were distributed using a system of "garages," which was an address of a house or cottage. Sometimes the location of the garage was the address of an evangelical priest where the presence of a foreign car would not be conspicuous. Šiklová would arrange the garage location ahead of a shipment, then meet the courier and give them the address where they would drive to meet the van and transfer the shipment. Each location was used a maximum of three times so as not arouse the suspicion of neighbors. Though the Palach Press Agency car was not changed often, Kavan always changed the registration plates and the drivers.[47]

The smuggling operation organized by Kavan and the Palach Press Agency functioned successfully for almost a decade. Relying on information provided by an informant, agents of Czechoslovak State Security (Státní bezpečnost, StB) launched *Akce Delta* (Operation Delta), aimed at stopping the underground transfer of materials to and from Czechoslovakia and punishing those with any connection to the illegal smuggling operation.[48] Operation Delta achieved results when on April 27, 1981, StB agents at Dolní Dvořiště on the Austrian border stopped a van crossing into Czechoslovakia. Border agents had been tipped off by an insider, a trusted person within Šiklová's inner circle of conspirators. "He knew a shipment was coming, he knew the date," Šiklová recalls. "The *Fízlové*[49] then stopped all cars at crossings and weighed them, so they discovered our car."[50]

Once the contraband in the van's compartments was confiscated, the StB acted swiftly. The drivers of the van, two French citizens—the twenty-nine-year-old attorney Giles Thonon and the twenty-four-year-old law student Françoise Anis—were taken into custody but were released and deported after two months of incarceration.[51] Days later, materials gathered for shipment out of the country by the same vehicle were discovered by the StB in Stará Boleslav, 32 kilometers northeast of

Prague. Items in the van mistakenly bore the addresses of the recipients of the documents and journals. The StB carried out house searches and made arrests on May 5–7, 1981.[52] As a consequence of the van's discovery, approximately fifty persons were arrested and interrogated. Šiklová was among the last to be arrested on May 8, 1981. After initial interrogations, eight persons remained in Ruzyně prison to await trial: in addition to Šiklová, Jaromír Hořec, Eva Kantůrková, Karel Kyncl, Ján Mlynárik, Jan Ruml, Jiří Ruml, and Milan Šimečka were incarcerated. The StB named the case "Šiklová and Company." The eight were charged under Article 98 of the penal code with *rozvracení a podvracení republiky* ("destruction and subversion of the republic"), which could carry a sentence of ten years.[53] The massive trial planned by the StB, by which it would "imprison all actors in samizdat publishing and smuggling networks," never came to fruition. It is reported that Jiří Pelikán, who at the time was a representative to the European Parliament, alerted the international media to the case, after which the StB dropped the matter.[54] Šiklová was released eleven months after her arrest in March 1982, along with Hořec, Kantůrková, Kyncl, and Jan Ruml. Mlynárik, Jiří Ruml, and Šimečka were released in May 1982.[55]

Only hours before her arrest, Šiklová had prepared a package of materials for transport. Knowing that her arrest was imminent, she made preparations for the care of her children and mother and reflected on her fate. "I don't reproach anyone abroad for anything. It had to happen sometime and maybe it will blow over," Šiklová writes in a letter to Prečan. "What Richard suggests—namely, to go immediately to some embassy and seek asylum, that they'll get things going abroad—is impossible for me, though it would probably be the sensible thing to do."[56]

In Ruzyně, enduring interrogations and awaiting trial, Šiklová found ways to use her time productively—for example, she taught German to prostitutes incarcerated with her.[57] Šiklová continued to reflect and write while in prison, producing some profound statements about her life leading up to the arrest and her motivation for her part in the smuggling operation. "What I miss most of all here is some meaningful activity, something which would fill this unreal misappropriated time; I can't sew, cook or clean here, so the only option left is to think. You can do that even in this small space," she writes in *Defense Mechanisms, or How to Survive Imprisonment*, dated July 20, 1981.[58] The document reveals Šiklová's commitment to acting for the benefit of others. "It's possible that something that occurred to me will be useful for other people of 'my type' too . . . or other friends who are sent to jail or find themselves in other exceptional situations, of which there is never any shortage. In any case it will help me now for I can write, think, do something which is perhaps meaningful, which isn't just for me alone."[59] In fourteen numbered paragraphs, and drawing on her knowledge of human psychology and philosophy, Šiklová provides eloquent insights into survival when one is placed in an exceptional situation such as prison.

One of the most profound documents produced by Šiklová in prison, or by any imprisoned dissident in the former Eastern bloc, is her own statement of defense. Šiklová drafted the statement after two months of interrogation in Ruzyně, producing what Prečan describes as a kind of "confession, in which she seemed to admit to everything, but in such a way as to make it difficult for anyone to sentence her without making themselves look ridiculous in the eyes of the world."[60] Šiklová's statement was published abroad in *Index on Censorship* with the title "Save These Books."[61] Šiklová addresses her remarks to her jailers—or, more accurately, to the Czechoslovak government, the StB, and state prosecutors. She pleads "not to allow the destruction of the books confiscated from the garage in Stará Boleslav. They are the result of much human endeavour, evidence of the writers' considerable self-sacrifice, for which credit is due. Please, put these books away in a safe, lock them up as 'libri prohibiti,' . . . but don't let them be destroyed! We have had enough unpleasant and sad experiences in this country with the destruction and burning of books."[62]

In a noble gesture, Šiklová expresses gratitude to the two French drivers of the van, Thonon and Anis, "for their truly internationalist help. I do not know these people, I have never seen them, but because of us, they spent two months in Ruzyně prison."[63] Šiklová eloquently justifies her own actions and those of other dissidents: "Throughout the sad history of our nation, we have always admired those who did not submit to the dictates of authority; those who, disregarding their personal safety, wrote, translated, hid, transcribed and distributed books and ideas, passing them on to subsequent generations." Šiklová goes further, linking her actions with the dissident activities carried out by the defeated Protestants after the Battle of White Mountain (1620) and the subsequent suppression of religious freedom in Bohemia: "What I did has always been done in this country, the only difference being that they used to carry banned books in carts from somewhere like Žitava, while today they are brought in a Peugeot from London or Paris.

That is merely a question of technological progress. The essence of our actions remains the same. Regrettably, the reasons why books have to be taken in and out of the country in secret also remain the same."[64] Proceeding to school her jailers—that is, the StB—on the value of differing opinions, Šiklová reminds them that the toleration of dissent by the state is both healthy and necessary, arguing that "no such society, in which everyone agrees and sings its praises, has ever existed. Such a regime would be condemned to stagnation and collapse according to the Marxist concept of history, because it lacked social contradiction 'as the principle of change and development'."[65]

Remarkably, even while incarcerated, Šiklová sought to remain a vital contributor to the intellectual life of her country and, thinking forward to the approaching centenary of Kafka's birth in 1983, penned a *Letter to Friends on Franz Kafka's Anniversary*. Identifying with Kafka's protagonist Josef K in *The Trial*, Šiklová writes, "Just as in Kafka's 'Trial' I have no idea when the trial will take place, by what particular laws we will be judged and when and who will decide whether, 'we may enter the courtroom.'" She continues, "Perhaps . . . all those parallels and the recent historical consequences, should form part of a Kafka memorial volume published in samizdat. Not even the most erudite Kafkologist in Paris, Vienna or Tel-Aviv could write on our behalf this part about the effect of Kafka's work on society. That can only come into existence here, in Kafka's city and birthplace."[66] Feeling a sense of urgency, Šiklová encourages her compatriots to move quickly to prepare a samizdat volume that "should be ready within a year so that something might possibly be sent to some conference or included in publications issued around the world to mark the anniversary. And so, dear friends outside, forgive me and get to work: a year and half, that's 'just about right' as we Czechs say."[67]

After her release from prison in March 1982, Šiklová resumed her activities as postwoman. Petr Pithart recalls, "Jiřina was of a higher calibre than me, however. She got out of prison, for example, and threw herself headlong into it again! She reasoned that the secret police would find it highly improbable that she would immediately begin to reoffend."[68] However, after the 1981 debacle, Prečan, Tigrid, and Pelikán, with Šiklová's assistance, found new pathways for smuggling materials to and from Czechoslovakia. The Austrian Path was established by Pelikán, with the help of US intelligence operatives. An Austrian schoolteacher drove a car with contraband materials to Czechoslovakia four times a year, and materials were received and distributed further by Šiklová.[69]

Prečan calls Šiklová's post-prison activities "the mass-transport miracle of 1983–88," the peak of the smuggling operation. Dissidents and exile publishers were assisted by diplomatic personnel and the diplomatic pouch. Šiklová collaborated with Wolfgang Sheur, the cultural attaché at the Embassy of the Federal Republic of Germany from spring 1983 to mid-April 1986. After Sheur was reassigned and left Prague in 1986, the Canadian diplomat Peter Bakewell took on the role.[70] "During Wolfgang's time it wasn't too difficult," Vaculík recalls, "it was easy to get to his place and, surprisingly, the secret police had specific working hours after which they did not keep physical watch of the house or of me."[71] Šiklová's letters to Prečan during this period under the coded signature of Osamělá Lotte (lonely Lotte) contained lists of documents and letters that comprised the shipments she sent out of Czechoslovakia. These letters, Prečan maintains, "testify to the great exchange of information between independent authors and dissidents in Czechoslovakia and their partners abroad. From this correspondence, which was, of course, two-way, one can reconstruct from the lists a substantial part of the shipments of literature (samizdat periodicals and books from one side, and émigré literature, foreign periodicals, and scholarly publications from the other), which flowed across the border in both directions."[72]

A partial explanation of Šiklová's motivation for her role in the smuggling operation is found in an interview published in *Listy* in 1980: "The significance of *Listy* is not only in the transmittal of current information, but also in its being lent out, taking the risk to read it and to pass it on and thereby to disobey 'civil obedience' and the herd mentality. Its significance is in some way the integration of readers into another, unofficial and informal community . . . . Lending *Listy* further means overcoming one's own fear, daring to belong to a certain group."[73]

In a 1998 interview, Šiklová elaborated, "My idea—and this I have been doing all my life—is that it is important to participate in life and not only to be passive."[74] Šiklová's perspective aligns with Václav Havel's maxim of "living within the truth." For Havel, "living within the truth" was the endeavor of a dissident to live life with the understanding that all the rights and freedoms stipulated in international and domestic law were in fact "real." Václav Havel defines the maxim in his essay "The Power of the Powerless" as "serving truth consistently, purposefully, and articulately, and organizing this service," which describes Šiklová's activities in the smuggling of literature.[75]

In 1984, Vilém Prečan, sensing the need to establish a permanent repository of exile and dissident literature outside Czechoslovakia,

FIGURE 8.2. Jiřina Šiklová in her Prague apartment (1998). Photo by Michael Long.

drafted a proposal for the establishment of a documentation center. Prečan sent his proposal and a set of by-laws to fellow exiles, including Pelikán, Tigrid, František Janouch, and Karel Schwarzenberg.[76] Tigrid responded, pledging his support and that of *Svědectví*. In 1986 Prečan received $50,000 in funding from the National Endowment for Democracy, established by US President Ronald Reagan. Additional funding for the center was provided by the Czechoslovak Society of Arts and Letters, the George Soros Open Society Fund, and the Charter 77 Foundation.[77] Thus was born the Documentation Center for the Promotion of Independent Czechoslovak Literature (Československé dokumentační středisko nezávislé literatury, ČSDS). The primary function of the ČSDS was "the collection of samizdat materials, their cataloguing and coding."[78] The collection contained "hundreds of manuscript volumes of *Edice Petlice*[79] and other book editions, samizdat periodicals, videotapes, audio cassettes, films, and photographs."[80] Prečan, who had been collecting samizdat from Czechoslovakia in his Hannover residence, asked Schwarzenberg if the center could be housed at the Schwarzenberg Castle in Scheinfeld, Germany. Schwarzenberg agreed, and all materials were moved from Hannover to renovated rooms of the castle.[81] In building the ČSDS collection, Prečan collaborated with other exile publishers, including Müller and Utitz at Index, the Škvoreckýs and 68 Publishers, Jelínek, Tigrid, Pelikán, as well as others in the United States and France, while also maintaining ties with Havel, Vaculík, Šiklová, and Šimečka in Czechoslovakia.

Exile publishing was made moot by the Velvet Revolution in Czechoslovakia, a series of events that began with a student protest on November 17, 1989, and ended with the downfall of the Husák regime and Václav Havel being proclaimed the president of an independent Czechoslovakia on December 29. With the long-awaited reestablishment of civil freedoms, so too ended the need for smuggled literature, encrypted messages and letters, and postwomen. Former dissidents became party leaders, members of parliament, ministers of culture and foreign affairs, and ambassadors abroad. The days of house searches, detentions, arrests, and interrogations by the StB became a thing of the past.

Within days of the collapse of Czechoslovakia's Communist regime, exile publishers made plans to cease operations. In November 1989, Müller and Utitz ceded rights to all Index publications to Czech publishers and returned permanently to Czechoslovakia.[82] Sixty-Eight continued to publish, although at a declining pace, into 2000. Pavel Tigrid transferred *Svědectví* to Prague in 1990 and published the last issue, no. 93, in 1992. Alexander Tomský transferred the operations of *Rozmluvy* and all publications from London to Prague in 1989. Jan Kavan, the founder and moving force behind the Palach Press Agency, returned to Czechoslovakia in the heat of the Velvet Revolution in November 1989 and became active in the opposition organization Občanské Fórum (Civic Forum). In 1990 Kavan was elected to the Federal Assembly. In the same year, the Palach Press Agency ceased operations.[83] Vilém Prečan returned to Prague in January 1990. In 1995 he was appointed a docent in the Philosophy Faculty of Charles University and in 2005 was named professor of history at Palacký University in Oloumouc, his birthplace.[84] Prečan transferred the ČSDS to the National Museum in Prague in 2003.[85]

Jiřina Šiklová continued her work as a sociologist with renewed vigor after 1989. She published numerous articles on dissidence and the pre-1989 opposition. She was a speaker at domestic and international conferences and symposia and gave lectures throughout Europe. Domestic and international journalists and researchers, including this author, continuously sought out Šiklová for interviews, wanting to learn more about her role in the illegal smuggling and distribution of literature, her activities during the Velvet Revolution, and her life and activities after 1989. She occasionally met with citizens from other countries with repressive regimes to instruct them on how to organize clandestine activities.[86] In 1989 Šiklová founded the Department of Social Work at Charles University and led the department until 2000. At the same time, she began the Gender Studies program, building a library and teaching classes in her Prague apartment until suitable space could be provided by Charles University.[87] In 1995 Šiklová received the Woman of Europe Award for her contribution to the integration of Europe. In 1999 she received the Medal of Merit of the First Degree from President Václav Havel, and in 2020 the Senate of the Czech Republic awarded her the Silver Medal in recognition of contribution to the establishment of civil society.

The details of how the miniature copy of Mlynář's *Mráz* became an artifact of the Keston Archive are either unknown or have been lost to time. Mlynář's brutally frank presentation of CCP machinations and his character evaluations of party and government functionaries guaranteed that *Mráz* could only be published by an exile publishing house.[88] Undoubtedly, Mlynář's manuscript for *Mráz* passed through Šiklová's hands to the van dispatched by the Palach Press Agency to be smuggled out of Czechoslovakia, then published by Index, and smuggled back into the country. This miniature volume of *Mráz* bears testimony to the decades-long struggle of scores of individuals—exiled publishers, writers, and dissidents in Czechoslovakia—who risked their lives and livelihoods to maintain their intellectual freedom under a repressive regime. Šiklová, in particular, exemplified "living within the truth." Many years later she recounted, "When the Czech secret police (StB) came to arrest me one night in 1981, and as they were leading me away in handcuffs, I quoted to my son the words of Jan Patočka: 'Our people have once more become aware that there are things for which it is worthwhile to suffer, that the things for which we might have to suffer are those things which make life worthwhile.'"[89]

Notes

1. Michael Long, *Making History: Czech Voices of Dissent and the Revolution of 1989* (Lanham, MD: Rowman & Littlefield, 2005), 7.

2. Francis D. Raška, *The Long Road to Victory: A History of Czechoslovak Exile Organizations* (Boulder, CO: East European Monographs, 2012), 74.

3. Alexander Tomský (1947), the Czech publisher, publicist, translator, and university educator, emigrated to the United Kingdom following the 1968

invasion of Czechoslovakia. He was a specialist on church-state relations, religion, and the Roman Catholic Church in Poland and Czechoslovakia at Keston College (1979–86).

4. Raška, *Long Road*, 161–66.

5. Raška, *Long Road*, 165.

6. Paul Wilson, "Josef Škvorecký Obituary," *The Guardian*, January 9, 2012, https://www.theguardian.com/books/2012/jan/09/josef-skvorecky (accessed October 10, 2021).

7. Wilson, "Josef Škvorecký."

8. Vilém Prečan, "K spolupráci dvou po srpnových exilových nakladatelství: Korespondence z let 1971-1987 s dodatky z roku 1996, in *Ročenka Československého dokumentačního střediska 2003* (Praha: Československé dokumentační středisko o.p.s., 2003), 121–25.

9. The *Listy* group was comprised of exiled reform Communists associated with the bimonthly journal *Listy* who had been prominent party functionaries before the Warsaw Pact invasion of 1968.

10. "Zemřel Adolf Müller, zakladatel exilového Indexu," March 29, 2002, *Český a slovenský svet*, https://www.czsk.net/svet/clanky/cr/mullerzemrel.html.

11. "Captain Bedřich Utitz," https://www.memoryofnations.eu. Pamět Národa (Memory of Nations) is a web-based archive containing oral testimonies about World War II and communism. It is administered by the nonprofit organization Post Bellum (founded in Prague in 2001) and its partners Czech Radio and the Institute for the Study of Totalitarian Regimes.

12. Luděk Jirka, "Samizdatové nakladatelství Index," *Český rozhlas*, September 20, 2010, https://plus.rozhlas.cz/.

13. Jirka, "Samizdatové nakladatelství Index."

14. Prečan, "K spolupráci," 127–32.

15. "Zemřel Adolf Müller."

16. Eva Behring, Alfrun Kliems, and Hans-Christian Trepte, *Grundbegriffe und Autoren ostmitteleuropäischer Exilliteraturen 1945–1989: Ein Beitrag zur Systematisierung und Typologisierung* (Stuttgart: Franz Steiner Verlag, 2004), 179.

17. The first English translation of Zedněk Mlynář's memoir, translated by Paul Wilson and titled *Nightfrost in Prague: The End of Humane Socialism*, was published in London in 1980. See also Michael Long, "Czech Dissident Zdeněk Mlynář's Memoir," in *Voices of the Voiceless*, ed. Julie deGraffenried and Zoe Knox (Waco, TX: Baylor University Press, 2019), 16–18.

18. Prečan, "K spolupráci," 127–32.

19. Jiří Pelikán (1923-99) was a politician and journalist. He was active in the Communist Youth Movement and was a member of the Czechoslovak National Assembly (1949-54), the director of Czechoslovak National Television (1963-68), and a supporter of Prague Spring reforms. He emigrated to Italy in 1969 and became an Italian citizen in 1977. He was elected twice to the European Parliament from the the Italian Socialist Party (1979-89).

20. Raška, *Long Road*, 49.

21. Prečan, "K spolupráci," 132.

22. Jiří Gruša (1938-2011) was a novelist and human rights activist. He was arrested in 1974 for distributing his first novel *The Questionnaire* in samizdat.

He was a signatory to Charter 77, had his citizenship revoked in 1981, emigrated to the FRG, and returned to Czechoslovakia in 1990 after the Velvet Revolution. He served as ambassador to the FRG from 1991 to 1997, and later as ambassador to Austria.

23. Vilém Prečan (1933) is a historian and political essayist. He was a researcher at the History Institute of the Czechoslovak Academy of Sciences in Prague starting in 1957 and was expelled in 1970. He was prosecuted by the state security forces for his part in the publication of the Czech "Black Book" of the Warsaw Pact invasion. He emigrated to FRG in 1976. From 1990 to 1998 he was the director of the Institute for Contemporary History, Czechoslovak Academy of Sciences.

24. Prečan, "K spolupráci," 133.

25. Prečan, "K spolupráci," 127.

26. Raška, *Long Road*, 135. Kavan had dual Czechoslovak and British citizenship.

27. Tereza Poláková, "Palach Press: Tisková a literární agentura: Studie o exilové agentuře a komparace její prezentace událostí s oficiálnimi československými médii," thesis, Univerzita Karlova, 2020, 26.

28. Poláková, *Palach Press*, 26.

29. Jiří Müller (1943) was a mechanical engineering student who was expelled from university in 1966, rehabilitated in 1968, arrested in 1971 for distributing leaflets explaining voters' rights, and imprisoned from 1971 to 1976. He was a Charter 77 signatory. He was prosecuted again in 1981–89 for political activities. After 1989 he was a representative for Civic Forum. He was a member of the Czech National Council from 1990 to 1992.

30. Poláková, *Palach Press*, 45.

31. Jiří Hájek (1913–93) was a politician and diplomat. He was the Czech ambassador to the United Kingdom (1955–58), a member of the Central Committee of the Communist Party of Czechoslovakia (1948–69), and the Minister of Foreign Affairs from April to September 1968. He was expelled from the Communist Party in 1970.

32. Poláková, *Palach Press*, 45–46.

33. Poláková, *Palach Press*, 46.

34. Raška, *Long Road*, 136.

35. Raška, *Long Road*, 31.

36. Raška, *Long Road*, 73.

37. Raška, *Long Road*, 166.

38. Long, *Making History*, 105.

39. "Jiřina Šiklová," Pamět Národa, https://www.pametnaroda.cz/en/siklova-jirina-1935.

40. Long, *Making History*, 103.

41. "Jiřina Šiklová."

42. Ludvík Vaculík (1926–2015) was a dissident writer and journalist, a progressive member of the pre-1968 Communist Party, and the author of "Two Thousand Words Manifesto to Workers, Scientists, Artists, and Everyone" (1968), in which he rebuked the Communist Party for losing sight of the

people's interests in exchange for maintaining power (Long, *Making History*, 2). He was a Charter 77 signatory. Peter Uhl (1941–2021) was a journalist, activist, and politician. He cofounded Charter 77 and the Committee for the Defense of the Unjustly Prosecuted (VONS). He served two prison sentences for dissident activities, the last (1979–84) for his involvement with VONS. He was a member of Parliament from 1990 to 1992.

43. Ludvík Vaculík, "Jiřina Š.," in *Kočka, která nikdy nespí*, ed. Vilém Prečan, trans. Gerald Turner (Praha: James Ottaway, Jr., 2005), 244.

44. Michal Plzák and Magdalena Čechlovská, eds., *Jiřina Šiklová: Bez ohlávky (rozhovory)* (Praha: Kalich, 2011), 183.

45. Milan Jaros, "Šiklová: Naučila jsem se koukat za sebe: S někdejší disidentkou o velkém dobrodružství, které nemohla s nikým sdílet," *Respekt*, June 21, 2015, https://www.respekt.cz/tydenik/2015/26/naucila-jsem-se-koukat-za-sebe (accessed January 28, 2022).

46. Jaros, "Šiklová."

47. Jaros, "Šiklová."

48. "Pašování samizdatů přerušila před 40 lety akce Delta," Pamět Národa, April 26, 2021, https://www.pametnaroda.cz/cs/magazin/stalo-se/pasovani-samizdatu-prerusila-pred-40-lety-akce-delta (accessed March 15, 2022).

49. *Fízl, Fízlové* (sing., pl.) is a pejorative term for agents of the StB. Though the precise origin of the term is unclear, a leading theory posits that the term is derived from the Austrian German colloquial term for "penis."

50. Jaros, "Šiklová."

51. Prečan, "From Some Remembered Correspondence," in Prečan, *Kočka, která nikdy nespí*, 234.

52. Prečan, "From Some Remembered Correspondence," 235.

53. Long, *Making History*, 107.

54. "Pašování samizdatů přerušila před 40 lety akce Delta."

55. Prečan, "From Some Remembered Correspondence," 238.

56. Prečan, "From Some Remembered Correspondence," 236.

57. Gordon Skilling, "To the Cat Who Never Sleeps," in Prečan, *Kočka, která nikdy nespí*, 242.

58. Prečan, "From Some Remembered Correspondence," 266.

59. Prečan, "From Some Remembered Correspondence," 267.

60. Prečan, "From Some Remembered Correspondence," 237.

61. *Index on Censorship* was founded in London. The first issue came out in May 1972. It was begun in response to the Soviet show trials of the defendants Yuli Daniel, Andrei Sinyavsky, and Alexander Ginzburg. It continues to publish works by writers who are repressed or banned in their home countries—for example, Alexander Solzhenitsyn, Vladimir Voinovich, Václav Havel, Tom Stoppard, and many others.

62. Jiřina Šiklová, "Save These Books," *Index on Censorship* 12, no. 2 (April 1, 1983), 37.

63. Šiklová, "Save These Books," 38.

64. Šiklová, "Save These Books," 39.

65. Šiklová, "Save These Books," 39.

66. Jiřina Šiklová, "Letter to Friends on Franz Kafka's Anniversary" (1981), in Prečan, *Kočka, která nikdy nespí*, 284.

67. Šiklová, "Letter to Friends," 285.

68. Petr Pithart, "Stronger Than Circumstances," in Prečan, *Kočka, která nikdy nespí*, 228.

69. Raška, *Long Road*, 157.

70. Prečan, "From Some Remembered Correspondence," 236.

71. Vaculík, "Jiřina Š.," 245.

72. Prečan, "From Some Remembered Correspondence," 236.

73. Pavel Orság, *Média československého exilu v letech 1948–1989 jako součast alternativní veřejné sféry*, dissertation, Palacký University Olomouc, 2011, 122. Quote found in *Listy*, no. 1 (1980), 5-7.

74. Long, *Making History*, 102.

75. Václav Havel, "The Power of the Powerless," trans. Paul Wilson, in *Living in Truth: Twenty-Two Essays Published on the Occasion of the Award of the Erasmus Prize to Václav Havel* (London: Faber and Faber, 1986), 87.

76. František Janouch (1931), a physicist, was the director of the Department of Nuclear Theory at the Institute of Nuclear Research, Czechoslovak Academy of Sciences (1960-70). He was exiled to Sweden in 1973. He founded the Charter 77 Foundation in 1978 to support Czechoslovak dissidents and the publication of dissident literature. Karel Schwarzenberg (1937), an entrepreneur and philanthropist, emigrated with his family from Czechoslovakia to Austria in 1948. He was the chair of the International Helsinki Conference for Human Rights from 1985 to 1990 and returned to Czechoslovakia in 1990), where he was the director of the Office of President Václav Havel (1990) and Chancellor of the Republic from 1990 to 1992.

77. Raška, *Long Road*, 152-54.

78. Raška, *Long Road*, 154.

79. *Edice Petlice* (Padlock Press, 1972-79), a samizdat journal of dissident literature founded and edited by Ludvík Vaculík.

80. Raška, *Long Road*, 154.

81. Raška, *Long Road*, 154.

82. "Zemřel Adolf Müller."

83. Poláková, *Palach Press*, 35.

84. "Vilém Prečan," March 29, 2022, Pamět Národa, https://www.pamet naroda.cz/cs/precan-vilem-1933.

85. Raška, *Long Road*, 157.

86. Reported by Jiřina Šiklová to the author in an interview in Prague in 1998.

87. Alena Wagnerová, "Three Days and Several Years in the Life of Jiřina Šiklová," in Prečan, *Kočka, která nikdy nespí*, 249.

88. Long, "Czech Dissident Zdeněk Mlynář's Memoir."

89. Jiřina Šiklová and Gerald Turner, "Courage, Heroism and the Postmodern Paradox," *Social Research* 71, no. 1 (Spring 2004), 135.

CHAPTER 9

The Unhappiest Barrack in the Soviet Bloc

Suicide, Well-Being, and Church-State Relations in Socialist Hungary

Patrick C. Leech

During the 1987 winter session of the National Assembly of the Hungarian People's Republic, the parliamentary body met to discuss the relationship between the state and the churches. Imre Miklós, a state secretary and president of the State Office for Church Affairs (SOCA), delivered a detailed statement. Notably, his comments consistently lauded the constructive, cooperative church-state relationship, noting that the churches actively contributed to Hungary's international standing via participation and leadership in global denominational and ecumenical forums, served as sites of Hungarian historical memory and culture, and conducted a variety of social welfare activities of the state. Miklós asserted, "Today it is only natural that—similarly to other communities—the churches also express their views on questions that are of concern to the entire people and that they take a share in the solution of social problems and promote social development."[1] This comment stands in sharp contrast to a view of the church held by state and party leaders decades earlier who, in alignment with Marxist-Leninist principles, systematically evicted religion from its role in the political, economic, social, and cultural life of Hungary through property confiscation, coercive antireligious policies, and prosecution of resistant church leaders. While the timing of this comment might appear to align with other shifts in the Soviet sphere, such as perestroika, in fact it is a result of a process that began at least a decade before.

The process by which the People's Republic of Hungary and the Hungarian Socialist Workers Party (MSZMP) came to embrace religion as a partner in addressing the country's social and moral problems is multifaceted and, at times, opaque.[2] The 1956 Uprising revealed the unpopularity of the previous party and the state's domestic illegitimacy; thus, the newly formed MSZMP, led by General Secretary János Kádár, quickly moved to reclaim dominance. Initially, they pursued harsh measures designed to root out "counterrevolutionaries" and to reestablish party control as the center of political, economic, and social power. Shortly after the 1959 execution of Imre Nagy and others convicted of treason during the 1956 revolt, the MSZMP felt securely in control of the levers of power.

In the early 1960s, the party shifted toward soft power policies to gain popular legitimacy. Kádár took full advantage of the cultural thaw and pursued social and economic policies that prioritized prosperity, ideas that Soviet Premier Nikita Khrushchev colorfully characterized as goulash.[3] Ideologically, goulash communism was a less-political form of destalinization that combined a flexible Marxist-Leninist ideology with various economic and social reforms. Practically, the leaders of the MSZMP, like their fraternal counterparts throughout the Soviet bloc, sought political stability through industrial development and economic advancement, although its approach was distinct. In 1966 the MSZMP introduced its signature economic policy: the New Economic Mechanism. The New Economic Mechanism, which went into effect on January 1, 1968, reduced the role of central planning and introduced various market-based mechanisms, including private enterprises and the reduction of price controls. Moreover, these economic changes coincided with social policies that relaxed some of the constraints on expression and dissent. This combination of social and economic programs formed the suite of policies also known as Kádárism. While not completely dissimilar to policies in other Warsaw Pact countries, Kádárism was widely seen as distinct, so much so that Hungary was known as the "happiest barrack in the Socialist bloc" due to its higher standards of living and greater tolerance of expression relative to its allies. These changes heralded a stable political system, improved economic standards of living, and expanded global economic and cultural interactions.[4]

Yet these political and economic measures provide only a partial picture. Concurrent with these developments, Hungary also experienced sharp increases in rates of suicide, divorce, and alcoholism that persisted into the 1990s. Such increases resulted in Hungary having the highest rate of suicide in the world.[5] In addition to the sheer human cost, the worsening of these problems troubled state and party leaders because Marxist ideology viewed social problems like alcoholism and suicide as symptoms of capitalism that would disappear with the advent of socialism. Yet, despite providing significant improvements in economic standards of living, the utopian promises of state socialism could not mass produce meaning, purpose, or happiness. So, when the ideologically correct solutions failed the state exhibited the same ideological flexibility it used with economics. Thus, even though the party kept its Marxist-Leninist ideology, persistent social problems led the state to partner with religious institutions for potential solutions.

Happiest Barrack or "Gloomy Sunday"?

On July 10, 1986, seventeen-year-old Csilla Andrea Molnár was found unconscious in her parents' home from an apparent overdose of lidocaine. A physician treating her observed that even though she briefly regained consciousness, "I could feel that she did not want our help. She wanted to die." Molnár was one of 4,817 suicides in 1986, yet hers received worldwide attention since she was Miss Hungary, having won the first nationwide beauty contest in 1985 and was second runner up in the Miss Europe contest in 1986. In 1969 when Molnár was born, Hungary was already experiencing a staggering annual rate of 33.1 suicide deaths per 100,000 people, the United Nations standard measurement of mortality rates.[6] Yet that rate would climb steeply until it peaked in 1983 at an annual rate of 45.9 suicide deaths per 100,000 people. The rate of suicide held steady for the next four years before entering a period of descent in 1988 (figure 9.1). Thus, Molnár's 1986 death occurred during the height of the suicide epidemic in Hungary. One factor that may have contributed to her death was the controversy surrounding the Miss Hungary contest, including critiques that such contests were exploitative and capitalist.[7] Like so many others, Molnár experienced the benefits of the social and economic changes of Kádárism, yet her death reflects a hopelessness rooted in the inability of state socialism to foster all aspects of human flourishing.

These developments were not unknown to party and state officials. In 1969 the Hungarian journalist Mihály Gergely wrote an extensive article examining the growing suicide crisis for *Kortárs*, a leading Hungarian journal. He sifted through official statistics, interviewed

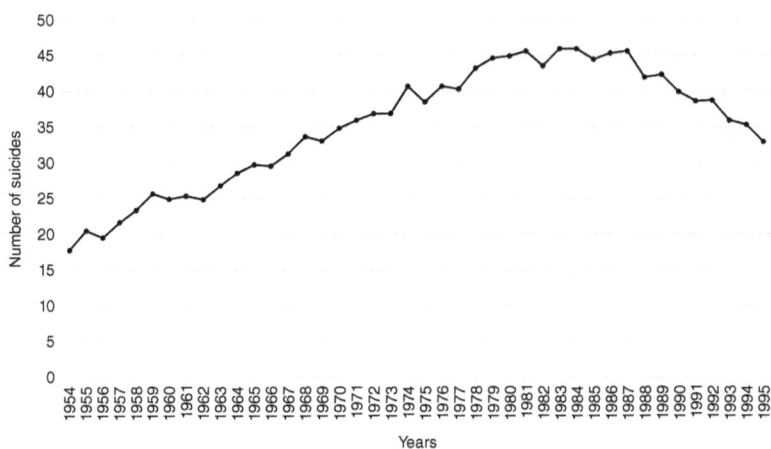

FIGURE 9.1.   Hungary, rates of suicide per 100,000 people, 1954–1995
Source: UN Statistical Office, *Demographic Yearbooks* (New York: United Nations, 1957, 1961, 1966, 1974, 1980, 1985, 1986, 1987, 1996). https://unstats.un.org/unsd/demographic-social/products/dyb/. Created by author.

medical and psychological professionals, parsed suicide notes, and consulted everything from theoretical texts to professional publications. He noted that historically Hungary experienced higher rates of suicide than did much of the world. For comparison, the 1961–63 average annual rate of suicide in Hungary was 33.9 deaths per 100,000 people, while for the same period the average rates of suicide in Poland, Czechoslovakia, and the United States were 28.2, 12.8, and 15.6 deaths per 100,000, respectively.[8] Yet high suicide rates were not unprecedented for Hungary. Gergely noted that between 1897 and 1932 the rate rose from 21 to 35.1 deaths per 100,000. During the postwar period the rate declined, reaching its lowest rate of the twentieth century (17.7) in 1954. Throughout the 1950s the rate stayed in the low twenties but started climbing as the decade closed. Thus, alarms sounded when the rate climbed to 26.8 in 1963 and then to 28.6 in 1964, rates not seen since the tumultuous interwar period. Throughout the rest of the 1960s, the overall suicide rate continued to increase, reaching 33.1 deaths per 100,000 in 1969.[9] Ultimately, Gergely concluded that the public needed a crisis hotline and more education about recognizing suicidal intentions, while professionals needed more and better mental-health facilities and treatment options. Overall, he makes clear that the public, professionals, party members, and policy makers were all aware and concerned about this social malady. He also reveals that they were ill equipped to address it.[10]

Two decades after Gergely's report, and a year after Molnár's 1986 suicide, the *New York Times* published an article about the Hungarian government's newest efforts to study the problem of suicide. The article echoes much of Gergely's reporting from 1969, including a discussion of Hungary's historically high suicide rates. The article noted that rates were even more staggering than they had been in the mid-1960s and quoted Dr. Béla Buda, a Hungarian psychiatrist who cited the nearly five thousand suicides a year and estimated ten times as many attempts. Strikingly, the strongest parallel comes from observations by Buda and his colleague, Dr. László Cseh-Szombathy, on the causes of suicides, which they ascribed to the "far-reaching social transformation that followed the installation of a Communist regime" in 1956 and the subsequent policies during which the "established family and community bonds were weakened or broken."[11] As Gergely noted, "From 1914 onwards . . . all generations have been war generations" who witnessed war, revolution, counter-revolution, the threat of thermonuclear war, and the related "suffering which followed, the disillusionment, the destruction of religious and traditional beliefs in the great upheavals of science and progress. This is the social background to suicide."[12] Tragically, these eerily similar verdicts point to a state that was as overwhelmed and ill equipped to foster well-being in 1986 as it had been in 1969.

While the composite suicide rate was very high, some parts of the population experienced even higher rates. Three subsets of the Hungarian population warrant a brief mention. First, Gergely noted that between 1961 and 1965, suicide was the fourth leading cause of death for Hungary's children aged ten to fourteen and the leading cause for adolescents aged fifteen to nineteen at rates that significantly surpassed their European peers.[13] Sadly, two decades later, a report on Hungarian children noted that between three hundred and four hundred children under the age of fourteen attempted suicide each year, although not many succeeded.[14] Second, other vulnerable populations such as those over sixty, women, unskilled and low-skilled workers, and those living in rural areas often experienced suicide rates higher than the national average.[15] Third, Gergely noticed that those who abused alcohol were significantly more likely to commit suicide.[16] Additionally, a 1993 study found that between 1950 and 1990 annual per capita alcohol consumption and annual rates of suicide were "connected in an intimate way, as the annual fluctuations in consumption [were] typically followed by significant parallel changes in suicide rates the following year."[17]

In all three circumstances—children, vulnerable populations, and high alcohol consumption—these individuals were particularly vulnerable to suicide.

While the statistics of suicide quantify the severity of the problem, they are not the only evidence. For example, there are many Hungarian cultural connections to suicide. Numerous major political and cultural figures died by suicide, including the statesman István Széchenyi, the geographer and politician Pál Teleki, and the poet Attila József—all of whom have streets, buildings, and other public spaces, named after them throughout Hungary. Similarly, in 1976 a famous Hungarian actor, Zoltán Latinovits, while struggling with his own mental health and preparing for a portrayal of József, committed suicide, reenacting József's unusual death.[18] The cultural association of Hungary with suicide reached international recognition with the success of the song "Szomorú Vasárnap" (1933). Translated as "Gloomy Sunday," this song about grieving for a recently deceased lover was recorded by Paul Robeson in 1936, made famous by Billie Holiday, and recorded by over seventy other artists around the world. It is also rumored to have contributed to dozens of suicides around the world, earning it infamy as the "Hungarian suicide song."[19]

These statistical and cultural connections between suicidality and Hungary have prompted numerous academic studies. While a meta-analysis of such studies is outside the scope of this chapter, as a whole they point to suicide as a complex phenomenon with numerous biological, environmental, economic, social, and cultural factors that complicate comprehension and comparison.[20] Nevertheless, what is clear is that Hungary experienced a significant increase in the rate of suicide between 1961 and 1988. Furthermore, these increases alarmed policy makers who were stymied as to solutions.

Marxist ideology asserted that resolving the fundamental inequities of the capitalist system would produce prosperity and flourishing. Yet even in a state with rising standards of living, instead of flourishing, Hungary experienced anomie. While this chapter highlights suicidality, Hungary also faced rates of alcohol consumption and divorce that often were the highest in the world.[21] Significantly, the increases in each of these social problems rose concurrently with the rising standards of living associated with goulash communism. Furthermore, despite intentional state intervention, these trends continued to increase into the 1980s. Taken together, these social maladies reveal that despite its best efforts, the Hungarian state could not manufacture meaning for people and that the traditional cultural institutions that could do so, such as churches, were absent.[22] Thus, Kádárism did not produce a socialist utopia; instead, Hungary became the unhappiest barrack in the Socialist bloc.

Changes in Church-State Relations

Culturally, religion, particularly Christianity, has played a critical role in the formation of Hungarian identity from the establishment of the Kingdom of Hungary in 1,000 CE under the now beatified King István I, and through the efforts of Protestant churches to foster a Hungarian national identity in opposition to the Catholic Habsburg monarchy during the nineteenth century. This blending of national identity and Christianity reached its peak during the interwar years when Christianity came to symbolize allegiance to the state and resistance to communism. While the upper levels of Hungarian society were quite open to assimilated Jews, the linkage of Christianity to nationalism increasingly cast the loyalty of Jews into doubt. During World War II, while Hungary allied with Germany, Miklós Horthy, regent of the Kingdom of Hungary, largely protected the Jews of Hungary. But a German military invasion in 1944 resulted in Nazi control and an abbreviated but highly efficient mass deportation and execution of Hungarian Jewry. The result was a postwar Hungary that was more religiously homogeneous and the association of fascism with Christian-nationalism. While Hungary was approximately 85 percent Christian, there was also dissatisfaction with the disproportionate political power of the Christian churches.[23]

This strong connection between Christianity and national identity represented a significant problem for Hungarian Communists after the creation of the Hungarian People's Republic in 1949. While precise figures are difficult to obtain, in 1949 approximately 60 percent of the entire population identified as Roman Catholic, a figure that included a small Uniate population. The Hungarian Reformed Church, a Calvinist denomination, was the largest Protestant denomination with slightly over 20 percent of the population. The next largest Protestant denomination was the Hungarian Evangelical Lutheran Church with around 5 percent of the population. Other Protestant denominations comprised less than 1 percent of the total population. Altogether, approximately 85 percent of the population in 1949 identified as Christian.[24] However, the latent postwar dissatisfaction with the power of the churches is evidenced by the public support for laws that expropriated church lands (1945), liberalized divorce (1947), secularized education (1948), and even enshrined freedom of religion and expression in the 1949 Constitution.[25]

While these actions were generally popular, the churches, particularly the Catholic Church, fought to retain their political position. This resulted in intrachurch divisions as some leaders, like the Catholic Cardinal József Mindszenty and the Lutheran Bishop Lajos Ordass, vocally opposed the Communist government established in 1949, while others, generally known as "peace priests," hoped to work within the new constitutional order.[26] Ultimately, the state arrested, tried, and convicted senior leaders like Mindszenty and Ordass for their opposition. These show trials, seen as coercive, were unpopular, as were the highly restrictive agreements the state imposed on the churches.[27] Yet by fall 1956, state control of the churches was sufficiently accomplished that leaders like Ordass and Mindszenty were being released.[28]

The release and reinstatement of dissident religious leaders during the 1956 uprising led to another round of crackdowns as the MSZMP exerted its authority over society. Yet the state also recognized that religion would not die quickly and thus opted for less hostile forms of control designed to maintain pressure while gaining legitimacy. For instance, in exchange for loyalty oaths from clergy, the state began supplying 25 percent of their salaries. Similarly, the state began allowing individuals to donate to religious institutions but capped donations to 1 percent of the individual's income. These measures represented a grudging acceptance of the reality of religious life despite persistent control mechanisms. Simultaneously, the state enacted measures that harassed congregants, including making the already limited opportunities for religious education more difficult, denying employment or promotions to admitted believers, and restricting access to higher education for believers and their children.[29] Thus while the government began to tolerate mild forms of nonsocialist social and cultural expression, it tightly controlled the window of tolerated forms of religious life. The intent of this dichotomy was to garner legitimacy for party governance via social and cultural tolerance while maintaining control over its most dangerous rival.

The first major shift in church policy came on September 15, 1964, when the Peoples' Republic of Hungary and the Holy See entered into an agreement that resolved many of the contentious issues between the two states. While it was not full, mutual, diplomatic recognition, this agreement marked the first time a Communist state and the Vatican brokered any agreement on the status of the Roman Catholic Church. The agreement created space for eventually resolving the status of Cardinal Mindszenty, established a process for the appointment of bishops and other members of the ecclesial hierarchy, and allowed for Hungarian bishops to participate in church affairs outside of Hungary, including the ongoing Second Vatican Council. Thus, Hungary became the flagship state of Pope Paul VI's *Ostpolitik* (Eastern policy). This agreement also marked the return of religious leaders of all denominations to participation in international denominational and ecumenical activities and even leadership. This agreement served the state's efforts to garner more legitimacy abroad. It also granted the state additional domestic support in checking the "quasi-underground church" and assistance in combating Hungary's social ills, such as suicide, alcoholism, and depression.[30]

The year 1971 marked the beginning of a new relationship between the Hungarian state and religious institutions, particularly churches. From 1956, Mindszenty's internal exile in the US Embassy spoiled Hungary's relations with both the Holy See and the United States, and served as an ever-present challenge to the domestic legitimacy of the state and the MSZMP. Pope Paul VI changed this in 1971 by announcing the retirement of Mindszenty over the objections of Mindszenty himself. In an unofficial agreement, the Hungarian government granted Mindszenty permission to leave the country, while the Holy See refused to grant him retirement in the Vatican. Additionally, neither side exercised its ability to appoint a replacement until after his death in 1975. This arrangement not only removed a vocal domestic opponent and the most prominent anticommunist church leader but also started the process for the establishment of diplomatic relations with the United States in 1978. This resolution of the Mindszenty affair greatly reduced domestic and international tensions for Hungary.[31] Additionally, in 1971 Imre Miklós was appointed president of SOCA. Under his leadership SOCA worked with church leaders to navigate challenges from internal dissenters, to participate in and lead international denominational and ecumenical organizations, and to have an expanded role for religion within socialist society. While resolving the Mindszenty affair had immediate results, the significance of Miklós's appointment would become clear only later.

The combination of goulash communism, the resolution of religion-related diplomatic and domestic questions, new state and church leadership, and an anomic society laid the foundation for a major shift in church-state relations.[32] One of the first indications of change came in 1976 when György Aczél, a key leader of the MSZMP with influence on cultural policies, published an article in the ideological journal *Világosság*. In it he posited a simple framework for church-state cooperation: since both ideologies would continue to exist and both "have to answer the same questions in the same world," it is therefore "possible" and "essential" that they work together "on behalf of humanity and in order to extinguish the flames of hatred and war."[33] Aczél, in a break with traditional Marxist ideology, asserted that religion would not soon wither but rather continue to exist for the foreseeable future, and as such could be a viable partner for a socialist state on areas of agreement despite fundamental ideological differences. This article foreshadowed the pronouncement of the alliance policy by János Kádár in 1977 that recognized the state's "co-operation on the basis of common interests and aims" with noncommunist entities. In that speech, Kádár explicitly cited the common interests of socialism and religion as "the basis of the normalized relations between State and Church in Hungary."[34] Based on the alliance policy, Miklós published an article in *Világosság* that announced a new relationship between the state and the churches and noted that the two could collaborate on areas such as international peace, "socialist national unity," caring for people, encouraging work, fighting "delinquency," and cultivating "progressive traditions of our national past."[35] This policy shift marked the origins of the "unique," mutual, cooperative church-state relationship that Miklós frequently discussed.[36]

The Church and Social Problems

As the relationship between church and state improved, there was a consistent inclusion of church leaders in forums to address various economic, social, cultural, and moral issues. For example, in December 1982 church leaders met with Imre Pozsgay, the recently selected General Secretary of the Hungarian Patriotic People's Front, the state's elected assembly. Official reporting of the meeting described it as a discussion of "current economic difficulties" and emphasized the agreement between all present on the proposed solutions.[37] The next month, an article by József Cserháti, Secretary of the Bench of Hungarian Bishops, in a Hungarian Catholic magazine asserted that given the settled nature of church-state relations, the church had a right to "ask for the trust" to openly work on social questions such as the economic situation, "the crisis in the family," and "disillusionment among youth."[38] Moreover, he asserted that "today's social situation undoubtedly requires the reopening of the inner resources of the Church."[39] A week later, Péter Bugár, a senior leader in SOCA, addressed a group of Catholic priests about the "great test" faced by Hungarian society and how the alliance policy was creating opportunities for cooperation.[40] A Radio Free Europe researcher observing these events described them as the "opening of safety valves to relieve social and economic tension" and as an "experiment aimed at improving both the national mood and public morality."[41] Here a pattern emerges of the state publicly working with churches on issues at the heart of Kádárism: economic prosperity and social well-being. What is particularly notable about these reports is the lack of specifics. Instead, problems are described as economic, social, or moral issues and the struggling populations are the young, the elderly, and the family. Such broad categories effectively include the entire populace and a wide range of challenges. The generalities implied an acute awareness of political sensitivities that required parsing and interpretation.

For example, on January 26, 1984, church leaders again met with Pozsgay to discuss "the social and economic aims" of the state. The church leaders expressed their support and emphasized the distress of pensioners, large families, and early career professionals.[42] One of the rare exceptions to the generic statements came from Imre Miklós in 1987. He described churches as "recognized institutions of the socialist society" and noted that they could advance socialism and humanism, encourage work, and aid "in the fight against crime, alcoholism and drug abuse, in the care of endangered youth on the fringe of society, and [in] charitable social work."[43] Even in Miklós's report, however, one notes the persistence of vague sloganeering and socialist encoded references to unspecified challenges.

Fortunately, contemporary observers can provide interpretive insights. For example, Zoltan Kovacs and Edith Markos, researchers for Radio Free Europe, utilized numerous Hungarian-language periodicals to assemble reports highlighting the ways that state leaders sought help from Hungarian churches in addressing a variety of economic and social challenges. They interpreted these events as official authorization for Hungarian churches to take on a greater role in social issues than would previously have been tolerated.[44] Similarly, John Eibner, a researcher at Keston College, wrote in 1985 that "the state has an interest in the existence of churches that are capable of taking up the challenge of social reform, and it promotes that interest by granting increased scope for public worship, evangelism, education, and social work." Eibner went further and noted that while previously the state expected political support from the churches, now that state was "also looking to the churches for help in solving the country's problems, e.g., high levels of suicide, divorce, alcoholism and corruption in public and commercial life."[45] While the institutional affiliations of Markos, Kovacs, and Eibner may raise questions about their bias, even Marxist scholars like János Jori concurred. In an interview about the increasing interest in religion in Hungary, Jori praised the "community-building capacity" of religion as life giving. In explaining the "stabilizing role" of churches, particularly in helping with "youth problems," he said, "Some of our young people feel a sense of helplessness and that, unfortunately, often leads to deviant habits, alcoholism, crime, or suicide."[46] When viewed through the comments of Kovacs, Markos, Eibner, and Jori, the statements of Hungarian leaders like Miklós and Pozsgay become clearer: portions of Hungarian society struggled with alcoholism, drug abuse, divorce, and suicide. While these problems afflicted only minorities of the population, they were significant enough to warrant the attention of the state; moreover, they were severe enough for the state to seek the assistance of churches to address them.

This interpretation is also supported by the actions of those churches in response to the invitation to help. During the 1980s, churches launched a variety of programs to aid alcoholics, drug addicts, the elderly, teens, and families by providing a variety of social services.[47] The Reformed Church even operated a mental-health hotline staffed by physicians and psychiatrists.[48] In support of these efforts, the state significantly increased its financial support of the churches and opened previously closed service opportunities, such as the establishment of a new Catholic service order, Sisters of Our Lady of Hungary.[49] One of the most striking examples was a state-sanctioned evangelistic tour featuring David Wilkerson, an American minister, and Nicky Cruz, a converted former gang leader, speaking to teens, parents, and doctors to discuss the problems of drug and alcohol abuse among teens.[50]

Whether considering statements from political leaders and outside observers, or the actions of the churches themselves, a pattern emerges that defines the social problems that both the state and churches faced: drug and alcohol abuse, family disruptions, petty crime, and social dislocation. These categories of problems were paired with specific populations of concern: children, adolescents, women, and the elderly. While suicide is not specifically in this list, it is nevertheless included, as family disruption, social dislocation, and alcohol abuse were three common causes of suicide. Similarly, adolescents, women, and the elderly were three populations with elevated risks for suicide.[51] Regardless of whether suicide mitigation was a stated purpose of these programs, the social services provided by churches addressed many of the root causes of suicide.

On November 19, 1989, a short article with the headline *VÉGRE!* ("FINALLY!") appeared in *Új Ember*, a Hungarian Catholic weekly newspaper. The article celebrated the significant drop in Hungary's national suicide rate in 1988. While the article cautiously explained the unequal improvements within vulnerable populations, it also struck a hopeful note that this marked a long-term trend.[52] The headline reveals that the Catholic Church, and likely other churches as well, was aware of and concerned about Hungary's suicide rate. The headline also implies that the churches had worked to address this problem.

Between 1960 and 1989, while Hungarians experienced economic prosperity due to Kádárism, they also experienced high levels of social dysfunction, most notably in escalating rates of suicide, alcohol consumption, and divorce. While Kádár's Hungary may have been the least restrictive barrack in the Socialist bloc, it was certainly not the happiest. This period also witnessed a gradual evolution in church-state relations with the most significant changes occurring after the 1977 adoption of the alliance policy, which allowed for noncommunist organizations to work with the state on areas of mutual interest for the benefit of the people. For the churches, this meant greater access to the public sphere followed by the invitation to provide social services to address crime, drug and alcohol abuse, juvenile delinquency, family planning and education, and elder care. While specific measures to address suicide are not mentioned, many of these problems were causes of suicide.[53] Moreover, the churches also provided some mental-health services and were clearly aware of the rates of suicide. Significantly, many of these initiatives began in the early 1980s, immediately before the rate of suicide stabilized from 1984 to 1988. Although measuring the immediate or long-term effects of social programs is quite difficult, one point seems relevant. Unlike most of the other social problems the churches sought to address, suicide represents an individual's sense of hopelessness in that moment, making it a more sensitive measure of immediate change. Hence, it is noteworthy that suicide rates plateaued at the same moment of the expansion of religious-based social services. Although it would be reductionist to credit the expanded role of religion with flattening the rising suicide rate, it does seem the cooperative church-state relationship may have provided a sense of hope for a different future.

Notes

1. *The State and the Churches in Hungary* (Budapest: Budapress, 1987), 5, Hungary General Subject Files, box 4, folder 15, Keston Center for Religion, Politics, and Society (KCRPS).

2. The Hungarian Socialist Workers' Party (*Magyar Szocialista Munkáspárt*, MSZMP) was the Soviet-aligned Communist party that governed Hungary from 1957 until 1989. It was established during the 1956 Uprising because the previous party, the Hungarian Working People's Party (*Magyar Dolgozók Pártja*, MDP), had been discredited in the eyes of the Hungarian people and Moscow. Yet the MSZMP, with János Kádár as its leader, initially owed its position to the Soviet Union and the Red Army, which were two of the root causes of the revolt in 1956. Thus, Kádár and the MSZMP sought to ease their own feelings of illegitimacy through generous, and often debt-funded, economic and social programs. These programs and the experimentation with greater tolerance for personal expression marked Hungary as anomalous among the Warsaw Pact countries, thus the "happiest barrack" appellation. These policies successfully garnered popular support for Kádár that lasted until his death in 1989. Yet that support was not extended to the party. Moreover, the debt-funded social and economic programs eventually resulted in Hungary seeking trade and loans from the West, which pressed for economic, social, and political reforms. As a result, the state enacted major political reforms, including a multiparty system in 1988. These reforms split the MSZMP between reformers and traditionalists, while the election of 1989 allowed public opposition to the Soviet-aligned government. While the MSZMP retained power into the early 1990s, it did so as a social democratic party.

3. The term "goulash communism" appears to have originated from a series of speeches given by Soviet Premier Nikita Khrushchev during a visit to Budapest in 1964. In his characteristically earthy style, Khrushchev repeatedly used the term for the traditional Hungarian beef stew, *gulyás*, to connect the policy shifts to promote economic prosperity with common citizen concerns. See Paul Underwood, "Khrushchev Says Primary Red Aim Is a Better Life," *The New York Times*, April 2, 1964, https://www.nytimes.com/1964/04/02/archives/khrushchev-says-primary-red-aim-is-a-better-life-in-gibe-at-peking.html; "Moscow's 'Goulash' Communism," *The New York Times*, April 3, 1964, https://www.nytimes.com/1964/04/03/archives/moscows-goulash-communism.html; David C. Humphrey and Charles S. Sampson, eds., "Document 20 'Summary Record of National Security Council Meeting No. 525,'" in *Soviet Union, Foreign Relations of the United States 1964–1968*, vol. 14 (Washington, DC: Government Printing Office, 2001), 20.

4. See Oscar Sanchez-Sibony, *Red Globalization* (Cambridge: Cambridge University Press, 2017); Cristofer Scarboro, Diana Mincyte, and Zsuzsa Gille, eds., *The Socialist Good Life: Desire, Development, and Standards of Living in Eastern Europe* (Bloomington: Indiana University Press, 2020); Theodora Dragostinova, *The Cold War from the Margins: A Small Socialist State on the Global Cultural Scene* (Ithaca, NY: Cornell University Press, 2021).

5. Mihaly Gergely, "Suicide in Hungary," *New Hungarian Quarterly* 42 (1971): 143–55; Gabriel Ronay, "Suicide in Hungary Now of 'Epidemic Proportions,'" *The Times* (London), March 16, 1972, Hungary General Subject Files, box 4, folder 10, KCRPS.

6. The rates cited in this chapter are compiled from annual cause-of-death statistics reported in multiple volumes of the United Nations Demographic Yearbooks, including a variety of demographic data as reported by each member state. For each cause of death, the tables include a count and a normalized rate of deaths per 100,000 population. Since the rate is normalized relative to population, it allows for easier year-to-year and international comparisons.

7. Associated Press, "Miss Hungary Commits Suicide," *Daily Telegraph* (London), July 12, 1986, Hungary General Subject Files, box 9, folder 3, KCRPS; United Press International, "Fatal Beauty—Miss Hungary Kills Herself after Having Trouble Coping," *Houston Chronicle*, July 12, 1986, NewsBank, Inc., Access World News, https://infoweb.newsbank.com/apps/news/document-view?p=AWNB&docref=news/0ED7AC530043F339; United Press International, "Seventeen-Year-Old Csilla Andrea Molnar, the Current Miss Hungary, Committed . . . ," July 11, 1986, UPI Archives Online, https://www.upi.com/Archives/1986/07/11/Seventeen-year-old-Csilla-Andrea-Molnar-the-current-Miss-Hungary-committed/7163521438400/.

8. Gergely, "Suicide in Hungary," 143.

9. Gergely, "Suicide in Hungary," 144.

10. Gergely, "Suicide in Hungary," 154–55.

11. Henry Kamm, "Hungary Seeks Way to Cut High Suicide Rate," *The New York Times*, July 30, 1987.

12. Gergely, "Suicide in Hungary," 153.

13. Gergely, "Suicide in Hungary," 145.

14. Judith Pataki, "Children in Eastern Europe: Hungary," Background Report, Radio Free Europe Research, October 26, 1987, 26–27, Hungary General Subject Files, box 9, folder 2, KCRPS.

15. Roger Boyes, "Misfits and the Elderly Pay Price for Success," *The New York Times*, February 8, 1984, Hungary General Subject Files, box 9, folder 3, KCRPS; Ole-Jørgen Skog and Zsuzsanna Elekes, "Alcohol and the 1950–90 Hungarian Suicide Trend: Is There a Causal Connection?" *Acta Sociologica* 36, no. 1 (January 1, 1993): 33–46, doi.org/10.1177/000169939303600103.

16. Gergely, "Suicide in Hungary."

17. Skog and Elekes, "Alcohol and the 1950–90 Hungarian Suicide Trend."

18. *Situation Report: Hungary, 10 June 1976*, June 10, 1976, HU OSA 300-8-47:22/3-20, Situation Reports, Publications Department, Records of Radio Free Europe/Radio Liberty Research Institute, Vera and Donald Blinken Open Society Archives at Central European University, Budapest, https://catalog.

archivum.org/catalog/osa:3b1739e9-8b87-45f9-8c47-4193e0c062bd;   Steven
Stack, Karolina Krysinska, and David Lester, "Gloomy Sunday: Did the 'Hun-
garian Suicide Song' Really Create a Suicide Epidemic?," *OMEGA—Journal of
Death and Dying* 56, no. 4 (June 2008): 349–58, doi.org/10.2190/OM.56.4.c.

19. Stack, Krysinska, and Lester, "Gloomy Sunday."

20. A simple search for "Hungary" and "suicide" in a university library database produced hundreds of medical, psychological, and sociological studies of
suicide for Hungary.

21. Gergely, "Suicide in Hungary"; Special Correspondent, "Hungary's
'Marriage School': Way to Boost Lagging Birthrate?," *The Christian Science Moni-
tor*, January 22, 1974, Hungary General Subject Files, box 9, folder 3, KCRPS;
Richard Bassett, "Hungarians Hit Bottle," *The Times* (London), February 4,
1986, Hungary General Subject Files, box 9, folder 3, KCRPS; Judith Pataki,
"Alcoholism in Eastern Europe: Hungary," RAD Background Report, Radio
Free Europe Research, July 30, 1987, Hungary General Subject Files, box 9,
folder 3, KCRPS.

22. Miklós Tomka, "Secularization or Anomy?—Interpreting Religious
Change in Communist Societies," in *Living in Truth: Catholics in Eastern Europe:
Report of the Pax Christi International Congress, Hilversum, October 31–November 4,
1989*, ed. Wilco de Jonge (Den Haag: Pax Christi Netherlands, 1989), 1–16.

23. Paul A. Hanebrink, *In Defense of Christian Hungary: Religion, Nationalism,
and Antisemitism, 1890–1944* (Ithaca, NY: Cornell University Press, 2006); Péter
Török, *Hungarian Church-State Relationships: A Socio-Historical Analysis* (Budapest:
Hungarian Institute for Sociologie of Religion, 2003); Leslie Laszlo, "Religion
and Nationality in Hungary," in *Religion and Nationalism in Soviet and East Euro-
pean Politics*, ed. Sabrina P. Ramet (Durham, NC: Duke University Press, 1984);
Yoko Aoshima, ed., *Entangled Interactions between Religions and National Identities
in the Eastern Borderland of Europe* (Boston: Academic Studies Press, 2020); Paul
Lendvai, *The Hungarians: A Thousand Years of Victory in Defeat*, trans. Ann Major
(Princeton, NJ: Princeton University Press, 2021).

24. Paul Froese, "Hungary for Religion: A Supply-Side Interpretation of the
Hungarian Religious Revival," *Journal for the Scientific Study of Religion* 40, no. 2
(2001), 253; "Hungary," Keston Institute, September 1974, Hungary General
Subject Files, box 4, folder 10, KCRPS.

25. "Hungary," KCRPS; John A. Coleman, S. J., "Spiritual Resistance in Eastern Europe," *Proceedings of the Academy of Political Science* 38, no. 1 (1991): 113–
28, doi.org/10.2307/1173817; Paul Mojzes, *Religious Liberty in Eastern Europe
and the USSR: Before and after the Great Transformation*, East European Monographs 337 (New York: Columbia University Press, 1992); Froese, "Hungary for
Religion."

26. Cardinal József Mindszenty was Archbishop of Esztergom and Prince-
Primate of Hungary, and as such was the leader of the Roman Catholic Church
in Hungary. He was also a strident monarchist who had been arrested by the
Communist government in 1919, the Nazi-aligned Arrow Cross Party in 1944,
and then by the Communists in 1948. Convicted in a show trial in 1949, he
remained in prison until his release during the 1956 Revolution. When the
Red Army re-entered Budapest on November 4, 1956, Mindszenty was granted

asylum in the US consulate. Bishop Lajos Ordass (née Wolf) was a bishop in the Evangelical Lutheran Church in Hungary. His vocal opposition to both the fascists and the communists led to his multiple arrests. He was convicted in a show trial in 1949 and remained in prison until the 1956 Revolution. In 1958 he was forced into retirement.

27. Keston College, "The Price of Prosperity: Church and State in Hungary," *Keston News Service*, March 22, 1984, Hungary General Subject Files, box 4, folder 15, KCRPS.

28. "Hungary," KCRPS; Coleman, "Spiritual Resistance"; Froese, "Hungary for Religion"; Török, *Hungarian Church-State Relationships*; H. David Baer, *The Struggle of Hungarian Lutherans under Communism* (College Station: Texas A&M University Press, 2006); Eniko Böröcz, "Lajos Ordass: A Christian and a Consistent Adversary of the Totalitarian Systems," in *Christianity and Resistance in the 20th Century: From Kaj Munk and Dietrich Bonhoeffer to Desmond Tutu*, ed. Sören Zibrandt von Dosenrode-Lynge, International Studies in Religion and Society 8 (Leiden: Brill, 2009), 203–32; András Fejérdy, *Pressed by a Double Loyalty* (Budapest: Central European University Press, 2016); Nandor Dreisziger, *Church and Society in Hungary and in the Hungarian Diaspora* (Toronto: University of Toronto Press, 2016); András Fejérdy and Bernadett Wirthné Diera, eds., *The Trial of Cardinal József Mindszenty from the Perspective of Seventy Years: The Fate of Church Leaders in Central and Eastern Europe* (Vatican: Libreria Editrice Vaticana, 2021).

29. Froese, "Hungary for Religion"; Michael T. Hickling, "The Christian Churches in Hungary," [c. 1972], Hungary General Subject Files, box 4, folder 10, KCRPS; "Focus on Hungary," *Crusade*, May 1977, Hungary General Subject Files, box 4, folder 10, KCRPS; Moira Cubie, "In Hungary Too . . . A Christian's Lot Is Not an Easy One," *Life and Work*, March 1980, Hungary General Subject Files, box 4, folder 10, KCRPS; Moira Cubie, Rev. Istvan G. J. Kardos, and Zsigmond Vad, "Second Post: The Church in Hungary," *Life and Work*, June 1980, Hungary General Subject Files, box 4, folder 10, KCRPS.

30. Krisztián Ungváry, "The Kádár Regime and the Roman Catholic Hierarchy," *Hungarian Quarterly* 48, no. 187 (September 2007), 83; Fejérdy, *Pressed by a Double Loyalty*; Nandor Dreisziger, *Church and Society in Hungary*, 133; Coleman, "Spiritual Resistance in Eastern Europe."

31. Hickling, "The Christian Churches in Hungary"; Mojzes, *Religious Liberty in Eastern Europe and the USSR*; Török, *Hungarian Church-State Relationships*; Lorenz M. Lüthi, *Cold Wars: Asia, the Middle East, Europe* (Cambridge: Cambridge University Press, 2020); Martin Mevius, "A Crown for Rakosi: The Vogeler Case, the Holy Crown of St. Stephen, and the (Inter)National Legitimacy of the Hungarian Communist Regime, 1945–1978," *The Slavonic and East European Review* 89, no. 1 (2011): 76–107, doi.org/10.5699/slaveasteurorev2.89.1.0076; Fejérdy and Diera, *The Trial of Cardinal József Mindszenty*; Margaret Murányi Manchester, "The Corporate Dimension of the Cold War in Hungary: ITT and the Vogeler/Sanders Case Reconsidered," *Journal of Cold War Studies* 23, no. 2 (May 28, 2021): 41–74, doi.org/10.1162/jcws_a_00983; Árpád von Klimó, "Anticommunism and Détente: Mindszenty, the Catholic Church, and Hungarian Émigrés in West Germany, 1972," *Central European History* 54, no. 3 (September 2021): 466–90, doi.org/10.1017/S0008938920001089.

32. These domestic factors were likely supported by international shifts, as they also closely parallel the end of brinkmanship, détente, and then glasnost. This idea is reinforced when considered in light of the annual intrabloc meetings of the State Offices of Church Affairs, a series of events mentioned in Lüthi, *Cold Wars*; and Böröcz, "Lajos Ordass."

33. György Aczél, "The State and the Churches in Hungary," trans. Ecumenical Council of Churches in Hungary, *Hungarian Church Press*, December 1, 1976, Hungary General Subject Files, box 4, folder 15, KCRPS; György Aczél, "The Socialist State and the Churches in Hungary (A Translation with Comment by the Hungarian Unit)," RAD Background Report, trans. RFE Research Hungarian Unit, Radio Free Europe Research, December 14, 1976, Hungary General Subject Files, box 4, folder 15, KCRPS.

34. János Kádár, "Some Lessons of Socialist Construction in Hungary," trans. Ecumenical Council of Churches in Hungary, *Hungarian Church Press*, March 1, 1977, Hungary General Subject Files, box 4, folder 15, KCRPS; János Kádár, *The Renewal of Socialism in Hungary: Selected Speeches and Interviews, 1957–1986*, trans. Mrs. Istvan Butykai et al. (Budapest: Corvina, 1987).

35. "Minutes of the British Council of Churches (BCC) Department of International Affairs (DIA) East-West Relations Advisory Committee (EWRAC)," February 14, 1978, Hungary General Subject Files, box 4, folder 15, KCRPS; Imre Miklós, "New-Type Relations: Development of the Relations between State and Churches in Hungary," trans. Ecumenical Council of Churches in Hungary, *Hungarian Church Press*, February 15, 1977, Hungary General Subject Files, box 4, folder 15, KCRPS; "Basic Concepts of Government Policy toward the Churches," *Osteuropa*, no. 7 (1977), Hungary General Subject Files, box 4, folder 15, KCRPS.

36. Darrell Turner, "Hungarian Official Calls Status of Religion in His Country Unique," *Lutheran World Information*, October 15, 1987, 39/87 edition, Hungary General Subject Files, box 4, folder 15, KCRPS; Keston College, "Hungarian State Secretary Says 'Small Steps' to Continue (Hungary)," *Keston News Service*, October 30, 1986, Hungary General Subject Files, box 4, folder 15, KCRPS; British Broadcasting Corporation, Monitoring Service, "Imre Miklós on Work of Churches under Socialism," *Summary of World Broadcasts*, April 15, 1987, Eastern Europe edition, sec. B. Internal Affairs—Hungary, Hungary General Subject Files, box 4, folder 15, KCRPS; *The State and the Churches in Hungary*.

37. British Broadcasting Corporation, Monitoring Service, "Church-State Discussions on Economic Prospects," *Summary of World Broadcasts*, December 7, 1982, Eastern Europe edition, Hungary General Subject Files, box 4, folder 15, KCRPS.

38. Zoltan K. Kovacs, "2. The Regime Calls on Churches for Help," Situation Report Hungary, Radio Free Europe Research, March 22, 1983, Hungary General Subject Files, box 4, folder 15, KCRPS.

39. Kovacs, "2. The Regime Calls on Churches for Help."

40. Kovacs, "2. The Regime Calls on Churches for Help."

41. Zoltan K. Kovacs; "Bishop Interviewed," *Tablet*, October 29, 1983, Hungary Denominational Files, ROM 33 Social Problems, KCRPS. Given the mission

of RFE/RL, there is room to question Kovacs's interpretation; nevertheless, the materials cited come from secular and religious publications in Hungary.

42. British Broadcasting Corporation, Monitoring Service, "Imre Pozsgay Meets Church Leaders," *Summary of World Broadcasts*, February 2, 1984, Part 2, Eastern Europe edition, sec. Hungary, Hungary General Subject Files, box 4, folder 15, KCRPS.

43. British Broadcasting Corporation, "Imre Miklós on Work of Churches under Socialism."

44. Kovacs, "2. The Regime Calls on Churches for Help"; Edith Markos, "Hungary," RAD Background Report, Radio Free Europe/Radio Liberty Research Institute, October 1, 1986, Hungary General Subject Files, box 4, folder 10, KCRPS.

45. John Eibner, "Kadar's Hungary: A 'Torn Curtain' Country," *Keston News Service*, October 31, 1985, Hungary General Subject Files, box 4, folder 15, KCRPS.

46. Brian Cooper, "While Church Attendance Declines Interest in Religion in Hungary Grows," *Baptist Times*, January 9, 1986, Hungary General Subject Files, box 7, folder 2, KCRPS.

47. "Bid to Help Drifters," *Guardian of Liberty*, April 1984, Hungary General Subject Files, box 7, folder 2, KCRPS; British Broadcasting Corporation, Monitoring Service, "Church-State Relations," *Summary of World Broadcasts*, January 7, 1984, Eastern Europe edition, sec. Hungary, Hungary General Subject Files, box 4, folder 15, KCRPS; "Hungarian Christians Report Encouraging Developments," *World Evangelical Information Service (WEIS)*, February 6, 1986, Hungary General Subject Files, box 9, folder 3, KCRPS; "Church Activities in Fight against Drug Abuse," *Summary of World Broadcasts*, August 3, 1987, Hungary General Subject Files, box 7, folder 1, KCRPS; Edith Markos, "New Measures to Combat Drug Abuse," February 25, 1987, Radio Free Europe/Radio Liberty Research Institute, Situation Report, Hungary, Hungary General Subject Files, box 9, folder 3, KCRPS; "The Churches' Social Work—in Hungary," *The Right to Believe*, 1987, Hungary General Subject Files, box 7, folder 2, KCRPS; "New Church-Linked Organisations for Helping Addicts," *Summary of World Broadcasts*, January 10, 1989, Hungary Denominational Files, ROM 33 Social Problems, KCRPS.

48. British Broadcasting Corporation, Monitoring Service, "The State of the Churches," *Summary of World Broadcasts*, February 2, 1988, Eastern Europe edition, sec. B. Internal Affairs—Hungary, Hungary General Subject Files, box 6, folder 11, KCRPS.

49. "The Churches' Social Work"; Edith Oltay, "Religious Orders Being Re-Established," in *Situation Report: Hungary, 4 October 1989*, October 4, 1989, HU OSA 300-8-47:27/1-15, Situation Reports, Publications Department, Records of Radio Free Europe/Radio Liberty Research Institute, Vera and Donald Blinken Open Society Archives at Central European University, Budapest, https://catalog.archivum.org/catalog/osa:65ee2a33-385d-4075-a194-92539156a87b.

50. Eurovangelism, "Dateline: Budapest," August 1985, Hungary General Subject Files, box 5, folder 18, KCRPS; "Hungarian Christians Report Encouraging Developments."

51. See Gergely, "Suicide in Hungary"; Skog and Elekes, "Alcohol and the 1950–90 Hungarian Suicide Trend."

52. B. B., "VÉGRE!," *Új Ember*, November 19, 1989, Hungary General Subject Files, box 9, folder 3, KCRPS.

53. See Gergely, "Suicide in Hungary"; Skog and Elekes, "Alcohol and the 1950–90 Hungarian Suicide Trend."

CHAPTER 10

The Russian Orthodox Church

Thirty Years of Post-Communist Development

Sergei Filatov

This essay is the result of my thirty-five years of research on religion in Russia. During and immediately after perestroika, Professor Dmitri Furman and I conducted sociological surveys on religion that covered the whole of Russia. This research was organized by the Analytical Center of the Russian Academy of Sciences, which no longer exists. In the course of this research, I came to the conclusion that an in-depth analysis of the religious situation in Russia could not be limited to surveys and the material already available in the public sphere, including church and state documents. A team of researchers (the number increasing and decreasing) gradually formed around me and conducted informal conversations with people who "did religion" (mostly clergy) about their convictions, plans, and the everyday organization of church life. From 1995 this research was carried out in collaboration with the Keston Institute and titled *Encyclopaedia of Religious Life in Russia Today* (1993–2022).[1] The team has interviewed more than a thousand clergy members belonging to all religious communities in Russia, though this chapter discusses only the Russian Orthodox Church.

These many years of research have enabled us to understand how the Russian Orthodox Church has evolved. The church to this day is still not fully aware of some of these changes. Around the time of the collapse of the Soviet Union, Russian Orthodoxy was dominated by primitive modes of thought, by various prejudices, and by nationalism. There was practically no community life at the parish level, no social work, and in general no forms of mutual help. There was no religious education, and the church was organized along strict authoritarian lines that mercilessly suppressed any dissent.

Religion and the Church during Perestroika (1986–1992)

The freedom gained by the church at the end of the 1980s gave a certain logic to its development, a process that did not depend for the most part on its leaders' personalities or on external circumstances. A dramatic, and in many ways unexpected, evolution fundamentally changed the life and mindset of the church. However, church ideology, which emphasizes the immutability of the Orthodox worldview, has prevented people from seeing the basic changes that have taken place.

Russia, it has been claimed, was more secularized than any other country when it gained religious freedom in 1990 with the adoption of the RSFSR's Law on Freedom of Conscience. In fact, a basic comparison of sociological data from questionnaires about the religiosity of Russia's population and the countries of Western Europe demonstrates that the most general indicators—belief in God, attendance at church services, belief in an afterlife, or in astrology, reincarnation, UFOs, and so on—among Russians were (and are) basically no different from the indicators of the most secularized countries of Europe.[2]

Like religiosity, Russia is also no different when it comes to respect for "traditional Christian values." The increase in abortions, divorce, prostitution, and tolerance of these, and the extent of the "collapse" of the institution of the family, are no lower than in the West.[3] However, the situation following the death of communist ideology with the collapse of the Soviet Union in 1991 and the end of Communist Party power is qualitatively different from the situation in 1917 when one integral dogmatic worldview was replaced by an equally integral and dogmatic worldview. Soviet ideology was replaced by a vague, amorphous, and eclectic worldview.

In religious terms, the spread of what came to be called "nontraditional beliefs" was prevalent during the pre- and post-perestroika period. The growth of the occult, of elements of Eastern religions, of interest in healers and all kinds of witchcraft, of belief in UFOs or in the Siberian Snowman, and the transmigration of souls, were already evident within Soviet territory in the 1970s. Before perestroika these "nonformal religions" prevailed essentially among the intelligentsia and young people—social strata that were particularly drawn to intellectual exploration. But there were others, too. In recent years evidence has emerged from various sources confirming that even members of the *nomenklatura*, the top Soviet social class, were interested in "nontraditional religion" and used the services of psychics and astrologers.[4]

It is significant that among the supporters of market reforms, most were not Orthodox believers or atheists but people with an amorphous, fuzzy religiosity. Those who believed in some sort of "supernatural force," UFOs, the transmigration of souls, astrology, and such, were more inclined to support democratic and market reforms than were Christians or atheists.[5] An eclectic, nondogmatic religious consciousness, religious entropy as it were, developed alongside the growth of interest in a market economy. Spiritual entropy well describes this sort of religiosity because only an insignificant number of people joined any sort of traditional or even nontraditional religious organization. Perestroika softened the ideological rigor of a system and promoted vague, undefined worldviews within society that succumbed easily to "the game without rules" that was characteristic of the post-Soviet market.

During the years just before and after the fall of Communism (1988–92), public opinion came to accept a form of religion that had no clear confessional content. At the same time as the enthusiastic celebration of the millennium of the baptism of Russia and the mass opening of churches were taking place, there was an explosion of interest in and sympathy for Catholicism and Protestantism (Western missionaries never evoked such interest and sympathy thereafter), and for Buddhism and Judaism. Almost all the newly formed churches, denominations, cults, and new religious movements (both those that originated abroad and that were home-grown) that exist today in Russia came into being during this time of unlimited interest and sympathy toward religion.

Government policies reflected public opinion. On a par with the way official representatives participated in the celebrations of the millennium of the baptism of Russia and with the removal of the ban on religious activity was the visit of Gorbachev and Yeltsin to the Vatican, the reestablishment of diplomatic relations with the latter, the creation of Catholic dioceses, the unhindered mass influx of foreign missionaries, and the forming of the warmest relations at a high level with some religious movements that had scandals associated with them in the West but were seen as exotic in Russia—for example, the Scientologists, the

Unification Church or "Moonies," the Indian spiritual leader Sri Chinmoy, and Shoko Ashara, the founder and leader of Aum Shinrikyo. For a Soviet person, whether the president of the USSR or simply a humble citizen, religion was terra incognita, and some could not differentiate between the Gospel and the unintelligible newspeak of Ron Hubbard, the founder of Scientology.

In 1990 the Russian Soviet Federative Socialist Republic Law on Freedom of Conscience, containing no limitations on religious freedom, was passed and remained in force until 1997. Church-state relations on a formal level resembled the American model. The main national church, the Russian Orthodox Church, subjected for seventy years to a system that officially had as its goal the destruction of religion, developed characteristics that in many ways were unique. In Russia during the years of Soviet power, any form of religious mission was banned, while bibles and other kinds of Christian literature were strictly limited and unobtainable for most people. As a result, the majority of Orthodox Russians had only a vague understanding of their faith. Not only was the traditional structure of the church and its basic organizational entity—the parish—destroyed, but participation in the parish community became alien. Most Orthodox believers were not required to have any direct contact with their parish priest; they came to church, prayed, received the sacraments, and often attended many different churches. They felt no obligation to build up any sort of relationship with other members of a parish. From Soviet times, Orthodox believers did not associate their choice of a church with the area in which they lived. Their selection of a church, and more importantly of a priest, depended on the latter's reputation and on the worldview of the believer. Furthermore, often this choice was the result of chance factors—the recommendation of friends and relations, or family tradition. There were believers, revered priests, and churches, but no relationship at all between parishioners or between a priest and his parishioners. For the clergy, such a situation was seen as normal. This type of religious life can best be described as atomized: at best, even regular churchgoers felt a need to relate only to the priest in whose church they worshipped.

During the Communist period, such an atomized form of religious life was all that was possible for most believers and clergy, as nothing else was permitted. Only a few felt able to oppose the authorities. These norms became the tradition, deeply embedded within church life. After the collapse of Communism, when organized religious life was no longer banned and activity within the community was welcomed (so long as this did not conflict with the interests of the authorities), within the Russian Orthodox Church in the early days this atomized form of religious life was generally maintained. In the vast majority of registered local religious organizations, there was no parochial life strictly speaking. The church was justifiably criticized for being an office for ritual services, used by visitors rather than parishioners.

During the perestroika years, omnivorous spiritual and mental attitudes affected the Russian Orthodox Church. It became normal for believers and clergy to encourage ecumenism as well as dialogue with Protestants, Catholics, and representatives of non-Christian religious movements, while some Orthodox clergy made no secret of their interest in the latter movements, in which they saw much that was positive— a view that later became totally unacceptable.

The Domination of Patriotic Folklore in Russian Orthodoxy

The period when Russia looked to the West and was open to all religions did not last long. During 1991–92 the Russian people fundamentally altered their attitude to religion, a change that was part of a global ideological reorientation within Russian public opinion. Disillusionment and apathy followed the euphoria about democratic and market reform and the expectation that the new interpretation of "a bright future" would be achieved easily and quickly. The realization that after the dissolution of the Communist Party there would be no paradise for Russia, and that democracy, with respect for the rule of law according to Western norms, would not be established quickly, led to convulsive, indeed emotional ranting, rather than to an intellectual search for a new identity.

The many surveys of those years show that if until mid-1991 no less than two-thirds of the population believed that Russia must follow the example of Western nations, imitating them in all they did, then already toward the end of 1992 an equal majority considered that Russia, as a fundamentally different civilization, had its own particular path to follow and that it should not measure itself against the West.[6] Democratic and liberal principles quickly lost their value. Isolationism and authoritarianism became the slogans of the day.

Loyalty toward the national church, the Russian Orthodox Church, replaced the interest among many Russians in anything that was "spiritual" and "godly." Orthodoxy started to acquire the significance of a cultural core value and to become a symbol of national identity. Up

until 2000 the number of people who identified as Orthodox in sociological surveys continually grew (to as much as 82 percent according to
some research).[7] From 1988 the church grew dramatically. The number of registered Russian Orthodox parishes increased from six thousand in 1988 to thirty-seven thousand in 2017, churches that had been
handed back to the Russian Orthodox Church by the government were
reopened and new ones were built, and the number of dioceses grew
from 38 to 303.[8]

Clergy expressed their patriotism in their sermons and public statements and condemned Russia's western neighbors for trying to impose
alien values and ideals on the Motherland. The glorification of military
feats came to the fore; the lives of saints (Russian saints in particular)
and historical essays in which the Russian Orthodox people coura-
geously resisted the foe became popular. In the 1990s in church circles
someone who called himself a Christian was looked upon with suspicion; after all, a Russian Orthodox believer always called himself Orthodox. Basically, after the vacillation of the perestroika years, the church
reverted to the ideology imposed by Stalin, an ideology of "patriotic service," which is summed up as praise for the authoritarian Russian state
and support for its unity and might. Such "patriotic service" looked
upon foreigners and internal opponents as enemies who would bring a
variety of ills upon Russia. In the mid-1990s at a point when Yeltsin's
regime started to become less and less democratic, the Russian Orthodox Church "overtook the steam engine" (the state), so to speak.

In tandem with the changes in public opinion, the state's policy
toward religion also changed. From 1992 the laws in force until then
began to be broken. At first this was done almost imperceptibly, tenta-
tively, as it were. But in 1997 the federal Law on Freedom of Conscience,
guaranteeing the separation of church and state, in reality was no longer effective when it came to its basic tenets. Church and state were no
longer separated, nor were schools separated from the church. Special
state organs (forbidden in law) dealing with religion were established
(admittedly, locally based) and the church was permitted to teach in
schools, introducing courses on Orthodox culture and similar topics.
The Moscow Patriarchate signed agreements on cooperation with law-
enforcement agencies and a few other ministries that gave the church a
significant presence within the army, the militia, and other state institutions. With the support of the Russian Orthodox Church's leadership, the new law "on freedom of conscience" was passed in 1997. This
in practice banned foreign missionary work and withdrew the basic

rights of those religious organizations that had existed for less than fifteen years, while forcing autonomous religious communities to join religious associations dating back to Soviet days.

A Silent Revival: Evangelical Evolution within the Russian Orthodox Church

Many observers in early 2010 and onward thought that the Russian Orthodox Church was ineluctably heading for a dead end and a gloomy future. However, new factors began to play a part in its life that gradually changed its character. What were these factors? The clergy, who for many decades had been cut off from their parishioners, found themselves in a totally different relationship with their flock in the years after the collapse of Soviet power. Now they were drawn into the lives of the laity and felt morally and materially connected to them. Furthermore, the laity themselves began to create a sense of solidarity within their church congregations, something very different from the anonymous participation in church services of the Soviet period. During perestroika and in the first years after it, members of the Russian intelligentsia joined the Russian Orthodox Church. These were people who had long been drawn to service within the church, but because they were educated had been banned from ordination by the Soviet authorities. At first there were relatively few such educated candidates for the priesthood, and at the start of their ministry no one noticed them, but with time, thanks to their idealistic motivation and education, they became more and more visible and played an increasingly important role in the church.

The majority of priests who were appointed during perestroika or soon after were poorly trained and many had no higher education at all, yet even such priests exercised great authority in the tiny number of overcrowded churches that were full of the newly converted. But this could not continue indefinitely. Most churchgoers were city dwellers who had at least a secondary education, and many of them had some comprehension of their faith. With time Orthodox believers increasingly started to seek out educated pastors and began themselves to develop a deeper understanding of Christianity. In the larger cities where there were more churches to choose from, churchgoers began to form communities with other like-minded believers.

The two patriarchs of the post-perestroika period, Aleksii and Kirill, concentrated mostly on two areas of church development—on building as many churches as possible and on improving clergy education. It is impossible to judge whether they were aware of the consequences of their choice of priorities, which promoted and speeded up evangelization. As the number of churches grew, so the proportion of church "visitors" (that is, those who rarely went to church and usually only on the main feast days) decreased and no longer dominated a congregation. The better educated, more pastorally minded, active priests, naturally attracted more believers and exercised great authority. The policies of the Russian Orthodox Church focused on raising the educational level of clergy and strengthened the prestige of education within church circles, while the uneducated, authoritarian *startsy* (elders) who dabbled in patriotic politics and occult practices gradually faded into the background, with their followers decreasing dramatically in number.

The early years following the collapse of the Soviet system were full of hope. There were many people who challenged the status quo, who opposed Soviet traditions and the ruling views within church and Soviet government circles. This was particularly true of the first years of perestroika, a period when Fr. Aleksandr Men (1935–90) was an important figure. The rejection of his writings by the majority within the church was usually justified on the grounds of what were termed his "liberalism" and "ecumenism." Until 2010 no book by him was stocked by church bookstalls, apart from a very few exceptions. If one carefully considers the criticisms against Men, it is surprising to discover how unconvincing they are. His critics thought up points and added ideas from their imagination in their efforts to appear serious. His analysis of the experience of other Christian confessions was termed ecumenism. He rejected none of Orthodoxy's dogmas, yet he was called a liberal. For some reason Protodeacon Andrei Kuraev labeled him a Catholic, though what exactly Men rejected in Orthodox teaching in favor of Catholic doctrine remained unclear. Some disliked Men's writings for the way they placed Christ and the Bible over and above tradition, the lives of saints, and church customs. In contrast, people who were unconnected or had little to do with the church read his work, available in secular bookshops. During perestroika many began to search for their identity through Christianity, and Men was just the person they were looking for. Many of those who were persuaded by his books to join the church, however, met with a cold response from churchgoers who criticized them for reading what they considered to be unacceptable material. It is interesting to note that during the first two decades after the collapse of the Soviet system, the number of Protestant congregations sharply increased. In part, this was probably because it was difficult for new converts to find Christ in the kind of Orthodoxy that then existed.

Men was a talented writer, and his published sermons reached hundreds of thousands, and even possibly millions of readers. As significant for the church was the pastoral work of a few especially revered priests, who either did not write anything or whose ministries were more important than what they wrote. Fr. Pavel Adelheim (1938–2013), even before perestroika, was highly respected not only at home in Pskov but also in Moscow and especially St. Petersburg. His pastoral ministry focused on the Gospel and on conversion to Christ. There were other priests, too, who promoted the evangelical work of the Russian Orthodox Church and began their ministry during the Soviet period. The most striking among them were Fr. Georgi Kochetkov (b.1950) and Fr. Gennadi Fast (b. 1954). Kochetkov founded within the Russian Orthodox Church the Transfiguration Brotherhood, which to date has attracted thousands of people. It emphasizes the importance of regular Bible study and stresses that a believer's life should conform to biblical teaching. From 1990 to 2000 Kochetkov was constantly attacked by many Orthodox clergy who criticized the nature of the Transfiguration Brotherhood and its evangelical approach. He was dismissed from his parish, was under a ban for a time, and suffered greatly from the continual attacks from within the church over many years. Fr. Gennadi (Heinrich before his baptism in the Russian Orthodox Church) Fast was born in a Siberian village into a devout German Protestant family. After graduating from the physics faculty of Tomsk University in 1978, he obtained a post in the Faculty of Theoretical Physics. Not long before he completed his studies he was converted to Orthodoxy and was soon expelled from the university for preaching the Gospel. In 1980 he was ordained. He did a correspondence course at the seminary and spiritual academy in Sergiev Posad. He served in several parishes in the Tuva Republic and Kemerovo oblast, but the most important part of his ministry was spent in parishes in the Krasnoyarsk region. He was persecuted from time to time by both the local authorities and by the church leadership. Fast's focus on the Gospel displeased both groups and was labeled "fanaticism, liberalism, and Protestant heresy." His Orthodox theological thinking was contained not only in his sermons and many lectures but also in some original theological essays. In 2010, after another conflict with his bishop, he was forced to leave the Krasnoyarsk diocese. The basis of this conflict concerned Fast's insistence that a candidate for baptism should first spend time studying the faith, a position rejected by his bishop. Since then, Fast has served in Abakan in Khakassia while continuing to teach in Krasnoyarsk, where he lectures at the university.[9]

Aleksandr Men, Pavel Adelheim, Georgi Kochetkov, and Gennadi Fast, as well as a few other priests, each in their own way put Bible study at the center of their ministry—the Gospel was the incontrovertible source of truth—and in various degrees they all used the Russian language in worship. From 1980 to 2000 they were treated as heretics (or near heretics) and were subjected to various kinds of punishment by the church authorities. And it was not just the church authorities who believed that these "reforming" ideas were reprehensible, but also the majority of clergy and laity. Yet there was one qualifying factor: the St. Petersburg diocese. It was the least subject to patriotic folklore from the time it was founded and, unlike any other part of Orthodox Russia, emphasized the importance of knowing and studying biblical texts. There is an old clerical saying, "In Moscow people pray, in St. Petersburg people study," which stems from the historic influence of the St. Petersburg Spiritual Academy and its seminary. After World War II when there were just a few parishes in the city, all the active clergy and laity were linked in one way or another to the St. Petersburg Spiritual Academy, and, unlike other parts of Russia, theological education there held pride of place even during the time of Stalin and Khrushchev.

Today every Petersburg parish is trying to set up some sort of educational center and to organize courses, while also trying to recruit the best lecturers from among the educated clergy and secular academics. At the heart of these teaching programs are biblical studies and church history, although courses are not limited to these and can include Russian and world history, the arts, philology, and the social sciences. Throughout the rest of Russia, the same phenomena can be found, but on a far smaller scale. Even in Moscow there are far fewer such centers, and as a rule the intellectual level is lower, but there, as in other dioceses, the direction is the same as in Petersburg.

Although it is difficult to measure the slow and almost unopposed trend toward biblical values and the retreat from a patriotic folklore type of mentality in the thinking of the church, its level can be assessed indirectly by the growth in the use of Russian rather than Church Slavonic in Orthodox worship. In principle, of course, a Christian whose faith is rooted in the Gospel but who prefers Church Slavonic in worship can exist, just as much as a radical nationalist can exist who is steeped in magic and occult practices but who prefers the comprehensible Russian language in worship. However, these are exceptions. Based on my observations, someone who searches for the truth in the Gospel seems to prefer a more comprehensible language for the exposition of Truth, whereas an Orthodox pagan will probably feel more at home when he hears beautiful but incomprehensible liturgical singing. The Russian language has come to be used more and more in the liturgy. In some parish churches, the readings from the New Testament are read only in Russian, while in some a few prayers in Russian are added as well. And as for the churches where such things never take place—the home of conservatives—the use of Russian is no longer condemned as heresy. Religious consciousness appears to be changing. Scripture seems to be gradually becoming more important and taking the place of tradition.

On March 23, 2019, an historical event took place in Tver when for the first time Metropolitan Savva of Tver and Kashin openly celebrated the liturgy in Russian. This took place in the Church of the Mother of God "Joy of All Who Suffer" in the Avaev medical center. Metropolitan Savva admitted after the liturgy that this was the first time he had celebrated in Russian, and although he loved and knew well the liturgy in Church Slavonic, he said that he had discovered new meaning in it. Today in this church the liturgy is regularly celebrated in church Russian—normal literary Russian—whereas before, such liturgies took place in secret. The previous Metropolitan Viktor had disapproved of this and even banned scripture being read in Russian, so that the church's priest in charge, Fr. Vyacheslav Baskakov, was regularly denounced.[10]

During my field trips to the Russian Orthodox Church dioceses with Xenia Dennen and Roman Lunkin, we have all observed the constant growth of interest in the Gospel and the development of different ways of reading, studying, and discussing scripture. Thirty years ago, youth clubs and other groups of active Orthodox believers relatively rarely studied the Gospel, and if they did so then this involved only a very few people. As the years go by, the Gospel is gradually moving from the periphery to the center of church life.

The Revival of Social Work

History has shown that a negative attitude to what was deemed an excessive interest in the Gospel was indissolubly linked with a similar attitude toward support for social work and other charitable activities. In the 1980s and the two decades following perestroika, most Russian Orthodox believers thought of social work as something remote that belonged to an imaginary world; it was foreign and non-Orthodox. I regularly heard clergy say that the church should encourage prayer, humility, fasting, patriotism, and regular attendance at the liturgy. These were the things that saved one's soul, whereas social work was not really needed and not the church's business. Indeed, concern about social work had been imported into the church, they believed, by newly converted members of the intelligentsia who had been influenced by Western churches. In the first years following his election in 2009, Patriarch Kirill paid little attention to charitable work. In his former position as Metropolitan of Smolensk he had preferred to encourage a rapid growth in the number of churches and monasteries, had focused on the development of seminaries and catechism classes for the younger generation (both in Sunday schools and state schools), and had supported the establishment of local sections of the International Russian People's Assembly at the provincial level.[11]

The change of attitude toward social work was not a conscious development, and it came about quickly and simultaneously at all levels of the church's hierarchical structure. The subject appeared on the church's agenda first in 2010, a year after Kirill was elected patriarch when he began to talk about compassion toward orphans, the sick, and the homeless. Thereafter a new movement began in the church, not initiated by the Patriarch but encouraged and ultimately controlled by him. In just four to five years a number of interesting social projects were set up in every diocese. Philanthropy suddenly became one of the most important activities of the church to the bishops and leading clergy, until by 2022 it was difficult to find a parish that was not involved in at least some form of social work.

Of course, even during the Soviet period there were some Russian Orthodox "Good Samaritans." During the first years of perestroika some social-work projects were set up in St. Petersburg, Moscow, and a few other towns; those in St. Petersburg were particularly important and clearly grew out of an interest in the study of scripture. In their sermons, Fr. Aleksandr Stepanov and Fr. Lev Bolshakov emphasized New Testament values as the focus of their ministry, and it was they who were the founders of social work in St. Petersburg. They were the first to begin helping the suffering by working in hospitals and among street children and the homeless. In the years just after perestroika most social projects focused on rehabilitating alcoholics and drug addicts.

Before the revolution, St. Petersburg had been the center of a temperance movement. This St. Petersburg tradition was then revived by

Stepanov when he started trying to help alcoholics and drug addicts. He began to achieve some success only in 2003 after he had disbanded a failed rehab center for former prisoners and children in care in Pushkinskiye Gory, about 100 miles from Pskov, and instead joined forces with the Christian Interchurch Diaconal Council (CIDC) to set up a drug rehab center that retained the infrastructure of the failed center. CIDC, known simply as Diakoniia today, works with professional psychiatrists, doctors, and other specialists.

In the 1990s the temperance movement, which had existed before the revolution in the form of brotherhoods, was revived in St. Petersburg and its environs. Currently there are more than twenty brotherhoods and other Orthodox organizations helping drug addicts in St. Petersburg. Apart from Stepanov, the best-known priest working in this field is Fr. Aleksandr Zakharov, who is known for his inability to get on with his church superiors and is constantly in conflict with them. Furthermore, he holds far-right political views and is a monarchist, unlike the majority of socially active clergy in St. Petersburg who hold liberal political views. This leads to his isolation from other church people involved in social work. However, when I interviewed liberal clergy, they acknowledged Zakharov's high moral qualities and the success of his original methods for treating alcoholics and drug addicts. At the start of perestroika, Zakharov served at the Church of the Epiphany on Gutuevsky Island, where he gathered and supported the temperance brotherhoods. During the 1990s this church became almost the main center for the city's temperance movement and his rehabilitation methods were recognized by the St. Petersburg diocese and successfully applied in almost all the other rehab centers in the area.

Zakharov's rehab center accommodated twenty-eight people, with four to a room. Rehab lasted six months and was followed by a period of adaptation to life in the outside world. For this, flats were rented where inmates had to spend another six months learning to hold down a job and keep a normal daily routine under strict supervision. About 30 percent gave up during this year. Spiritual direction played a key part in Zakharov's system:

> The goal of the first six months is to replace a person's set of values. For most people the purpose of life is pleasure, and for an addict the strongest and most intense pleasure is destructive. My aim is to awaken in them a sense of themselves as immortal souls, to instill in them the fear of God. They begin to pray to God,

whom they probably don't believe in. Prayer takes place regularly and through prayer they start to understand how godforsaken they are. I totally banned alcohol, tobacco, and swearing from the center.[12]

Stepanov, consumed with his growing charitable center, concluded that Zakharov's rehab center was the best in the diocese, and so decided to hand over to him the rehab center in Pskov oblast that he ran with the help of Diakoniia. But because Diakoniia had links with Western churches, Zakharov, a conservative with anti-Western views, faced a problem. How could he work with them? Nevertheless, he decided to do so after concluding that Diakoniia was doing a great deal of good. In his words:

> In Pskov oblast Diakoniia has worked out a program called Metanoia, which is based on the Alcoholics Anonymous Twelve Steps program. We have adapted it a bit on the basis of our experience. I had a rebellion on my hands from my parishioners who were dead set against Diakoniia as something out of America that produced nothing good. But I argued that the Americans would work in Russia anyway and that it would be better if we helped to assimilate them into Orthodoxy. Volunteers from Diakoniia in recent years have helped with the agricultural work as well as on a professional level.
>
> The community has been reorganized into a rehab center. Qualified doctors and other specialists have been brought in to help and have put in place the continuous monitoring of the clients. Over the last four years, 250 people from fifty cities have been helped. Director Rydalevskaia affirms that 70 percent of the clients remained free from drugs for at least a year after rehab (there is no data on longer periods).[13]

Thanks to Stepanov and Zakharov, both pioneers with a strong focus on evangelism, today additional substantial rehab centers have been established in the St. Petersburg Metropolia that includes the St. Petersburg, Vyborg, Gatchina, and Tikhvin dioceses.

In addition to the temperance movement, work to help orphans and children in need was developed in the St. Petersburg diocese during perestroika and expanded in the post-Soviet years. The most significant children's project was called "The Orthodox Children's Mission of St. Seraphim of Vyritsa," in the village of Vyritsa, a favorite place for holiday homes outside Petersburg. During World War II, Vyritsa was occupied by the Germans, who set up a camp for abandoned children from around Leningrad. A monk named Seraphim (1866–1949), canonized in 2000, got local residents to collect clothes and food for these young prisoners. Four people played a key part in the creation of the Mission: Fr. Ioann Mironov, Feodosi Ambartsumov, and two brothers, Kirill and Mefodii Zinkovsky.

At almost the same time as Stepanov started to help children in need, the Zinkovsky brothers, both seminarians, and Ambartsumov (assistant to the rector of the St. Petersburg Spiritual Academy and later an ordained priest) did likewise. All three were distinguished graduates of the Academy. The Zinkovsky brothers had graduated from the Physics and Mechanics Faculty of the St. Petersburg Polytechnic Institute in 1992 with doctorates, and in 1995 they entered the St. Petersburg Seminary, from which they graduated in 1999. During these three years, they trained in children's work in Cyprus, and in 1999 they joined the Spiritual Academy, where during their first year they took monastic vows and were ordained as deacons. In 2001 they completed a three-month theological course in Oxford and served at the Russian Orthodox Cathedral of the Dormition in London with Metropolitan Anthony of Sourozh. In 2002 they were ordained as priests and, after receiving their degrees in theology, were appointed to teaching posts at the St. Petersburg Spiritual Academy, where Mefodii taught dogmatics and Kirill patristics.

The Children's Mission began when Ambartsumov was asked to organize a meeting between the theological students and abandoned children in care.[14] For Ambartsumov, the great grandson of the martyred Fr. Vladimir Ambartsumov, this meeting between street children and students was life changing. It led to regular visits to the children's home by Academy students and teachers who organized lessons for the children and recruited volunteers to help in other children's homes and orphanages. Eventually in 2010 the Zinkovskys set up the Orthodox Children's Mission of St. Seraphim of Vyritsa, with Mefodii as chairman of the charity. In 2011 the two brothers resigned from their teaching posts at the Spiritual Academy and went to live in Vyritsa, where the next year Ambartsumov and his wife joined them. The following year, the Mission started courses to train volunteers under the directorship of Kirill Zinkovsky. Initially most of the volunteers were students and teachers from the Spiritual Academy. In time the number of volunteers grew dramatically, so that today more than four hundred people from the St. Petersburg area are involved in the work and visit over forty children's homes.

The Vyritsa center aimed to find people who would adopt the orphans and give them a home. An Orthodox community of families with many children was established there and included Ambartsumov and his wife, who adopted nine children. In 2012 a building was constructed that housed five families who fostered fifteen children, including many disabled children. Some were home-schooled within the center, while others attended the local school. By 2021 the center consisted of three houses that accommodated fifty adopted children and their parents. The children received specialized medical and emotional care and were encouraged to play games that involved lots of exercise, and concerts, plays, and special guest visits were organized for them. The center also had a facility that focused on the development and socialization of the children, where the antisocial behavior of some children could be managed.[15]

Another important aspect of social work in St. Petersburg involved care for terminally ill children. Fr. Aleksandr Tkachenko, the priest in charge of the Cathedral of the Descent of the Holy Spirit, set up children's hospices and was widely acclaimed for his innovative work. Before his ordination he studied in the Faculty of Biomedical Electronics at the Leningrad Electrotechnical Institute and the St. Petersburg Seminary. During this latter period of study, he spent some time in the United States and United Kingdom learning about hospital chaplaincy. In 1997 he was ordained and, while serving in the St. Nicholas Epiphany Naval Cathedral in St. Petersburg, began to help families with disabled children. He started with just a small group of people who cared for six to seven families with seriously sick children. As this work became widely known, more and more anxious parents started turning to Tkachenko. He soon realized that much more was needed. Thus, in 2003 he and his colleagues founded a charity that they named the Children's Hospice. A team of doctors, nurses, psychologists, and social workers selected a group of children who needed palliative care and organized systematic help for them and their families in their homes with a visiting team of teachers and psychiatrists. In 2006 a health care unit was set up. The number of teams visiting children at home grew and began to include specialist doctors. The Petersburg city authorities gave Tkachenko a building in 2007 that had once been the country house of the Kurakin family and more recently had housed the Nikolaev orphanage. Here on June 1, 2010, the St. Petersburg Autonomous

State Health Care Institution, or Children's Hospice, was finally opened with Tkachenko as the general director. Exactly one year later he opened another children's hospice in the village of Lakhta for children from other regions who were being treated in St. Petersburg, and soon thereafter further children's hospices were set up near Moscow and in Tatarstan. Tkachenko believes there are about forty thousand to two hundred thousand children in need of hospice care. Today hospices are being built in Belgorod, Ekaterinburg, Oryol, Sevastopol, and Simferopol, and there are also plans for a large palliative-care facility in the Khanty-Mansiysk autonomous region.

Tkachenko is one of the pioneers of children's hospices in Russia and the world. The first children's hospice was opened twenty-five years ago in England, the second in Canada, and the third was the St. Petersburg hospice.[16] Today Europeans come to St. Petersburg to learn about the Russian Orthodox hospice experience and to use this knowledge when setting up similar facilities. Tkachenko has been innovative in his approach, using his experience of working with sick children and their parents to create a special environment, an oasis where an ill child can experience joy.[17]

A relatively new type of social work being developed by the Russian Orthodox Church focuses on support for young pregnant women. At its best, this involves the provision of long-term accommodation, material help, and teaching domestic skills. Homes for pregnant women and mothers with small children who have nowhere to live are currently being planned by several parishes and other Russian Orthodox organizations.

The Russian Orthodox Church's social work has its problems and deficiencies; it is certainly not ideal, and compared to that of the Protestants and Catholics is underdeveloped. Nevertheless, in the current context, it should be noted that this work has involved the whole church and has produced examples of the highest standards in spheres that the government has not touched.

Secular and Church Authorities Face the Challenge of the Gospel

The most obvious and painful problem facing the Russian Orthodox Church is that of governance—how to organize the internal administration of the church and the church's relationship with secular authorities. Since the Soviet era, senior ranks have had unlimited power over their subordinates: the Patriarch over the bishops, the bishops over the clergy, the clergy over the laity.[18] Soviet atheist authorities usually advanced the careers of those candidates among the clergy who were not the most worthy, to put it mildly, and to this day, such self-promoting people still exist, people whose moral qualities definitely would have prevented them advancing in their careers had they not been nurtured (in the Soviet era) by militant atheists.

During the perestroika years and immediately after, the church leadership was disorganized and the Patriarch and other leading churchmen were openly criticized by dissidents, particularly Fr. Gleb Yakunin. During perestroika Yakunin was appointed the priest in charge of a church despite his critical stance, but when perestroika came to an end he was defrocked in October 1993 "for refusing to obey the requirement that Orthodox priests should not participate in parliamentary elections."[19] In 1997 Yakunin was excommunicated "for the unauthorized wearing of a pectoral cross."[20] By the mid-1990s any criticism of church leaders or of government policies was firmly suppressed, much like suppression during the Soviet period. In December 1997 Patriarch Aleksii II announced at the yearly gathering of bishops in Moscow:

> Particularly objectionable were the speeches of a few priests when the matter of the direction of the new law "on freedom of conscience"—so important for the church—was being decided. Although the position of the church leadership was stated most clearly and unequivocally, these priests put forward through the mass media their opposing views, which conformed to the interests of totalitarian religious communities who are the enemies of the Russian Orthodox Church. Basically, we were not confronted with an honest error, but rather by a conscious and focused attempt to undermine the authority of the Russian Orthodox Church within society. This is most accurately defined as betrayal.[21]

As each year passed, the Russian Orthodox Church publicly supported the actions of the government and during elections supported the pro-government candidates. The election of Patriarch Kirill (Gundyaev) in February 2009 led to a slight change in the behavior of the senior church leadership. The Patriarch and other Orthodox Church leaders gradually stopped supporting individual politicians in their public statements and instead made eloquent and strong pronouncements about stability, unity, and loyalty to national tradition, while at the same time criticizing revolutionaries and radical oppositionists. The strongest support for the government and rejection of the opposition was expressed by the Patriarch, who represented the Russian Orthodox Church, during public protests over election fraud. On December 17, 2011, at the end of the liturgy in the Cathedral of Christ the Savior, the Patriarch spoke out:

> We know into what a messy bloodbath was turned the life of our twentieth-century forefathers when, fighting for these small human truths, a father rose up against his children and children against their father; when love and friendship were destroyed; when rivers of blood flowed and people, crazed by this blood, did all they could to affirm their small, human, and frankly insignificant truth without regard for anything else! Yes, and perhaps in reality there was no truth at all but only pride and the desire for power! Many millions of human lives were lost and a great country fell apart. There is not enough time to describe all the suffering that was inflicted in the twentieth century in the name of those human truths. . . . Today the minds of people are not guided by God's Truth, but by information technology that is used by all who insist on their human truth. We know what this leads to in some countries where blood is again being spilt. How important it is that we, the heirs of a great Russia, who underwent the terrible trials of the twentieth century, should today learn the lessons of the past and not repeat the mistakes of those who in the 1990s drastically altered the life of our people, and we mustn't repeat other mistakes too! What else needs to be done, what else needs to be said to deflect our people from actions that could destroy people's lives as well as God's Truth?[22]

Thus, the Patriarch called the protesters to think again and to obey the authorities. In April 2012 during a fellowship meeting at Christ the Savior Cathedral in Moscow, Russian Orthodox Church leaders brought together thousands of people from all over the country and condemned the group Pussy Riot, who had staged a performance critical of Vladimir Putin and the Patriarch. Patriarch Kirill's speech censured more strongly than ever all "revolutionaries."[23]

In recent years (prior to war with Ukraine) there is evidence of a gradual and unofficial weakening of internal church authoritarianism. A number of priests, with varying degrees of frankness, have risked criticizing the church's internal state and its leaders and have not been punished by church authorities. The most striking example is

Protodeacon Andrei Kuraev, who was one of the church's leading official intellectuals until 2010 when he became a strong critic of the situation within the church and of the Patriarch himself, whom he accused
of being illiterate, cruel, greedy, and a liar. Despite this, he retained
his post as a professor at the Moscow Spiritual Academy until 2013,
and until 2014 he continued to lecture in the philosophy faculty of
Moscow State University. Furthermore, he continued to serve as a dea-
con in one of Moscow's churches. On December 29, 2020, Moscow's
Episcopal Ecclesiastical Court passed a resolution to defrock Kuraev,
but it was not immediately ratified by the Patriarch.[24] How different
is this outcome to what would have happened twenty years previous,
when a priest would have been stripped of everything for the slightest
misdemeanor. Furthermore, there was the sensational event of 2019,
when two hundred priests of the Russian Orthodox Church publicly
supported those who were imprisoned for demonstrating against the
manipulation of the Duma elections and against the banning of opposition candidates from standing, an event known as "the Moscow case."
Not one of the signatories was punished by the Moscow Patriarchate
leaders!

The church's internal financial arrangements provide the most significant evidence of corruption within the church administration. These
arrangements are all kept secret; there is no accountability. The Russian
Orthodox Church in practice adheres to no legal standards or written
corporate regulations in such matters. The attempts of a few researchers to examine the Patriarchate's finances contain so many gaps, pre-
suppositions, and admissions of a lack of information that the value of
such research is extremely low.[25] At the same time the enormous varia-
tions in material well-being are obvious to all: there are impoverished
country parish priests who have no resources for educational or social
projects, and there are "princes of the church" who make no secret of
their opulence. During the perestroika years such a situation within the
church was considered quite normal, whereas now church leaders feel
they must justify their wealth or hide it. The Patriarch's decision during
the coronavirus lockdown to dispense with the usual church collections to support the Patriarchate was evidence of this change. Such a
concession would never have been allowed in the past.

At all events, during the Stalin-Khrushchev-Brezhnev era, the Russian Orthodox Church, represented by its leaders, would have supported
unreservedly the political authorities; no one deviated from such a position. But in recent years a few initial, perhaps rather tentative, changes

have taken place in the church's position regarding the government's policies. Before the collapse of the Soviet Union, the church gave complete autonomy to the Ukrainian Orthodox Church in October 1990, granting it "independence and autonomy in its governance," which included complete freedom to appoint its bishops and establish and abolish dioceses. Since then, the Russian Orthodox Church leadership has not made any serious effort to interfere in the life of the Ukrainian Orthodox Church Moscow Patriarchate. Patriarch Kirill has spoken at length and often about Russian civilization or the "Russian world," which includes Ukraine. In his view the "Russian world" adheres to the same Orthodox values and, consequently, to the same political values. However, in relation to Ukraine, the Patriarch has never referred to the spiritual harmfulness of parliamentarianism or the importance of rejecting the separation of powers and the institution of political parties. He has emphasized how essential are peace, the search for mutual understanding, and the preservation of the church's unity. At the beginning of March 2014 when Crimea was annexed by Russia, Patriarch Kirill said not a word in support of this and even absented himself from the ceremony when the documents formalizing this act were signed.

Until 2022, the Patriarch never once supported, but also did not condemn, the annexation of Crimea. For a leader of the Russian Orthodox Church not to support the government in matters of foreign policy is unheard of, either in tsarist, Soviet, or post-Soviet Russia. Many critics in the West and within Russia have censured the Patriarch for not condemning Putin's policies on Ukraine. Nevertheless, changes in the relationship of the church with the government and the growth of the church's independence are evident. Without waiting for the Kremlin to recognize the 2014 election of Petro Poroshenko as Ukraine's president, Patriarch Kirill congratulated him. The religious, Orthodox wing of militant Russian patriotism stayed silent and, at least in the public arena, the church tried to soften Russian public opinion on relations with Ukraine. In early February 2020, the church's Interconciliar Assembly published a sensational document that had been debated earlier in June 2019. The document proposed placing a ban on blessing weapons of mass destruction—that is, the whole of that "nuclear shield" that, as Russian nationalists teach, defends the homeland like "the Mother of God's girdle (*poyasa*)" from the surrounding wicked world. The authors stated that the blessing of something that leads to the destruction of an unlimited number of people is not supported "by the tradition of the Orthodox Church."[26]

The invasion of Ukraine by Russian forces in February 2022 put the Russian Orthodox Church in a difficult position. During the first days of the war, an "appeal from Russian Orthodox Church priests calling for reconciliation and an end to the war" was published on the internet. It was signed by 293 priests. Surprisingly, none of them were punished. But this was almost the last time that a large group of clergy—among them were influential clergy and some in top church administrative posts—publicly spoke out with a declaration of political opposition. The influence of activist, militaristic, and authoritarian forces began to grow within the church. No doubt Putin put pressure on the Patriarch to support the government's actions. On March 6, Forgiveness Sunday, Kirill seriously tarnished his reputation: for the first time in many years, he made a speech in which he clearly supported Russia in the conflict with Ukraine. He said: "For eight years attempts have been made to destroy what exists in Donbas, where the so-called values supported by those who want world power are rejected fundamentally. Today there is a loyalty test for attaining such power, a sort of admission ticket into the 'happy' world of excess consumption, a world of apparent 'freedom.' And do you know what this test actually is? It's both very simple and also horrible—it's a gay parade."[27] It should be noted that the Patriarch sees the conflict as part of the battle between traditional Christianity and the anti-identity policies of "new liberalism." His view is unlike the reasons for the invasion put forward by official Russian government circles—for example, the danger of NATO at Russia's borders, the spread of radical nationalism in Ukraine, discrimination against Russians living in Ukraine, and concern about the security of the population in the unrecognized Donbas republic. The Patriarch emphasized that this is an ideological war, not an interethnic and intergovernmental war. Of course, his is not a totally independent stance, but if compared with how the church enthusiastically and unreservedly supported all government policies—especially its foreign policy—during the Communist period and tsarist period, we see here a significant difference.

The church's position on Ukraine was at first expressed in a prayer that called for peace and an end to enmity. It was said during every liturgy and had been authorized by the Patriarch in 2014. The clergy, whose authority is still respected, addressed hundreds of thousands of their parishioners with the words: "Strengthen Thy faithful flock in the land of Ukraine with Thy might, fill the eyes of the erring with Thy divine light that they may comprehend Thy truth, quench their bitterness, quell enmity and confusion toward our country, and empower the peacemakers that all may perceive Thee, our Lord and Savior. Turn not Thy face from us, O Lord, grant us the joy of Thy salvation. Be merciful unto us as Thou wast unto our forefathers, turn Thine anger into mercy and grant Thine aid to the Ukrainian people, who are in dire straits, suffering."

However, as the war continued, the Church's position on the Ukraine question grew closer and closer to that of the government. In September 2022, the Patriarch authorized a prayer "On Holy Russia" that focused on the Ukrainian tragedy and replaced the prayer for peace. Now the prayer was about Russian victory: "Come to the aid of Thy people, O God, and through Thy might grant them victory." Furthermore, the Patriarchate began to persecute those who would not pray for victory, although only a few months earlier it had demanded prayers for peace. On May 11, 2023, the ecclesiastical court of the Moscow diocese defrocked Fr. Ioann Koval, the priest in charge of the Church of the Apostle Andrew the First-Called. The reason for this punishment was that he had changed a word in the prayer "On Holy Russia." In the line "Come to the aid of Thy people, O God, and through Thy might grant them victory," he replaced "victory" with "peace." Fr. Aleksei Uminsky, the priest in charge of the Moscow Church of the Holy Life-Giving Trinity in Khokhlovsky Lane, was dismissed and defrocked unexpectedly and with exceptional speed in January 2024, after the required bureaucratic process had been completed. This punishment was imposed on Uminsky because he did not read the prayer for the victory of Russian forces during the liturgy. Uminsky was well known for his defense of human rights and his pacifist views. Of all Moscow priests, he was one of the most authoritative, and perhaps the most authoritative.

Until the end of 2023, it was possible, although with difficulty, to see timid signs of peace-loving independence in the Russian Orthodox Church in relation to the situation in Ukraine. Since January 2024, the church has fully and unconditionally supported the Russian government's policy on Ukraine, and moreover supports all matters of foreign policy.

During the past decade the Russian Orthodox Church had clearly taken the first (and therefore the most difficult) steps toward removing elements inherited from the Soviet era from the ideology and organization of church life. These steps were taken with no fanfare or serious conflict. We are witnessing a quiet evolution, but apparently this has not been noticed by the church's elite or its members. The war in Ukraine and the increased authoritarianism within Russia itself has frozen the evolutionary processes within the church. Those elements pushing for reform are no longer heard. Nevertheless, this freeze is only superficial. The biblically based reform movement has just about disappeared from the public sphere, but it is continuing to grow in the life of the church and in the consciousness of believers.

I have paid more attention in this chapter to the early results of this quiet evolution because they emerged unconsciously. Soviet anachronisms are obvious, whereas that which is being born within the church is not obvious. If, to put it mildly, Orthodox believers are not fully aware of the changes taking place in the church, then this is even more true of secular society. Patriotic folklore ideology has taken its toll on the Russian Orthodox Church. The democratically inclined part of Russian society, who were sympathetic toward the church during the perestroika years, turned away from it in the mid-1990s. Anticlerical criticism is growing and accuses the church of being servile to secular power, of corruption in its financial affairs with unacceptable wealth among its top bureaucracy, and of lacking contact with the people of God. The clergy, as each year passes, mention with growing concern that they are losing the young people. The church, however, is in fact evolving in the direction desired by young people and by the democratically minded part of society, but this evolution is slow and quiet. That is the nature of things. A child cannot be born in just three months after conception, however desirable this might be.

Translated by Xenia Dennen

Notes

1. The results of this research were published in Michael Bourdeaux and Sergei B. Filatov., eds., *Sovremennaia religioznaia zhizn' Rossii: Opyt sistematichesk-ogo opisaniia*, vols. 1–4 (Moskva: Logos, 2003–2006); Michael Bourdeaux and Sergei Filatov, eds., *Atlas sovremennoi religioznoi zhizni Rossii*, vols. 1–3 (Moskva-SPb: Letnii sad, 2005, 2006, 2009); Sergei Filatov, ed., *Religiozno-obshchestvennaia zhizn' rossiiskikh regionov*, vols. 1–3 and 5 (Moskva: Letnii sad, 2014, 2016, 2018, 2021).

2. Roman Lunkin and Sergei Filatov, "Sekuliarizatsiia i mezhkon-fessional'nyiye razlichiia: Stanovlenie dvukh ideologicheskikh podkhodov," *Sovremennaia Evropa*, no. 3 (2018): 102–13.

3. M. B. Denisenko and Zh-P. Dalla Zuanna, "Seksual'noe povedenie ros-siiskoi molodezhi," *Sotsiologicheskie issledovaniia*, no. 2 (2001): 81–90; M. M. Bulygin, B. P. Brui, T. F. Gorbunova, "Osnovnye mediko-demograficheskie parametry rasvitiia detei i podrostkov Rossii," *Problemy sotsial'noi gigieny zdra-vookhraneniia i istorii meditsiny*, no. 6 (2001): 14–21.

4. Dmitri Furman and Kimmo Kääriäinen, "Religiia i tsennostnye orien-tatsii rossiiskoi elity," in *Novye tserkvi, starye veruyushchie—starye tserkvi, novye veruyushchie: Religiia v postsovetskoi Rossii*, ed. Dmitri Furman and Kimmo Kääriäinen (Moskva-SPb: Letnii sad, 2007), 230–60, 232–35.

5. Sergei Filatov and Dmitri Furman, "Religiia i politika v massovom soz-nanii," *Sotsiologicheskie issledovaniia*, no. 7 (1992), 10–11.

6. Sergei Filatov, "Traditsionnye religii, 'russkaia tsivilizatsiia' i suveren-naia demokratiia," in *Religiia i konflikt* (Moskva: Rosspen, 2007), 16–18.

7. Dmitri Furman, Kimmo Kääiäinen, and Vyacheslav Karpov, "Religioznost' v Rossii v 90-e gg. XX–nachale XXI v., in Furman and Kääriäinen, *Novye tserkvi, starye veruyushchie*, 43.

8. Patriarch Kirill gave a figure for the number of Russian Orthodox clergy and churches in *Svezhie Novosti na RBK*, November 29, 2017, https://www.rbc.ru/rbcfreenews/5a1e7eb99a7947948fdc00c8.

9. Xenia Dennen, Sergei Filatov, and Roman Lunkin, "Krasnoyarskii krai," in Filatov, *Religiozno-obshchestvennaia zhizn' rossiiskikh regionov*, vol. 2, 472–74.

10. Sergei Pushkov, "Pervaia v Tveri arkhiereiskaia liturgiia na russkom," *Tverskaia zhizn'*, March 28, 2019, https://tver.bezformata.com/listnews/arhierejskaya-liturgiya-na-russkom/73822816/.

11. S. Filatov, "Bezopasnost' v sotsial'noi doktrine i prakticheskoi politike Russkoi pravoslavnoi tserkvi," in *Bezopasnost' kak tsennost' i norma: Opyt raznykh epokh i kul'tur*, ed. S. Panarin (St. Petersburg: Intersotis, 2012), 107–19.

12. Interview with Sergei Filatov, September 10, 2018.

13. Aleksei Reutskii, "Zgliani v svoe serdtse: Posle reabilitatsii v tsentre 'Sologubovka' ustoichivaia remissiia nabliudaetsia u 70% narkozavisimykh," *Journal of the Moscow Patriarchate*, no. 3 (2017): 82–88.

14. Later, after ordination, Ambartsumov became the priest in charge of the Church of the Mother of God "of Tenderness" in Gzhatskaia Street. In 2022, the church leadership highly valued the work of the Zinkovsky brothers: Kirill was appointed rector of the Moscow Spiritual Academy (i.e., the church's top academic institution) and was consecrated Bishop of Zvenigorod, while Mefodii was made rector of the Nikolo-Ugreshsky Seminary and abbot of the Nikolo-Ugreshsky Monastery.

15. E. Milovidova, "Kommunalka, v kotoroi khorosho. V Vyritse deistvuet priemnyi tsentr dlya priemnykh semei," *Voda zhivaia*, no. 11 (2017): 45–57.

16. M. Akhmedova, "Imeyushchii delo s zhiznyu," *Ekspert*, no.1 (February 27, 2017): 81–97. Interview in Blagovest-info with Fr. Aleksandr Tkachenko, direc-tor of the Children's Hospice and the priest in charge of the Church of the Descent of the Holy Spirit on the Apostles on Dolgoozyornoi Street. "To Help Your Neighbor Is the Christian Ideal," *Blagovest-info*, August 21, 2017, http://www.blagovest-info.ru/index.php?ss=2&s=5&id=74496.

17. Akhmedova, "Imeyushchii delo s zhizniu."

18. Pavel Adelheim, *Dogmat o Tserkvi v kanonakh i praktike* (Pskov: bez izd., 2002).

19. "Ukaz Sviateishego Patriarkha moskovskogo i vseia Rusi Kirilla zashtatnomu sviashcheniku Glebu Pavlovichu Iakuninu," http://krotov.info/acts/20/1990/1993_10_03.htm.

20. "Akt ob otluchenii ot Tserkvi Gleba Pavlovicha Iakunina," *Pravoslavnaia entsiklopediia*, January 11, 2014, https://www.sedmitza.ru/lib/text/429346/.

21. "Doklad Sviateishego Patriarkha moskovkogo i vseia Rusi Aleksiia na Eparkhial'nom sobranii g. Moskvy," *Journal of the Moscow Patriarchate*, no. 3 (1997): 58–68.

22. "Slovo Sviateishego Patriarkha Kirilla posle bogosluzheniia v Khrame Khrista Spasitelia," December 17, 2011, Russkaia Pravoslavnaia Tserkov: Ofitsial'nyi sait Moskovskogo Patriarkhat, http://www.patriarchia.ru/db/print/1837473.html.

23. "Slovo Sviateishego Patriarkha Kirilla na bratskoi trapeze," April 22, 2012, Russkaia Pravoslavnaia Tserkov: Ofitsial'nyi sait Moskovskogo Patriarkhat, http://www.patriarchia.ru/db/text/2183143.html.

24. Kuraev was eventually defrocked by Patriarch Kirill in April 2023. In April 2024, the Patriarch of Constantinople revoked Kirill's decree, reinstating Kuraev. On ratification of defrocking, see the article on the official site of the Russian Orthodox Church Moscow diocese, "Ukaz No U-02/69 ot 28 aprelia 2023 goda//protodiakonu Andreiu Kuraevu," April 28, 2023, http://moseparh.ru/ukaz-u-0269-ot-28-aprelya-2023.html. On reinstatement, see "Soiuz pravolslavnykh zhurnalstov," and "Konstantinopol'skii Patriarkh vosstanovil v sane Protodiakona Andreia Kuraeva," April 8, 2024, https://spzh.live/ru/news/79602-konstantinopolskij-patriarkh-vosstanovil-v-sane-protodiakona-andreja-kuraeva.

25. Nikolai Mitrokhin and Mikhail Edel'shtein, *Ekonomicheskaia deyatel'nost' Russkoi Pravoslavnoi Tserkvi i eiyo tenevaia sostavliaiushchaia*, ed. Lev Timofeev (Moskva: RGGU, 2000); Zhan Toshchenko, "Ekonomicheskiye pritiazaniia religii," *Novaia gazeta*, July 2009.

26. Bishop Savva (Tutunov) of Zelenograd, deputy administrator of the Moscow Patriarchate, stated that a priest must not bless weapons of mass destruction and referred to the conclusions on this subject of the Commission on Ecclesiastical Law set up by the church's Interconciliar Assembly: "This week saw the conclusion of two years' work on the document 'On the Russian Orthodox Church's Blessing of Weapons,' a subject proposed by the Presidium of the Interconciliar Assembly, according to RIA Novosti. In the opinion of the commission, within the framework of church tradition one can talk about blessing a soldier who is carrying out his duty in defense of the Fatherland . . . personal weapons may be blessed only because they are connected to the person who is being blessed. On this basis, weapons of mass destruction and personal weapons must not be blessed, wrote Bishop Savva on his Instagram page." RIA Novosti, June 21, 2019, https://ria.ru/20190621/1555783722.html. See also "V Russkoi Tserkvi zaiavili, chto oruzhie massovogo porazheniia ne dolzhno osviashchat'sia," PRAVMIR, June 20, 2019, https://www.pravmir.ru/russkaya-pravoslavnaya-tserkov-oruzhie-massovogo-porazheniya-ne-dolzhno-osvyashhatsya/.

27. "Patriarshaia propoved' v Nedeliu Siropustnuiu posle liturgii v Khrame Khrista Spasitelia," March 6, 2022, Russkaia Pravoslavnaia Tserkov: Ofitsial'nyi sait Moskovskogo Patriarkhat, http://www.patriarchia.ru/db/text/5906442.html.

A Biography of Michael Bourdeaux and Keston College

Xenia Dennen

I met Michael Bourdeaux three years before Keston College was founded. It was 1966 and I had just taken my final exams at Oxford University. Professor William Fletcher had recently established the Centre de Recherches in Geneva to study the religious situation in the USSR and had engaged Bourdeaux in 1965 as one of his researchers. I came into the field on Bourdeaux's coattails as his assistant, funded by the Centre. Professor Fletcher's organization was a dry affair that studied only official sources and the Soviet press and did not explore the fascinating field of samizdat that was taking off in 1966 with the burgeoning of the dissident movement following the trial of the writers Andrei Sinyavsky and Yuli Daniel.[1]

Michael Bourdeaux had visited Moscow briefly in early August 1964 and had had an extraordinary encounter. He heard from Russian friends that the Church of St. Peter and St. Paul on Preobrazhensky Square had been blown up in the early hours of July 18, and he went off there to see what he could find out. As he peered through the fencing that surrounded the pile of rubble, he noticed two rather short women, one trying to lift the other so that she could peer through a crack in the fencing. Waiting until they had walked away from the site, he went up to them and asked, "Can you tell me what happened?" One of them jumped, he thought from fear, but when he offered to leave them in peace, they said, "No, we need you. Please, follow us!" Keeping his distance, Bourdeaux followed them to a small wooden house on the outskirts of Moscow. Once inside, he told them that he had recently read a collection of documents about the persecution of the monks at Pochaev Monastery in Ukraine, which had been signed by two women, Feodosia Varrava and Efrosinia Shchur. Could they tell him more about what was happening to the church? At this point one of the women started crying: "We are Feodosia Varrava and Efrosinia Shchur!" Bourdeaux was stunned. In his memoir he described the moment:

> I couldn't speak. I waited for them to go on. "We brought those documents to Moscow last year, hoping to find a foreigner to give them to. It was difficult, but eventually we found a French school-teacher from Paris. We never heard whether she was able to take them back with her."
>
> "She did [Bourdeaux replied]. I've seen a copy and read them. This was the reason why I came to Moscow: to try and find out whether what they said was true and to ask for more information. This is my first evening."
>
> "It's ours too. We arrived today and immediately heard about the destruction of the church, so we went there—and found you! We were wondering how this time we would contact a tourist who would take our new documents."
>
> "What do you want me to do with them? What can I do for you?" I asked. The reply was instantaneous and decisive: "Take the documents back, then be our voice and speak for us."[2]

That was the moment Keston was born, at least in Bourdeaux's mind. Meeting Professor Fletcher soon after that dramatic encounter in Moscow, Bourdeaux jumped at the opportunity to work for his Centre de Recherches, believing that this would fulfill his wish to help the churches in the USSR. It did not. Professor Fletcher's outfit produced a publication that in Bourdeaux's words "could almost have come from a group of automatons," and Professor Fletcher's Centre died at the end of 1969.

Michael Bourdeaux was the son of a Cornwall baker whose pasties were considered the best in the county. He was educated at Truro School, where his gift for languages became apparent, and during National Service he had the luck, thanks to an enlightened RAF Group Captain, to get into the Russian interpreters' course. And that is where his lifelong love of Russian culture and literature began.

After National Service, Bourdeaux went up to read Russian at St. Edmund Hall, Oxford, followed in 1959 by a year at Moscow University as part of the first student-exchange program organized by the British Council. This was an important year in the history of religion in the Soviet Union: Khrushchev's antireligious campaign started in 1959 and continued until his fall in 1964. Consequently, Bourdeaux saw the effects of that campaign firsthand: he witnessed the mass closure of churches and discrimination against religious believers. After the year in Moscow, now convinced that he should be ordained, he enrolled at Wycliffe Hall, Oxford, to study theology, which led eventually to his ordination as an Anglican priest in 1961. Thereafter he served for a few years in Anglican parishes, but all the time longed to focus on studying the religious situation in the USSR, a concern that was dramatically reinforced by his 1964 encounter with Feodosia Varrava and Efrosinia Shchur. By 1965 he had published his first book, *Opium of the People: The Christian Religion in the USSR*, and that year he began his period of work for Professor Fletcher.

During 1969, Sir John Lawrence, Professor Leonard Schapiro, Professor Peter Reddaway, and Michael Bourdeaux began discussions that led to the founding of the Centre for the Study of Religion and Communism, later renamed Keston College. Sir John had been a press attaché in the Soviet Union during the Second World War, and he had edited a remarkable publication, *Britansky Soyuznik* (The British Ally), the only uncensored publication to be produced in the Soviet Union from 1917 until the advent of Gorbachev. He became Keston's first chairman and served in that role until 1983. Leonard Schapiro was Professor of Political Science at the London School of Economics and Political Science (LSE). He had trained as a lawyer, but turned to politics when he became convinced that the Western world needed to understand the true nature of the Soviet Communist system. According to Peter Reddaway, a lecturer in Soviet studies at the LSE when Keston was founded, Schapiro said, "Revolution is pitiless, shapeless, and nearly always seems to provide a cure which is worse than the disease."[3] Schapiro saw that religion was not included in Soviet studies and felt this was a serious gap that a research center, as envisaged by Bourdeaux, would fill. Bourdeaux commented in his memoir, "He was convinced that our approach was sufficiently academic to be able to hold its own in any university company."[4] Thanks to him, Bourdeaux was awarded a fellowship at the LSE's Centre for International Studies, his first academic appointment and the first academic appointment in the United Kingdom in communism and religion. Reddaway, who in

1985 was appointed director of the Kennan Institute in Washington, DC, became a close friend and collaborator of Bourdeaux. Thanks to these four men and a fundraising campaign, the new Centre for the Study of Religion and Communism (CSRC) was founded in 1969 and in 1970 was registered with the Charity Commission as an educational charity as well as a membership organization under the Department of Education. It had a distinguished governing body and gradually began to build up its membership.

CSRC's charitable status banned it from involvement in political activity or campaigning. It was both an academic institution focused on the serious study of religion in Communist countries and a popularizing organization that publicized its findings. It published books, the academic journal *Religion in Communist Lands* (later renamed *Religion, State & Society*), a news service, and the popular magazine *Frontier*. From the outset it collected official and unofficial material—samizdat documents, newspaper cuttings, antireligious posters, letters, books, journals, articles—all of which now form the remarkably rich Keston Archive. Those words spoken to Bourdeaux in 1964 in Moscow—"Be our voice"—became CSRC's motto for all of CSRC's work: the documents published would speak for themselves. In Bourdeaux's words: "The work would be grounded in scholarship and integrity towards our sources, whatever their provenance. Thus, we would be faithful to the 'voice' of those who were silenced. Important, too, was to evaluate the controlled and censored opinions of those under constraint who spoke for the official churches from within the system. We would also evaluate official atheist sources."[5]

At first, CSRC's focus was on the USSR, but with time and the addition of staff with all the required languages, the work expanded to cover all the countries of Eastern and Central Europe. Thus today the archive contains large collections of Polish, Romanian, Czech, and Hungarian material in addition to its massive collection of material in Russian from different parts of the Soviet Union.

CSRC took a balanced approach: it supported diplomacy but always believed that the truth should be told. It was accused by the left wing in the West of being "anticommunist," of not understanding the positive aspects of socialism, and it was attacked by the right wing because it refused to take up an anticommunist crusade on behalf of the persecuted, as was done, for example, by the Romanian pastor Richard Wurmbrand or Joe Bass's Underground Evangelism. CSRC covered all religions in Communist countries without bias toward any one in particular; religious liberty and freedom of conscience were its watchwords. Within professional ecumenical circles, and the World Council of Churches (WCC) in particular, CSRC was an irritant because it spoke the truth to power and published the facts about religious persecution and discrimination. Long after Bourdeaux had accused WCC members of "selective indignation," the Romanian Orthodox theologian and former gulag prisoner Fr. Dumitru Staniloae, a member of the WCC's Central Committee, went up to Bourdeaux and said, "Michael, you were right all along—and you are still right now."[6]

CSRC's name was changed to Keston College when Bourdeaux's team of researchers moved from their workspace in his home to a former Church of England school building outside the village of Keston, south of London, which Bourdeaux heard was for sale in the autumn of 1972. After negotiating with the relevant education department and securing a loan from the Church of England's Rochester diocese, CSRC's trustees were able to buy the building. It bordered on Keston Common and the woodlands beyond, where many émigré Russians who subsequently visited the building remarked on the number of wonderful mushrooms and thus felt totally at home! In Bourdeaux's words, "Keston College immediately suggested itself as the new name. In the old sense of the word, a 'college' was a collegium of scholars doing the same work."[7] These former school buildings were extremely dilapidated with no functioning heating system. A memento of those days is a photograph of Bourdeaux at his desk wearing his Russian *shapka*! In 1991 after Keston College had moved to Oxford, the organization was renamed the Keston Institute.

Keston's history is linked in many ways with the birth and development of the dissident movement in the USSR. After the partial cultural thaw during the Khrushchev period, by 1965 the writers Sinyavsky and Daniel had been arrested and their trial was staged the next year. Two years later in 1968 the trial of Yuri Galanskov and Aleksandr Ginzburg triggered a new major human rights samizdat publication, the *Chronicle of Current Events*, which devoted most of its first issue to this trial, and which, in Andrei Sakharov's view, marked the birth of the Soviet dissident movement.[8] Sakharov and many other Soviet dissidents were concerned about religious believers as much as about other victims of injustice and emphasized that freedom for the churches was an integral part of the struggle for human rights. The *Chronicle of Current Events* regularly published information about the persecution of religious believers, while Sakharov's Human Rights Committee, founded in 1970, took up, for example, the case of the Russian Orthodox writer Anatolii Levitin-Krasnov and that of five Adventists who had been put on trial.[9] Particularly important for Keston, as a source of information, was the formation in 1977 of the Christian Committee for the Defense of Believers' Rights, founded by the Russian Orthodox priest Fr. Gleb Yakunin, who was to become a close friend of Bourdeaux. This organization gathered information from all Christian denominations within the USSR and in under three years had sent out 423 documents.[10]

Although Keston, because of its charitable status, could not organize campaigns on behalf of imprisoned religious believers, its role was nevertheless significant: it gathered the information, checked its reliability, and distributed it. Keston became famous within the UK's national press as an organization with a spotless reputation. As it was said, "If it comes from Keston it can be trusted." In addition to its academic journal, magazine, and news service, Keston worked closely with Amnesty International and regularly published lists of religious prisoners with all the known information about them, their sentences, and the addresses of the labor camps where they were held.

Keston publicized the well-known case of the poet Irina Ratushinskaya, who was arrested in 1982 at age twenty-eight for disseminating her religious poetry and sentenced in 1983 to seven years in strict regime labor camps, with a subsequent five years of internal exile. Keston kept abreast of her situation through telephone calls to her husband. The Keston staff member who rang him made sure she was talking to the right person by quoting a few lines from Ratushinskaya's poetry, which he then completed. Keston regularly updated the national press on her fate, and when she was released in 1986 following the appointment of Gorbachev as Communist Party leader in 1985, she and her husband flew to Heathrow where Keston staff turned out in force to meet them. As a thank you for Keston's support, Ratushinskaya composed the following poem:

> Believe me, it was often thus:
> In solitary cells, on winter nights
> A sudden sense of joy and warmth
> And a resounding note of love.

> And then, unsleeping, I would know
> A-huddle by an icy wall:
> Someone is thinking of me now,
> Petitioning the Lord for me.

My dear ones, thank you all
Who did not falter, who believed in us!
In the most fearful prison hour
We probably would not have passed

Through everything—from end to end
Our heads held high, unbowed—
Without your valiant hearts
To light our path.[11]

Dramatic change resulted from the advent of Gorbachev and his realization that the Soviet polity was dying, its economy unproductive and its political system in need of reform. Dissidents were freed from prisons and labor camps while ideas and information began to be freely exchanged. Hostility to religion, however, was still evident in November 1986 when, via the Soviet newspaper *Pravda vostoka* (November 25, 1986), Keston picked up Gorbachev's speech in Tashkent, in which he sharply denounced Communist Party members for participating in religious ceremonies and emphasized the need to wage war against all religious phenomena. But the next month there was a symbolic gesture, auguring future reform: this was the release of Sakharov from exile in Gorky (Nizhny Novgorod). During 1987 there were amnesties of political and religious prisoners, and Soviet press articles were published portraying religion in a positive light. Then came a statement in late June 1988 at the 19th Conference of the Communist Party when Gorbachev criticized disrespect toward a "spiritual worldview" and condemned "administrative methods" used against religious believers. As a result of this change in policy, the Russian Orthodox Church was allowed to organize remarkably elaborate celebrations for the Millennium of Russian Orthodoxy that year.

With perestroika and the eventual collapse of the communist system, Keston had a crisis of identity. What was its role now that policies on religion had changed and religious believers were no longer in prison? By 1991 Keston had moved to Oxford but could no longer afford many staff members. So the pruning began and Keston had to rethink its mission. It concluded that research on religion in Communist countries was still important and that Keston's archive was vital for such research, and it also embarked in the late 1990s on a major project to study all religions in the Russian Federation based on field research. In 2007 Baylor University in Texas agreed to house the archive in a newly created Keston Center for Religion, Politics, and Society.

The Keston Archive was Bourdeaux's great love and is a particularly important part of his legacy: it contains the stories of many remarkable people who defended the freedom of mind and spirit in the face of a political system that claimed total control over all aspects of human life. For myself, I continue to find that the lives of these heroes are a source of inspiration, like water in a desert. As Antoine de Saint-Exupéry wrote in *Le Petit Prince*: "What makes the desert beautiful is that somewhere it hides a well."

Notes

1. Leopold Labedz and Max Hayward, eds., *On Trial: The Case of Sinyavsky (Tertz) and Daniel (Arzhak)* (London: Collins & Harvill Press, 1967).

2. Michael Bourdeaux, *One Word of Truth: The Cold War Memoir of Michael Bourdeaux and Keston College* (London: Darton, Longman & Todd, 2019), 86–87.

3. Peter Reddaway, *The Dissidents: A Memoir of Working with the Resistance in Russia, 1960–1990* (Washington, DC: Brookings Institution Press, 2020), 106.

4. Bourdeaux, *One Word of Truth*, 124.

5. Bourdeaux, *One Word of Truth*, 125.

6. Bourdeaux, *One Word of Truth*, 195.

7. Bourdeaux, *One Word of Truth*, 133.

8. Peter Reddaway, ed., *Uncensored Russia: The Human Rights Movement in the Soviet Union* (London: Jonathan Cape, 1972), 72–94. In his article "An Anxious Time," Andrei Sakharov wrote: "The defence of human rights has become a universal ideology, uniting people of all nationalities and the most varied beliefs on the basis of humanitarian concerns . . . In the USSR the human rights movement in its present structure was formed by the end of the 1960s, when the first issue of the *Chronicle of Current Events* came out." In *The New York Times*, June 8, 1980, and the *Chronicle of Current Events*, no. 57, Amnesty edition, 47.

9. See the *Chronicle of Current Events*, no. 21, Amnesty edition, 278, on this committee's defense of Levitin-Krasnov, and the *Chronicle of Current Events*, no. 53, Amnesty edition, 22, for its defense of the five Adventists.

10. See Jane Ellis, "The Christian Committee for the Defence of Believers' Rights in the USSR," *Religion in Communist Lands* 8, no. 4 (Winter 1980): 279–91.

11. Irina Ratushinskaya, "Believe Me" (1986), in *Frontier* (March–April 1987), 13.

Contributors

Wallace L. Daniel is a Distinguished University Professor of History at Mercer University in Macon, Georgia. A historian of modern Russian religious and intellectual history, he is the author or editor of six books, most focusing on civil society, the intelligentsia, and the Russian Orthodox Church in the Soviet and post-Soviet eras.

Julie K. deGraffenried is Associate Professor and Chair of the Department of History at Baylor University in Waco, Texas. The author or editor of three books, she is a historian of Soviet Russia with a research focus on children and childhood, conflict, and visual culture. Recent publications address religious policy in the Cold War USSR and depictions of the family in children's media during the Great Patriotic War.

Xenia Dennen is one of the four founders of the Keston Institute in 1969 and has been the institute's chairperson since 2002. She established and edited the journal *Religion in Communist Lands* beginning in 1973. She has traveled extensively conducting fieldwork for the multivolume *Religious Life in Russia Today*.

Sergei Filatov is a Senior Fellow of the Institute of Oriental Studies, Russian Academy of Sciences, Russia. He is the author of more than two hundred publications and is the editor-compiler of the multivolume *Religious Life in Russia Today*. His research interests focus on the sociology of religion and its intersections with freedom of conscience and human rights.

April L. French is an independent historian who studies the theology, everyday practice, and dissidence of religious believers in the Soviet period, including evangelical Christians and the Russian Orthodox priest Father Aleksandr Men. She works at the University of Wyoming.

Mark Hurst is a Lecturer in the History of Human Rights at Lancaster University. His research focuses on campaigns conducted by human rights organizations during the Cold War, and more broadly in the history of human rights, political dissent, and activism.

Zoe Knox is Associate Professor of Modern Russian History at the University of Leicester and a Fellow of the Royal Historical Society. Her research explores issues of religious tolerance and intolerance in the modern world, particularly as these relate to religion under Communist regimes and in Soviet and post-Soviet Russia.

Patrick C. Leech is a PhD candidate in the Department of History at Baylor University. His work focuses on the history of Hungary in the context of the Cold War, specifically as expressed in Hungarian diaspora communities. He recently completed a Fulbright in Budapest.

Michael Long is Professor of Russian at Baylor University and Department Chair of Modern Languages and Cultures. His research interests include dissidence and human rights in the Eastern bloc and the restoration of cultural monuments in Georgia.

Barbara Martin is an independent postdoctoral researcher, formerly at the University of Basel. Her research, which was funded by an Ambizione Grant of the Swiss National Science Foundation, focuses on the national-religious revival in the Russian Orthodox intelligentsia of Moscow and Leningrad from the 1970s to the 1990s.

Joshua T. Searle is Professor of Mission Studies and Intercultural Theology at the Theologische Hochschule Elstal and an ordained pastor in the Baptist Union of Germany. He serves as a co-founder and trustee of the charity Dnipro Hope Mission. The author of four books and dozens of academic articles, his research focuses on public theology, especially in the post-Soviet space.

Bishop Rowan Williams, Baron Williams of Oystermouth, PC, FBA, FRSL, FLSW, is an Anglican bishop, theologian, and poet, writing and teaching extensively on philosophy, theology, and aesthetics. He is the former Archbishop of Canterbury (2002–12) and, since then, has held positions at Oxford, Cambridge, and University of South Wales.

INDEX

Figures are indicated by "f" following page numbers.